The Yale Series of Younger Poets

THE YALE

YOUNGER

POETS

ANTHOLOGY

Edited by George Bradley

Yale University Press   New Haven and London

Designed by James J. Johnson and set in New Caledonia and Bulmer types by
Tseng Information Systems, Durham, North Carolina.
Printed in the United States of America by Vail-Ballou Press, Binghamton, New York.

Library of Congress Cataloging-in-Publication Data

The Yale younger poets anthology / edited by George Bradley.
    p.   cm. — (The Yale series of younger poets)
    Includes index.
    ISBN 0-300-07472-7 (alk. paper). — ISBN 0-300-07473-5 (pbk. : alk. paper)

    1. American Poetry—20th century.   I. Bradley, George. 1953–.
II. Series.
PS613.Y35   1998
811'.508–dc21   97-35444

A catalogue record for this book is available from the British Library.

The paper in this book meets the guidelines for permanence and durability of the
Committee on Production Guidelines for Book Longevity of the Council on Library
Resources.

10 9 8 7 6 5 4 3 2 1

Contents

The Modern Series

Preface

IRST BOOKS of verse bear a family resemblance. They typi-
cally range far afield, for young authors are eager to lay claim
to sophistication, and one of the ways they go about this is
by exploring exotic terrain. Many a first book of American poetry
takes its readers to Europe, and it is not unusual for the audience to
find itself wading through the Amazon basin or clambering up the
Himalayas. First books of verse seek to establish the newcomer's
credentials, and thus often contain formal exercises. Sonnets were
once pro forma, and sestinas, too, have had their vogue. First books
frequently imitate, and the most promising among them do so with
enthusiasm. Their authors have been inspired by a particular poet
or school, and they wish to take their places alongside the model.
First books of poetry are most often written by the young, and
so are naturally youthful in sensibility: brash, impressionable, self-
absorbed, of decided opinions. A youthful outlook is no hindrance
to art, of course; in fact, it's often a great help. The god-like self-
confidence, the ignorance of failure, the contempt for compromise,
the impulse to investigate, the bubbling energy and outsized ambi-
tion of adolescence are great allies for any writer. The sensibility of
so fine a poet as Shelley might be termed essentially adolescent. So

might that of the *Iliad.* The bad attitude of Achilles constitutes our culture's first book of poetry.

The Yale Series of Younger Poets to date is made up of ninety-two first books, and all of them are represented in this selection. An anthology devoted to first books necessarily embraces a limitation—by definition even the best of these authors cannot be represented by his or her mature work—but such a volume will have its music, too: the fever pitch of sheer desire, the hymn of true belief. The strength of initiate ardor is not to be dismissed. A sufficient aspiration is the sine qua non of poetry, and the youthful poems collected under this cover offer aspiration undiluted. Thoreau said that the young man dreams of building a palace, whereas the middle-aged man takes up the same materials and decides to build a woodshed. There are no woodsheds here. Here instead are ninety-two plans for the palace of art.

This is not the first time someone thought of a Yale Younger Poets anthology. As far back as 1939 the idea was proposed, and it has been brought up since once every ten or fifteen years. The project has seemed a daunting one, however, and it has only become more so with time. One problem has been that the styles of poetry found in the Younger Poets Series have grown so various as to make impartiality almost impossible. Still, I have tried to avoid excessive partisanship, recognizing that the Yale series is by now a venture larger than the confines of personal preference.

Yale University Press has been generous in the space allowed, and that has helped. I have been permitted to select at least a few lines by every poet published in the series, although those who preceded Stephen Vincent Benét's arrival as editor in 1933 are provided primarily to give a sense of the series' origins and so are not represented at length. The Yale Younger Poets published since that time have been given several pages each, and I believe each is included in sufficient quantity to give an adequate idea of his or her early work.

In weighing the merits of the Yale Younger Poets, I have looked to the quality of their Yale volumes, and the relative space I have given them does not necessarily reflect my assessment of their subsequent careers. Here it is the first book that counts. Feeling that it is any poem's first duty to interest the reader, I have (where there is a difference) made it a principle to select what I believe to be the strongest work from each volume, rather than the most characteristic or the most educational. One entry—that of Joan Murray—will no doubt occasion surprise. It is the longest in the anthology both because I feel her book to be one of the very best the Yale Series has yet published and because her work is long out of print.

During my selection of poetry for this anthology, I have been alone with my thoughts, but I have received much help with the rest of the project. I wish to thank the many Yale Younger Poets, too many to mention by name, who have written me detailed letters and engaged in long conversations by phone. The Yale series inspires loyalty and affection in its poets, and I have been able to draw on those feelings in generous amounts. In producing my Anglo-Saxon Chronicles of the Yale Series of Younger Poets (and then Benét was king, and then MacLeish was king, and then Auden was king . . .), I am grateful for the time and attention given me by people especially knowledgeable about Yale University Press and the Yale series; among these are Chester Kerr, Louis Martz, James Mooney, and Tina Weiner. Others who have been of great help include Cornelia Fitts, who freely shared her recollections of her late husband, and Jorie Graham, who ascertained which of the Yale Younger Poets have been associated with the Iowa Writer's Workshop. For my modicum of understanding as regards the business side of publishing poetry in this century, I am indebted to Ronald Wallace's excellent introduction to his anthology of university press verse, *Vital Signs*. I also owe a debt of gratitude to Edward Mendelson and the Estate of W. H. Auden, to James Cummins of the Elliston Poetry Collection at the University of Cincinnati, to Bridget Burke, Curator of the Arts of the Book Collection at the Yale University Library, and particularly to the good-humored and professional staff at the Manuscripts and Archives Department of the Yale University Library. For assistance in tracking down biographical information concerning poets so obscure as to never have been born or died (insofar as may be determined from the public record), I thank several of the staff and interns of Yale University Press for their energy and interest: Isaac Cates, Brooke Conti, and most especially Mary Francis. The assemblage of so many facts as make up this anthology will surely involve errors, but my mistakes would have been grossly multiplied were it not for their research.

Also, I would like to thank my wife and child for their patience through the many months in which this book was prepared. One is what one does, and they bore admirably with the stranger created by long days in the archives. Finally, and above all, I thank my editor, Richard Miller, whose conception this *Yale Younger Poets Anthology* was, who participated in some of the research entailed, and who has never been less than encouraging. He provided me with every opportunity to do as best I might, and if the result proves to be a useful volume, he deserves much of the credit.

December 1997
Chester, Conn.

Introduction

THE YALE SERIES OF YOUNGER POETS was founded in 1919, a year that had seen the end of civilization and the beginning of modern poetry. World War I, which America had entered in medias res, officially ended on November 11, 1918, and many of its survivors felt the cultural assumptions based on the ideal of *humanitas*, which had been taken for granted for nearly five hundred years, had been swept away in an ocean of blood. One result of this sanguinary sea-change was to give new force to modernism, a movement to be embodied above all by T. S. Eliot's *The Waste Land*, published in 1922. Another result, though it took place across an actual ocean and sprang from reactionary rather than revolutionary artistic instincts, was the project of several university men to encourage the first efforts of the poetical young veterans come home to Yale. Modernism and the Yale series were two ideas occasioned severally by the Great War.

Civilization survived, of course, to end again on numerous occasions since; and modernism would have to begin all over on this side of the Atlantic, where it remained an innovation confined to several small magazines and an elite group of poets for the better part of a decade. Yet American poetry is still traveling along a trajectory dictated by the events of those years, because Eliot's gloomy and self-dramatizing assumptions (that book-learning had become archaeology, the sifting of cultural potsherds; that shared notions of meaning and form had collapsed, leaving artists to the uneasy improvisations for which each would henceforth be individually responsible) remain those of many of our poets today. American poetry in the 1990s is conspicuously divided into factions drawn along regional, ethnic, and ideological lines, and there appears to be little that these competitors are willing to share. Yet they do share a paradox, for Eliot's despairing recognition that cultural norms are no longer held in common has become common currency. Nowadays, our poets are likely to celebrate as a healthy diversity what Eliot once deplored as confusion, but regardless of the positive or negative valence attached, cultural fragmentation is taken for granted. Eliot could not have countenanced the place at which we have arrived, but we have come here under his impetus all the same.

It is a journey that may be followed in the development of the Yale series, albeit sometimes at a certain remove. The sort of poetry being published by the series in any given period is at least as dependent on the predilections of the editor in charge as it is on the condition of poetry at large; but an editor chooses and does not invent, and one can choose only from that which is available. The manuscripts submitted to the series are inevitably an expression of their times, the reflection of artistic fashions, of political ideologies, of historical incidents. If art at its most ambitious is precisely an effort to rise above context, still no art can do so entirely. So it is that the story of the Yale Series of Younger Poets in many ways parallels the story of twentieth-century American poetry as a whole.

Like the Great War, the modernist movement would come to be recognized as irreversibly significant, and the writing of poetry would be forever altered. The Yale men who initiated the Yale Series of Younger Poets, however, had formed their literary tastes in an earlier time, back at the turn of the century. George Parmly Day, who founded Yale University Press, was Yale class of 1897; his brother Clarence, who conceived of the Younger Poets Series, was

Yale class of 1896; and Charlton M. Lewis, the series' first editor, had earned his Ph.D. at Yale, also in 1896.

If the aftermath of World War I appears distant today, the years leading up to the war have been substantially obscured by the watershed itself. To understand the assumptions that shaped the Yale Series of Younger Poets, one has to reimagine an unvivid era. In the ebb and flow of artistic movements, the Belle Epoque was slack tide. Georgian poetry was the order of the day, and John Masefield was publishing the books that would make him the most popular poet writing in English during the decade surrounding the war. The qualities most often praised in poetry reviews were nobility of sentiment, euphonic harmony, and moralist content. Those qualities would reach their apogee in the poems of Rupert Brooke, who was destined to die in the war and become the Sir Philip Sidney of the hour, at once the ideal poet and the type of true manhood. One must also imagine a time in which poetry still enjoyed considerable prestige. To an extent now difficult to grasp, the appreciation of poetry was culturally central and formed a basic intellectual credential. Culture meant refined books, and poetry was central because literature *was* poetry. Prose fiction had replaced verse romance as the stuff of mass-market publishing in the mid-nineteenth century, but it did not begin to be extensively taught in the universities until after the war. In the pre-war years, the core curriculum remained poetry, above all classical poetry: Virgil and Horace, Homer and Pindar and Sappho. Ancient Rome and Athens could not, of course, be visited in the here and now; but England could be reached, and it represented the next best thing. England was the most powerful country on earth, and English letters exercised a corresponding dominance. T. S. Eliot had not gone to England purely because of a youthful urge to see the world. Would-be authors were drawn to London in those days, as surely as they are called to New York City in our own.

The Yale Series of Younger Poets was the natural outgrowth of this neoclassicism and anglophilia, ideals which had underpinned Yale University Press from the start. When George Parmly Day founded the press in 1908, together with his wife, Wilhelmine, he did so partly in order that Yale University might enjoy some of the prestige and influence that Oxford University derived from its publishing operations. George always credited his brother Clarence with the idea for Yale's poetry series, but such an idea would not have seemed unusual at a time when a press with high literary aspirations could not overlook the genre. Also, since English opinion ruled the academies, the fact that Oxford University Press was publishing a similar series, called Adventures All, provided a persuasive example. Additionally, both George and Clarence Day were poets themselves, after a fashion. George remained an amateur, but Clarence was a professional author. Several volumes of affectionate memoirs, most notably *Life with Father* (1932), would form the basis of his reputation, but he also published verse. It was light verse, couplets and quatrains that might be described as proto-Thurberesque, particularly so because Clarence accompanied them with casual drawings of considerable charm.

One such combination of drawing and verse (see illustration at right) demonstrates that Clarence Day recognized the predisposition of Yale English professors toward rear-guard action. He shared this predisposition, however, insofar as we can judge by the poetry series that resulted from his prompting. In any case, the glory that was Greece certainly exercised a direct influence upon the first editor of the Yale series, Charlton Miner Lewis.

Lewis was the son of the prominent classicist Charlton T. Lewis, who had compiled *Harper's Latin Dictionary* (1879) and was a long-time member of a club devoted to the literature and language of ancient Greece. Like the brothers Day, Charlton M. Lewis was intimately associated with Yale, where he taught in the English department from 1896 until his death in 1923. In 1919, Lewis was the obvious choice to edit a poetry series for Yale University Press, because poetry was an area of his academic expertise, and poetry manuscripts submitted to the press were already being referred to him. Lewis's recommendations shaped the Yale Series of Younger Poets even before it began, for among the authors who published with Yale University Press under Lewis's aegis early on were William

When eras die, their legacies
   Are left to strange police.
Professors in New England guard
   The glory that was Greece.

—from *Thoughts without Words* (1928), by Clarence Day

Alexander Percy, Stephen Vincent Benét, and Archibald MacLeish. These three would edit the Yale series for a total of twenty years, from Percy's appointment in 1925 until MacLeish's resignation at the close of World War II.

In 1917, the press published an anthology called *A Book of Verse of the Great War,* edited by W. Reginald Wheeler and carrying a foreword by Charlton Lewis. The germ of the Yale poetry series is perhaps to be sought in this volume, because the series initially embodied the encounter of neoclassical education with wartime experience. Six of the first seven poets selected for the series had served in the Great War, and the eighth, Viola White, had spent time in France nursing the wounded. Lewis's taste in war poetry first defined the series, and his foreword to this wartime anthology is as close as we are likely to get to his thinking at the time. Here is his caveat regarding the difficulty of creating significant poetry out of the patriotic impulse:

> A critical curse rests upon the poetry of patriotism and war. The passion of patriotism is common to all right-minded men, and criticism wants the uncommon. Criticism requires that a poet's vision be new and peculiar; whereas race-consciousness and martial glory have been familiar themes ever since Pharaoh's chosen captains were drowned in the Red Sea. The poet whose sole aim is to rekindle these old ardors will be fortunate indeed if he escape the ninety-nine ways of banality; and even the hundredth way, unless he is a consummate artist, will hardly lead him to the very peaks of Parnassus.

Lewis knew where the pitfalls lay, in theory, but he was a harsher judge in theory than in fact. Perhaps he suspended his judgment to a degree, wanting to encourage the literary young men who returned from the war to sit in his classes at Yale. One of those men was Howard Swazey Buck, who had driven an ambulance for the French army at Verdun and written a small cycle of war poems called "The Tempering: Leaves from a Notebook." The collection won the Albert S. Cook Prize for poetry at Yale in 1918, and it was published as a pamphlet by Yale University Press. Another literary young veteran was John Chipman Farrar—he had been an aviation inspector in France—and he, too, was a Cook Prize winner. Early in 1919, booklength manuscripts by Buck and Farrar arrived at Yale University Press, and Lewis was given them both. He sent back Buck's "unread"—it was passed on to another—but he did render judgment on Farrar's book. No doubt it was all pro forma, because Lewis and the press were already familiar with the work of each poet. At any rate, both books were accepted for publication, though it was almost a year before they actually appeared. The first title page in the series—that of Howard Buck's *The Tempering*—gives the publication date as 1919, but in fact the book was not released until January 17, 1920. Somewhat delayed, then, the Yale Series of Younger Poets was under way.

Just why Buck's volume was designated first in the series instead of Farrar's is no longer clear, but that primacy has brought his name a continued attention that his poetry itself could not have attracted. This is not to belittle Buck. His was schoolboy verse, and it is not his fault if the series his volume initiated has gone on to greater things. Moreover, he was not alone in his humble ability. No survey of the Yale series can avoid the assessment that its early volumes were banal, even if Lewis's ninety-nine ways to banality rather overestimates their variety. Put simply, these authors tried to say too much and thereby said too little. The first Yale Younger Poets knew that they were witnesses to history, and they believed they had been touched by fire as surely as Oliver Wendell Holmes, Jr., and his Civil War companions had been before them. The early Yale poets were incapable of effectively communicating their wartime experience, however, because in art skill must precede meaning, and skill was what they lacked. Instead, their slim volumes are filled with what seems in our more cynical age to be unconsidered piety and patriotism, most of it couched in unexceptional imitation of the classical verse in which these authors had been tutored. Above all, the early Yale Younger Poets struggled to measure up to extraordinary events, and perhaps their frequent resort to platitude should be thought of as an attempt to ensure sufficient sincerity.

The triteness of these books is not just a matter of youth, how-

THE YALE SERIES

The Tempering

Howard Buck

OF YOUNGER POETS

ever, for most of the English war poets were young, too. The American verse resulting from the First World War will not bear comparison with the best that England produced, possibly because English poetry as a whole still retained the greater vitality, possibly because the English war effort involved so much of that country's population that the chances of its comprehending at least some poets of genuine ability were greater. For whatever reason, one finds no David Jones, Siegfried Sassoon, Wilfred Owen, Robert Graves, or Edward Thomas among the Yale Younger Poets. Of the sixteen volumes Charlton Lewis selected before his death in 1923, Hervey Allen's is probably the least hackneyed, in part because he was willing to question conventional responses to the Great War.

The first books in the series appeared in January 1920, and those of two other Yale students, David Hamilton and Alfred Bellinger, followed in the spring. Thereafter the series settled into a pattern of publishing four volumes a year, two in May or June, two in November or December. Darl Macleod Boyle, whose book appeared in the fall of 1920, was the first non-Yale man to be included. Viola Chittenden White's publication in the spring of 1921 made her the first woman in the series. All of these selections resulted from Lewis's semi-annual reading of accumulated manuscripts, which also took place in the spring and fall.

Once the manuscripts available to Lewis on the Yale campus were exhausted, the Yale Series of Younger Poets became a nationwide contest. It did so in a desultory fashion, however, without much publicity and with the rules developing on an ad hoc basis. Such as they were, those rules were first articulated by Lewis in the summer of 1920. Here is a statement by Lewis which appeared that August in the the *Detroit News:* "The Series is by no means limited to students, either at Yale or elsewhere. All four volumes thus far issued are by Yale men, but one of those accepted for the Fall issue is by a student at Leland Stanford. Anyone is eligible provided he (or she) is young and comparatively unknown. The age limit is understood to be about thirty." The rules would evolve through the years. What it meant to be "comparatively unknown" would be defined, length limitations would be imposed on manuscripts, and the age limit would eventually be extended to forty. The spirit of the contest was made clear from the start, though, for each of the little volumes in the series carried this statement of purpose: "The Yale Series of Younger Poets is designed to afford a publishing medium for the work of young men and women who have not yet secured a wide public recognition. It will include only such verse as seems to give the fairest promise for the future of American poetry,—to the development of which it is hoped that the Series may prove a stimulus."

These were high hopes, as genuinely noble in sentiment as anything the books themselves contained. As to whether such hopes were likely to be met, opinion was divided. The early volumes in the series received mixed reviews. "These young poets sing of France and of war," said the *Dallas Morning News* (July 27, 1920), "but their songs are not martial. They are quiet-hearted. Something better than promise may be found in each volume." The *New London Day* (October 9, 1920) was not so easily pleased: "The Younger Yale Poets—contrasted with heaven knows what older ones—are if anything, startling in their simplicity: they are very young, and they realize it." The most judicious assessment came from William Rose Benét in the *Yale Review* of October 1921. William Benét was good-humored, but unimpressed. After reading the books of Thomas Chubb, Darl Boyle, Theodore Banks, and Viola White, he found it "almost impossible to remember which of these four authors wrote any dimly remembered poem. And their poems *are* so dimly remembered. There is so little finality of phrase, so much that one has heard sung in more or less the same tone and manner. . . . Poetry, after all, is not a manner. It is either the actual innermost being of the person or it is merely a pose that means nothing. Yet these younger poets are just breaking their first lances—so why be so harsh about it? I won't. I wish them all the good luck in the world. And I hope they'll all learn thoroughly to put what they think in the way they actually think it and not in the way they think precedent demands that it ought to be put." The reviewer would not see the sort of poetry he was looking for in the series until his brother,

Stephen, took over as editor a decade later. Still, if the poets who constituted the series in its early years were greeted most often with forbearance, the series itself was soon recognized as providing a valuable service, and the attractive and affordable book design by W. A. Dwiggins generally received high praise.

Sixteen slim volumes dressed in blue (the book jackets reminded some reviewers of the French army uniform) had become part of the Yale series by the winter of 1923, when Charlton Miner Lewis died at age sixty-seven. In assessing Lewis's tenure as series editor, one may say that although his dyed-in-the-wool academic taste did not prompt him to search out work of high caliber, he did reasonably well with what came in over the transom. None of the young authors he selected would become a good poet; but quite a few of the first Yale Younger Poets went on to make a career in letters. Some of them—Howard Buck, Thomas Chubb, Theodore Banks—became professors of literature and published in their field. John Farrar co-founded the publishing houses Farrar and Rinehart and Farrar, Straus & Giroux. Alfred Bellinger became an expert numismatist and wrote studies of ancient coinage. Viola White was appointed librarian at Middlebury College and wrote as a naturalist about Vermont. Paul Tanaquil—the pen name of Jacques Georges Clemenceau Le Clercq—translated from the French. (He also fathered Tanaquil LeClercq, the ballerina and wife of George Balanchine.) Medora Addison composed children's verse. Hervey Allen became a best-selling author of historical novels (his *Anthony Adverse*, a lengthy yarn set in the Napoleonic era, made him the James Michener of 1933); and Harold Vinal edited a literary magazine called *Voices*, where he sold critiques at fifty cents per poem, with a five-cents-per-line surcharge on anything over sixteen lines. (Possibly thereby, he earned the ridicule of e. e. cummings, who sent him up in "POEM, OR BEAUTY HURTS MR. VINAL.") Amos Wilder published a second book of poetry with Yale University Press, but most of his attention was given to writing books of theology. The least obscure name in the group today is that of Oscar Williams, who became a sort of godfather in poetry circles, editing anthologies with an iron hand. His *Pocket Anthology of American*

Verse and *Immortal Poems of the English Language* were once ubiquitous.

Lewis's list did not exactly provide the "fairest promise for the future of American poetry," but he had at least assembled a group literary enough to continue producing books of one kind or another. Given that the manuscripts he received consisted mostly of undergraduate belletristics, he did a creditable job. There was no guarantee that anyone else would get a chance to improve on this record, though, for at the time of Lewis's death the series had no more than four years of tradition behind it, and it was not a conspicuous success. Certainly the little books did not sell well. Volumes of poetry by unknown authors did not fare any better in the 1920s than they do today, and the early Yale Younger Poets were no exception. When Paul Tanaquil's third book was proposed for publication in a modest run of five hundred copies, Norman Donaldson, the press's sales manager at the time, went on record as opposed. "I have no idea how to sell them," he said flatly.

Fortunately for the Yale series, it had become the pet project of at least two in-house editors at the press. One was Leslie Soule, who was soon to leave Yale. Soule loved poetry indiscriminately, and prior to his departure he wrote a memorandum to George Parmly Day recommending that the series be continued and arguing its unique value: "While plenty of prizes are offered elsewhere for single poems, this contest requires real and continued effort." The other was Wilson Follett, who had dubious taste but enormous enthusiasm. Thus, he supported Tanaquil's third book, saying that the author was on his way to becoming a "very great poet indeed," a rash statement to make about anyone and an astonishing judgment in this case. Follett's love of poetry sustained the series, however, for his high opinion of unremarkable work both assured the series' survival and secured its first editor from outside the Yale community. William Alexander Percy would be appointed in 1925 on Follett's recommendation, but in the interim, while the fate of the series remained undecided, there were two editors pro tem. These interim editors came from the same source that had pro-

vided the press with Lewis: the Yale faculty readers who were so-
licited for peer review. Professor Frederick Erastus Pierce served
as series editor in 1923 and chose two poets in the spring con-
test, Marion Boyd and Beatrice Harmon. The manuscripts Pierce
selected were of a piece with the sixteen previous volumes, and
they were published without delay in the fall of the year. So far,
the series had not skipped a beat. The next interim editor, how-
ever, was Edward Bliss Reed, who was made of different stuff. He
held the position for one year only and selected a single book, but
his impact on the series was considerable. Professor Reed was not
content with the contest as he found it.

The press had asked Reed to fill in as editor on the understand-
ing that he would not have to do so for more than one year. At the
end of that time, in November 1924, he summarized his experience
in a letter. Reed said that he read twenty-eight manuscripts, made
notations on all but three, and spent at least fifty-six hours in the
process. Far from selecting four manuscripts for publication that
year, he had a hard time endorsing one. At last he resigned him-
self to Elizabeth Jessup Blake's *Up and Down,* an offbeat collection
of poems about the Middle East, which he later referred to as a
"rather mediocre volume which I recommended for publication,
possibly unwisely."

Having found the job of editor demanding and the quality of
manuscripts poor, Reed volunteered a few suggestions, and the
Yale Series of Younger Poets as it exists today still reflects his ideas.
He proposed that the series editors be paid, and he recommended
they be changed frequently to keep from going stale. He suggested
that the series be publicized by alerting teachers of poetry at lead-
ing universities. And he felt it was time that the contest have some
official rules. Not one to leave legislation to others, Reed drew up
a set of guidelines and enclosed them with his letter. They were
passed around the press for comment and substantially accepted,
so that by the time William Alexander Percy took over the editor-
ship a few months later, the contest rules were already spelled out.
Here they are:

1. The Yale Series of Younger Poets is open to writers of American citizenship, who are under thirty years of age and have not previously published a volume of verse.
2. Manuscripts for this competition are due May 1 and November 1 in each year. The best manuscript submitted in each competition is, if recommended by the Editor, published at the expense of the Yale University Press, the author receiving the usual 10% royalty on all copies sold in the United States.
3. The format of this Series calls for a volume of from fifty to seventy-five pages with but one sonnet or short poem to a page. A page of solid verse contains forty lines.
4. It is permissible to include poems previously published in periodicals or newspapers, if the consent of such journals is given for such republication.
5. An unsuccessful manuscript may be revised and resubmitted after one year has elapsed since it was first placed in competition.
6. The Yale University Press does not guarantee to issue a volume as the result of each competition, if, in the opinion of the Editor, no manuscript submitted is worthy of publication in this Series.
7. Contestants should address manuscripts and correspondence to the Editor, Yale Series of Younger Poets, Yale University Press, New Haven, Connecticut.

A couple of points bear comment. Reed was ahead of his time in publishing one Yale Younger Poet for the year, but the press did decide to cut back to two. Also, the restriction of "one sonnet or short poem to a page" (the words are not Reed's) is telling, for the phrase shows the sort of manuscript that press personnel of the era expected. The clutter of sonnets and quatrains filling so many of the early volumes in the series was no irritant in that era. Such a manuscript was considered normal and was perhaps implicitly favored. The proviso that no manuscript need be published if none was considered adequate is also worth noting, for that is precisely what has happened on several occasions. Finally, for the first time American citizenship here becomes a qualification for the Yale Younger Poets prize. Auden later opened the contest to any poet writing in

English, but it has since been restricted to American nationals once again. This is no doubt for the best, for American poetry is nothing if not various. As Professor Reed foresaw, it has been hard enough to find editors competent to judge the many strains of our indigenous art. It wants an agile intelligence to be at once broad-minded and discriminating. The next editor to attempt the task would be a regional writer who might have stepped from a Faulkner novel, William Alexander Percy.

Aged forty, with graying blond hair and fierce blue eyes, Percy was short and slight and every inch a Southern gentleman. Called "Mr. Will" by his friends and family, he had been born to the gentry in Greenville, Mississippi, the son of a senator and the scion of generations of planters. A man of public charm, Mr. Will could be quite irritable in private, yet he inspired loyalty and affection. Percy's own affections were given to literature and to gardening, and when not in the rosebed or the library of his home on Percy Street, he could be found in the law offices of Percy & Percy. He was a world-traveler, the first of several series editors the press would be continually tracking down in foreign countries, and he had expensive tastes. A person whose wedding reception took place in Percy's second home in Sewanee, Tennessee, recalls Mr. Will saying in a reflective mood, "My only regrets in life are things I didn't buy. I ought to have *plunged* on that Bokhara carpet."

Nowadays, William Alexander Percy is remembered as the cousin and guardian of the novelist Walker Percy and as the author of an autobiography, *Lanterns on the Levee* (1941). In 1925, what small reputation he had was as a poet, the author of three volumes of verse, all published by Yale University Press. His taste in literature ran to the Romantics, and he was good at conveying his enthusiasm to others. "He could read you a poem of Keats that, by the time he finished reading it, made you want to run home and be with Keats by yourself." (So says Shelby Foote, an intimate of the Percy family.) Percy's own poetry is carefully polished, mellifluous, and filled with classical allusion. Much of it reflects his experience of the Great War, in which he had served with determination. His verse is similar, in fact, to that of the earliest Yale Younger Poets, and his appointment as series editor represented more a continuity of style than a new direction.

Percy happened to be in close contact with the press around the time of Charlton Lewis's death. His third volume of verse was in the works, and he was also editing a book for the press, a selection of poems by Arthur ("we are the movers and shakers") O'Shaughnessy. When Pierce and Reed returned to their scholastic discipline, Percy was at hand. It was not a difficult decision. Though he was the first editor to live outside of New Haven and the first who was not a Yale man—he had been educated at the University of the South and Harvard Law School—still, the hiring of William Alexander Percy was essentially another inside appointment.

In March 1925, Percy was sounded about his willingness to edit the series. While professing uncertainty of his critical ability and concern regarding the time the job might demand, Percy nonetheless declared he would be proud to undertake the editorship on a trial basis for whatever money had been paid in the past. But there had been no money paid in the past. It was decided to let Percy establish his own fee after he had discovered for himself just what the job would entail, and it was agreed that the press would pay his postage and stenographic expenses. In the event, Percy set the editor's fee at two hundred and fifty dollars per annum.

The first thing Percy did as editor was to set about publicizing the series' existence. The press was already thinking along the same lines—Reed had recommended such action—and notices requesting attention were sent to the leading literary magazines of the day: *Poetry, Contemporary Verse, The Fugitive, Voices* (Harold Vinal's magazine), *The Measure, Verse.* The press also ran a few advertisements in *The Literary Review.* The publicity was needed, because the Yale Series of Younger Poets was still a local event. This can be seen from a letter written to the press in August 1925 by Jacques Le Clercq, who was then in San Francisco: "In the East and among Yale men the Series is of course well-known. But you would be surprised how little-known it is in the West." Above all, publicity was needed because something had to be done to bring in more submissions. There were only eight of them waiting for Percy when he took over.

The obvious answer was to go looking for manuscripts, and Percy asked if he might do just that. He had heard from John Farrar (the former Yale Younger Poet had begun his successful career as a publisher) about "a young Negro by the name of Countee Cullen." Percy was told that the press would be happy to have him bring in any manuscript he thought worthy of publication, and he sent off a letter to Cullen, then at Harvard. There was no reply. One possibility is that Cullen's first book of poems, which appeared the same year, might already have been accepted for publication, making him ineligible for the Yale series. Be that as it may, the fact that Percy had been given free rein to drum up submissions was important, for it established a precedent. As late as the first years of Auden's tenure (1946-47), editors who had read all the finalists and found them wanting were permitted to search out a better manuscript if they could.

With no Countee Cullen and only eight entries on hand, none of which he admired, Percy needed help. He got it from Bernard Raymund, another former Yale Younger Poet who kept an eye on the series. Raymund, who was teaching at Ohio State University, recommended the manuscript of a young woman just graduating from that school and soon to be employed by the *American Insurance Union Magazine.* No other submission arrived that struck Percy as any better—by the end of May there were still only twelve— and so on May 21 he made Dorothy E. Reid's *Coach into Pumpkin* his first selection for the Yale Series of Younger Poets. His letter to the University Council's Committee on Publications is interesting as an indication of just who made up the literary pantheon in 1925. It reads in part: "Being young [Reid's] work still shows echoes (echoes, so far as I can judge, only of the moderns, Millay, Teasdale, Emily Dickinson, Eleanor Wylie and de la Mare), but the echoes are faint. . . . So far as she is concerned the Victorians do not exist." Today we think of the 1920s as the decade of Eliot and Hart Crane and Marianne Moore, but it didn't seem so at the time. The school of sentiment still commanded the field. Stevens' aphorism, that "sentimentality is a failure of the emotions," was not the abstract attack of a man firing off rounds in the air. It was a pointed response to a competing idea of poetry.

Percy's lead-off selection did not occasion much comment (though the *American Insurance Union Magazine* did run a very nice article), but nonetheless things looked promising for the Yale series in 1925. The editorship had been taken off campus and placed on a professional footing, a publicity campaign was under way, and the new editor had brought fresh energy to the job. Within two years, though, disaster struck. It was a natural disaster, and one of biblical proportions.

"This county is a wreck and a desolation." Percy's letter of June 22, 1927, is written on Red Cross stationery and written in haste. He had his hands full directing the relief effort during the worst flood the Delta region in Mississippi had ever known. Percy's autobiography contains a gripping and appalling chapter about the deluge, "a torrent ten feet deep the size of Rhode Island . . . seventy-five hundred square miles of mill race in which one hundred and twenty thousand human beings and one hundred thousand animals squirmed and bobbed." The bobbing survivors were Percy's responsibility. As chairman of the National Red Cross Mississippi Valley Flood Relief for Washington County, he had somehow to shelter and feed a displaced population of over forty thousand people in his jurisdiction alone. The problem was out of all proportion to anything he had faced before, but he was not raw to the job, for he had helped cope with the flooding of previous years.

With no way of feeding the thousands of scattered survivors, Percy decided to evacuate whomever could be located and persuaded to leave. The white population was rescued first, taken off in a flotilla of borrowed boats to the high ground at Vicksburg. On his own testimony, Percy was preparing to evacuate the black population, too, when he was dissuaded by a group of prominent landowners, chief among them his father. The planters did not want the blacks allowed out of the county, fearing that they would have small reason to return and the Delta plantations would be left without labor. Faced with such pressure, Percy let himself be convinced.

The blacks were moved up on the levee, where such livestock as could be saved had already been transferred. On that narrow strip of dry land, with the swollen river rushing by on one side and the vast floodplain stretching away on the other, something like a refugee camp was formed, as many as thirteen thousand trapped people unprovided with shelter, clean water, or food.

Reports vary on the conditions in that camp, but clearly by any measure they were unhealthy. They were also coercive. When relief supplies eventually arrived, it was the blacks who had to unload the material, and in contrast to practice elsewhere, they were made to do so without pay. They were also forced to work for free in the cleanup of Greenville. But the blacks strung along the levee (the camp extended for seven miles) were not in a helpful mood. Some of them had only recently been conscripted at gunpoint during the futile struggle to stave off the rising water, and here, too, the labor gangs were organized by white guards carrying guns. Furthermore, blacks were not allowed to leave the camp until claimed by the owners of the plantations on which they sharecropped. The situation was explosive, and it came to a head when a black laborer was killed by a white policeman. A riot nearly ensued, and Percy acquired a bad odor in the Northern newspapers.

The great flood of 1927 spurred a major demographic shift, because the black population of Mississippi had finally had enough. Many laborers left to look for work in Northern cities, the very exodus the Percys had hoped to avoid. Those who stayed were worse off than ever, and with the onset of the Depression their situation became desperate. We shall meet these Delta blacks again, in Margaret Walker's Yale Younger Poets volume, *For My People*.

The impact of the 1927 flood on the Yale Series of Younger Poets was considerable. Percy's performance as editor ceased to be characterized by the vigor of his first days on the job. More immediately, though the spring contest that year closed May 1, it was weeks before the manuscripts could get through to Greenville and months before Percy had time to look at them. Contestants began to be curious, then restive, some of them finally irate. One incensed aspirant actually threatened legal action. The press sent

out explanatory notes as the inquiries accumulated, but Percy did
not reach a decision until August 31. Even then he could not quite
make up his mind. He asked the press to pick between two manu-
scripts (the press opted for Mildred Bowers) and set sail for a
lengthy vacation in Japan.

Percy's inability to reach a decision was chronic. The previous
spring he had left it up to the press to choose between Thomas
Hornsby Ferril and Lindley Hubbell, with the result that both were
printed, Hubbell as the winner of the autumn contest. Through-
out his tenure, Percy behaved as if he were assisting the in-house
editors rather than vice-versa, and it often devolved upon the press
to decide which of the several submissions Percy favored might be
declared the winner. One result of this abdication of editorial pre-
rogative was that the press ceased to act upon Percy's recommen-
dations unless they were strong, feeling that there was no point in
losing money just to satisfy lukewarm opinion. Neither of Percy's
two suggestions for the fall 1928 contest was given the go-ahead.

The lack of approval was not only a matter of cost. The press
was becoming unhappy with Percy's editorial taste. Eugene David-
son, assisted by Roberta Yerkes, was by this time the in-house
editor most involved with the series, and his notions were other
than Wilson Follett's or Leslie Soule's. We can see as much in a
brief exchange jotted at the foot of Percy's letter of June 9, 1931,
which recommended either of two poets for possible publication.
"Mr. Davidson—and which do you like better?" is written in one
hand; in the other, "Neither Sir—E.A.D." No winner was declared
for that spring. There had been only one winner in 1930, and there
would be only one winner declared in 1932, Percy's last year as edi-
tor. Thus, the series arrived at its current publication schedule of
one volume per year. Edward Bliss Reed's vision had come to pass,
though more by accident than by direction.

Percy's choices were tentative, and they were also often late.
Like many series editors to follow, Percy suffered bad health, and
illness delayed his decision in the fall contests of 1927 and 1929.
The same happened in the fall of 1931, but by then he saw a way
out of such problems. He resigned in a letter of January 1932,

composed with characteristic self-deprecation. "I have been over-whelmed with a number of worries of all sorts and under the cir-cumstances I do not trust my own literary judgment, so the work has gone slowly," he wrote. "This leads me to think in this harassed and troubled world of ours it will be reasonable to anticipate simi-lar delays in future contests. I therefore believe it is only fair to you and the contestants for me to resign the position as editor of the Series." Paul Engle's volume was Percy's last selection as series edi-tor, and Eugene Davidson's in-house comment regarding it was not flattering: "Many of the poems are commonplace with not much originality of line or of idea . . . various of our Yale undergraduate publications print poetry that is better than this." For whatever rea-son, Percy and the press parted ways, and the Southern gentleman settled down on the floodplain to tend his garden and write his trou-bling memoirs, a record of outer and inner conflicts obliquely faced.

Percy's selections for the series differ little from those of Charl-ton Lewis. To be fair, he did not have an impressive pool of manu-scripts to choose from, and it is not as if he passed over genius. As it is, none of Percy's poets remains well known, although quite a few of them continued to publish and were successful career-ists in their day. Dorothy Reid went on to write children's verse. Thomas Hornsby Ferril published a good deal of poetry and sat on any number of panels and councils, becoming a sort of tribune for Midwestern arts. Paul Engle was a professor at the University of Iowa and founded the Iowa Writer's Workshop, making his mark on American poetry as a teacher. Lindley Hubbell metamorphosed into Hayashi Shuseki, an expert in the repertory of Noh theater and a naturalized citizen of Japan. Ted Olson became a journalist, and his 1970 article in the *New York Times Book Review* offers this clear-eyed appraisal of the series' beginnings: "Those early volumes with their classical allusions and archaic language, were presum-ably the kind of poetry that Yale professors approved and expected young people to write." Percy approved of such poetry, too, the dif-ference between him and Charlton Lewis being that Percy lived long enough to realize he was out of step with the times. He had allowed as much to the press early on: "it may very well be that another editor more in sympathy with radical tendencies in poetry would be better suited to the work you are trying to do."

Upon Percy's resignation, the press was again left to decide just what it wished to make of the Yale Series of Younger Poets. The series still did not have much forward momentum, and the transition between judges had not yet become routine. A reckoning was due, and Eugene Davidson was quick to provide it, writing an extended memo to George Parmly Day which he delivered within a week of Percy's resignation.

At the time, Davidson had no special fondness for the series, and he did not varnish a thing. "The list as a whole has not been a very distinguished one," he stated, pointing out that only four or five out of the thirty writers that had so far been selected had gone on to establish themselves as poets. He wondered whether the series might not best be dropped, but if it was to be continued, he thought that it ought to be officially reduced to one publication per year, and that the volumes ought to be updated in appearance. More important, Davidson also thought that a poet of high reputation should be invited to edit the series. He had four candidates in mind, all of them based in New York or New England: Edwin Arlington Robinson, Stephen Vincent Benét, Louis Untermeyer, and Robert Frost.

George Day was not ready to kill off his brother's brainchild. He was willing to take advice, though, and he allowed Davidson to send off a letter of invitation to the first name on the list, which was Robinson's. This proposal contains the first mention on record of the in-house screening of manuscripts. Davidson suggested that the press weed out the inferior manuscripts from the yearly average of one hundred submissions and forward only the ten or twelve most promising to Robinson. He also inquired whether Robinson would be willing to write a "critical preface of a few pages for each volume you might select, giving your estimate of the poetry and some of your reasons for choosing the manuscript." Robinson was having none of it. In a swift and brief reply, written in a hand so exquisite as to be nearly illegible, he stated crisply that there were a "number of reasons why it would be impossible for me now to take the editorship of the Younger Poets." If the press was seeking a New England sensibility, it had found one, about as sociable as dry ice. A pause of several months ensued while the press sucked burnt fingers, and none of the other illustrious poets on Davidson's list was contacted.

Finally George Day took over, going back to the well. He turned to an old friend and Yale man, Lee Wilson Dodd, who had become an established playwright. Over the years, Dodd had read manuscripts for Yale University Press, and the press had published some of his verse. As of the moment, he was a Yale instructor living in New Haven, and he was thus at hand. He was not, however, in good shape. In fact, he was on his deathbed, from which position he promptly accepted the editorship.

Dodd's letter of acceptance in November 1932 was his only act as series editor. Come spring, Dodd was dead. His determination to take on new assignments regardless of bad health was opportune, though, for had George Parmly Day selected an old friend in better condition the series might well have continued undistinguished and sputtered to a halt the moment the director lost interest. Instead, Davidson had time to collect himself for a second try, and upon Dodd's demise he proposed to the Committee on Publications the names of five candidates for series editor: Archibald MacLeish, William Rose Benét, Stephen Vincent Benét, T. S. Eliot, and Wilbur Cross. The committee approved, but with one change. It moved the third name to the top of the list.

Stephen Vincent Benét was attractive to the committee on at least two counts: he was an author at the peak of his career, and he was closely connected to the university. Benét was Yale class of 1919, and while still an undergraduate he had published a book of verse, *Young Adventure*, with Yale University Press. A novelist and short-story writer as well as a poet, his Civil War epic *John Brown's Body* had won the Pulitzer Prize in 1928. Stephen's older brother, William Rose Benét, was also closely connected to Yale University and Yale University Press; but William Benét would not win his Pulitzer until 1942, and his reputation rested more upon his criticism than his poetry. Both Benéts were at the center of the Northeastern literary establishment—William was among the founders of the *Saturday Review of Literature* and had been married to the late Elinor Wylie—and neither would have found a trip to New Haven an inconvenience. They were the sons of a career army officer and had grown up a bit of everywhere, but they were living in New York City now, and Stephen summered in Connecticut.

In 1933, Stephen Vincent Benét was thirty-five years old. A gentle, balding man, Benét had not inherited a military bearing. Rather, he spoke softly and had a benign air about him. Edward Weismiller, whom Benét made the youngest Yale Younger Poet ever, at the age of nineteen, remembers him this way: "He was a round man, with round glasses on a round face with round cheeks. He smoked non-stop, without ever taking his cigarette out of his mouth. The cigarettes were held precisely at the center of his pursed lips and bobbed as Benét spoke around them, the ash dribbling down the vest of his three piece suit. He smiled a lot, and it seemed to me that everything he said in his kind way was incredibly wise." The round, smiling man was invited to edit the series on June 7, on the same terms offered Robinson, and he was glad to accept.

Within two weeks of Benét's appointment, he and Davidson met in New York to talk matters over. They decided to abandon the old design format for the series, with its board covers and picture of Yale's Harkness Tower, and go to a jacketed cloth binding in a larger size. Benét also told Davidson that he would try to improve the submissions. "He plans to write letters to various literary editors that he hopes will enable us to get better material for the Series, and also some publicity," Davidson reported to Day.

Benét's letters got results. The level of talent among the contestants skyrocketed. The submissions in the spring of 1934 included the manuscripts not only of that year's eventual winner, James Agee, but also of Muriel Rukeyser, May Sarton, and Lincoln Kirstein. There is no way to be sure just whom Benét contacted in his effort to elicit such work, but it seems likely that Agee's submission was prompted by Archibald MacLeish. (Benét certainly knew it was coming, because he wrote the press asking that someone keep an eye out for it.) In any case, the foreword to Agee's volume was written by MacLeish, a guest appearance for which Benét himself offered to pay. Benét, who as series editor was a benevolent presence, wished to put money into the poet's pocket, too, and he told the press he wanted one hundred dollars of his fee given to Agee as a cash award. Davidson balked. The Yale Younger Poets prize had never included cash, the volumes were published without any money asked of the authors, the royalties were up to professional standards, the fact of publication made poets happy enough, the editors worked hard and deserved their payment. But Benét insisted he could do without the full fee, saying, "After all, I'm old and tough." Faced with mild determination, Davidson relented. He supposed that an award might be created to account for the hundred dollars, and he suggested it be named for the benefactor. Benét didn't like the sound of that. "If you call it the Benét Prize, I'll feel as if I ought to have ivy planted on me," he wrote back, preferring to remain anonymous. So it was that a fiction was arrived at, whereby the Yale Younger Poets throughout Benét's tenure (and afterwards in MacLeish's) received part of the editor's fee but were told that the gift derived from "The Henry Weldon Barnes Memorial Fund." Davidson never did like having such generosity enforced upon the press, and each year thereafter he asked whether the editor chose to persist in giving money away.

One hundred dollars the richer, James Agee had his Yale book published in September 1934. *Permit Me Voyage* differs from anything prior to it in the series. It is one of those first books of verse which are interesting without being very good, for although none of the poetry stands up today, one can still see the great ambition in it. Agee's is a large book of poetry, if not a large poetic talent.

Large poetic talent was not long in coming. A letter of July 6 or 7, 1935 (Benét seems to have lived in a bit of a fog and was often unsure of the date) finds the editor asking about a manuscript he had seen the year before and would like to have back again. Benét had been forwarded seventy-three manuscripts (about half the total submitted), having told the press to send him all submissions that were not simply unprofessional, but he had not seen anything to excite him. "So I'm trying to get the girl whom I thought of as second last year to put her back in again," he writes. The girl whose manuscript he retrieved was Muriel Rukeyser.

Rukeyser was twenty-two years old and on fire. Born and bred in New York City, she embraced the startling possibilities offered by the machine age, and she had a real affection for urban landscape. That affection included an intimate knowledge of the city's composition. Asked in childhood the meaning of that character-building word *grit*, she had answered: "Number-four gravel." As a writer, she pursued all avenues at once. Captivated by the young medium of the movies, she wrote enthusiastic film reviews. Socially aware, she wrote angry poems about lynchings and the Scottsboro boys. Politically active in a politicized age, she contributed to such publications as *Labor Defender* and *Proletarian Literature*. And it didn't stop at the typewriter. Rukeyser pursued ideas actively. She actually went to Scottsboro and was arrested; and her Yale volume, *Theory of Flight*, is based in part on experience gained in training for her pilot's license.

Theory of Flight is the first book in the series that can still be read with genuine interest today. It crackles with energy and is fervid with both political and artistic commitment. The aggressive product of an aggressive intelligence, Rukeyser's poetry embodies Eliot's tenet that modern poetry must often be difficult. Oddly punctuated, long and long-lined, the poems charge on, their sharp imagery and bald pronouncement giving them a tone somewhere between manifesto and lyric. *Theory of Flight* is a modernist landmark, one of the first books to combine the manner of Eliot and Pound with Leftist politics, and it made an impact. Rukeyser is the first Yale Younger Poet whose work was to exert significant influence on a subsequent generation of writers. Her Yale volume is one of the better books she ever produced, and her career as a whole inspired such poets as Adrienne Rich and Anne Sexton. Rukeyser's work may be understood as a bridge from the public politics of the thirties to the personal politics of the sixties. And right from the start, Rukeyser's work drew attention. *Theory of Flight* is one of the books that put the Yale Series of Younger Poets on the map.

Rukeyser's book sold over five hundred copies within half a year, which was modest but nonetheless a distinct improvement over earlier sales in the series. The series' sales continued to go up, too. Benét could appreciate poetry that espoused art for art's sake,

THEORY OF FLIGHT   BY MURIEL RUKEYSER

WITH A FOREWORD BY STEPHEN VINCENT BENÉT

NEW HAVEN · YALE UNIVERSITY PRESS · 1935

but his own taste ran to verse that was willing to dirty its hands with the number-four gravel of this world. He liked poetry that involved itself in human struggle, and that taste proved popular. Five of the ten Yale Younger Poets volumes Benét chose went into multiple editions, and some of them sold in the thousands. Rukeyser's book sold more than fourteen hundred copies, and Benét's final selection would sell over five thousand copies, making its author Yale's best-selling poet for two decades.

That best-selling poet was Margaret Walker, whose *For My People* would prove to be another influential volume in the series. Walker, the daughter of a Methodist minister, was born in Birmingham, Alabama, and had grown up both there and in New Orleans. She left the Deep South, however, to gain an education, and she went a long way in pursuit of it. She attended Northwestern, graduating in 1935, and several years later she applied to the University of Iowa's Department of Graduate English. She wanted to be a writer, and she had heard that at Iowa one could earn a degree by substituting a manuscript of fiction or poetry for an academic thesis. Her application was accepted, and she traveled out to Iowa City in the fall of 1939. There her arrival came as a surprise to some. When the dean of the School of Letters first encountered the young black woman, he was taken aback. "*You're* Margaret Walker?" "Yes." Pause. "Well, all I can say is you write a good letter."

Walker was in the school, but staying in was another matter. She had little money and less idea how to pay her tuition. Help came from Paul Engle, by then a professor at Iowa, who was determined that Walker stay on. Knowing that her father was a minister, Engle talked the local Methodist church into lending her money. When that ran out, he arranged for her to get a job on campus funded by the National Youth Administration. The monthly salary came to thirty dollars, which still left Walker eighteen dollars short of the tuition fee, but her mother made up the difference, and she was able to continue.

Walker wanted to write, and what she was writing then were poems of protest. Using an extended line reminiscent of the Bible, she described the harsh conditions that racism and poverty had created for her people, the black population of the Deep South. The poems no longer quite shock, but they remain disturbing, and Engle, for one, was uncomfortable with them. He told his protégé that her work was "heavy," and he suggested that she write some poems about folklore using ballad measure. Fifty years later, the suggestion sounds all too predictable, and it must be said that Walker's long-lined poems of prophetic anger are the ones that have stood up best. But Walker found a freedom in the lighter verse—if nothing else, it gave her time off from her more weighty concerns—and she has continued to employ the ballad form in subsequent books.

While at Iowa, Walker submitted her manuscript for the Yale Younger Poets prize repeatedly. By this time, Benét had succeeded in drawing attention to the series, and the contest was becoming a magnet for poetic hopefuls. The literary community looked forward to the announcement of the Yale prize with interest, and winning the award guaranteed attention. In 1939, for example, an editor at *The Atlantic Monthly* wrote to Benét soliciting work sight unseen, explaining, "I have been so constantly impressed and delighted with the volumes in this series, that I am confident any poet you choose would be worth presenting to our readers."

Walker had submitted a manuscript to the series before, in 1937. She needed a favorable response from an established press in order to earn her master's degree from the Iowa English department. Because of this requirement, she kept resubmitting her book, in 1939, 1940, 1941. She received some positive letters from Benét, and on the basis of his favorable comments she did get her degree. Still, the book kept coming back, and Walker grew discouraged. She began to suspect that Yale University Press was not interested in publishing a black writer, regardless of Benét's opinion. In 1942, she did not enter her manuscript.

Meanwhile, in Connecticut, Benét was unhappy with what he was reading. He was summering in Stonington that year (the press liked to describe him as driving down to New Haven with his laundry under one arm and a satchel of manuscripts under the other . . . it may even have happened once), sifting through the submissions. Once again, there were some capable writers among the contestants—Jean Garrigue among others—but none of the material struck Benét as outstanding. Where was that book with the "Delta" poem he remembered from the previous year? He decided to prompt a resubmission, as he had done with Muriel Rukeyser. He sent a telegram to Iowa City, got the manuscript he wanted, and then telegraphed the press in turn. He was mailing in his selection, a book by Margaret Walker: "I have recalled it as this year's lot was not promising."

Published in October 1942, the forty-first book in the series, Walker's *For My People* went through six cloth editions with Yale and has been in print elsewhere ever since. Like Rukeyser's volume, *For My People* has had an impact on a wide spectrum of writers. Readers often react to Walker's book as they do to Whitman's *Leaves of Grass* (a book that strongly influenced her), feeling that if it speaks *for* one people, yet it speaks *to* people everywhere, engaging each of us on grounds at once aesthetic and moral. *For My People* is standard in black studies curricula, but writers involved in the agon of social change in all areas have taken it to heart. Walker's book is expressly concerned with racial constraint, but it has traveled beyond ethnic barriers.

Walker came east after her book was accepted, visiting the press in New Haven and Benét in New York. She didn't feel entirely comfortable at the press—she still wasn't sure her book had been welcome—but Benét was a different matter. He had asked her to stop by his home in the East Seventies of Manhattan early one afternoon, but Walker was rarely on time for anything, and on this occasion she was spending the day with some friends from college. She arrived late, several hours late, and it was only years afterward that she learned Benét had planned a party in her honor. The other guests had long departed, but Benét asked her in without a question. He offered her a drink, but the minister's daughter declined, so he decided to break the ice by showing her round the place. It was a writer's lair, with books stacked floor to ceiling in every room, a look at where a life devoted to literature might lead one. Later, as they went over her poems together, Walker noticed his hands as he turned the pages. His letters had been written in an unsteady script, and now she knew why, for his fingers were painfully twisted with arthritis. After they reviewed her work, it was time to go, and the magical afternoon was over. Walker left feeling that she had not just made an important connection but had found a friend as well. As Weismiller had discovered before her, Benét was both wise and well intentioned. She looked forward to meeting with him many times again, but she never did. Benét died five months later, in March 1943.

Stephen Vincent Benét was editor of the Yale Series of Younger Poets for a decade, and he utterly transformed it. He found the series a publisher's hobby given over to inconsequential work, and he left it the most prominent venue for new poets in the country. When he arrived, the contest was attracting almost no entries of note; when he left, talented poets with real prospects were submitting work every year. Where the Yale volumes had received haphazard attention, they now were eagerly anticipated and reviewed in major newspapers and quarterlies as a matter of course. Before Benét took over, the work published in the Yale series consisted of faint imitations of standard styles, those of Whitman and Frost at best, those of Sara Teasdale or Rupert Brooke at the too frequent worst. By contrast, the work Benét ushered into print was usually up-to-the-minute in both manner and content. None of this happened by accident. Benét had known what he wanted from the start. In the early 1930s, the young poet of greatest reputation writing in English was W. H. Auden, and the politically engaged work Auden was then producing was exactly the sort Benét found of interest. In a letter to Eugene Davidson, dated with typical imprecision "July 3rd or 4th" of 1934, Benét had written: "I don't see why, eventually, the Series shouldn't be something in which all the budding Spenders and Audens would want to publish *first*." Benét died young, at forty-four, but not before he had achieved his purpose. The series in particular and American poetry as a whole are much the richer for Benét's devotion. Other and even more famous editors and books have come to the series since, but the Yale Series of Younger Poets stands as Stephen Vincent Benét's monument.

Of the ten poets Benét picked, almost all became successful writers. Shirley Barker, his first choice, wrote a good deal of fiction. James Agee is well known for *Now Let Us Praise Famous Men,* his text accompanying Walker Evans' photographs, as well as for writing several screenplays, including *The African Queen.* Edward Weismiller has published poetry and also a novel: *The Serpent Sleeping,* a spy story based on Weismiller's experience in the O.S.S., is a tale of compromise and betrayal that anticipates John Le Carré. Joy Davidman wrote novels, poetry, and film scripts; she has gained a measure of attention because of her marriage to C. S. Lewis, depicted in his memoir *Surprised by Joy* and subsequently in the film *Shadowlands.* Reuel Denney became quite a prominent sociologist, a co-author, with David Riesman, of *The Lonely Crowd.* Norman Rosten wrote for radio when radio was the big time, as well as publishing poems, essays, novels, and a memoir of Marilyn Monroe. Jeremy Ingalls has published four more books of poetry, along with stories, essays, and a play in verse; yet another of the Yale Younger Poets who have specialized in Asian studies, she has also translated Chinese and Japanese literature.

The Yale volumes Benét chose reflect his own preference for poetry that is engaged in the hurly-burly of human affairs, but they also show the stamp of their impassioned and ominous times. The thirties were a decade swept by political movements and shadowed by the gathering clouds of war, and much of that fever and sense of crisis made its way into these books. Rukeyser and Davidman both espouse the political left; Denny and Ingalls each show an acute awareness of imminent bloodshed; and Walker warns that cataclysm overseas will soon be mirrored by social upheaval at home. Benét's Yale Younger Poets are energetic and opinionated, and some of their opinion is extreme; yet for all their many fierce ideas, the group forms a whole. They have an integrity beyond that of editorial taste, a coherence imposed by overwhelming events. Even so abstracted an intellect as Wallace Stevens acknowledged this imposition: "In the presence of the violent reality of war, consciousness takes the place of imagination." Benét's choices have been described as popular poets, and in a sense they are, but they might be better described as poets unavoidably conscious of a violent reality.

That violent reality was long past the sticking point by March 1943. The Russians had just retaken Stalingrad, and in the Pacific, U.S. Marines were mopping up on Guadalcanal. Stateside, there was a war on, and Yale University Press was feeling its effects. The Depression had been no kinder to the publishing industry than it had to the rest of the economy, and the financial condition of the press had been weak even before the war began. Recent volumes in the Yale Series of Younger Poets had sold comparatively well, but even so the series was not a moneymaker. The war revived the economy in many areas, but academic publishing was not one of them. For one thing, paper was in short supply: rationed, expensive, often of poor quality. For another, the reading public had other claims on its attention. The Printing Office of the press was thousands of dollars in the red and would not show a profit again until after the war. Moreover, the press management would soon be at a crossroads, because George Parmly Day was approaching the age of retirement. Against this background, Day, Donaldson, and Davidson, the in-house triumvirate responsible for the Younger Poets Series, wanted the next series editor to be a sure thing. Benét had clearly done a fine job, and they hoped to find someone as like Benét as possible.

Candidates were not lacking. There were even volunteers. Within days of Benét's death, Oscar Williams sent Davidson a letter asking to be considered for the job. That so aggressive a careerist as Williams was interested in the position is proof in itself that the Yale series had by this time acquired a considerable reputation. There were volunteers, but to get the person they wanted, Donaldson and Davidson had to exercise persuasion. They wanted Archibald MacLeish, and he was an extremely busy man. MacLeish had been a close friend of Benét, graduating a few years ahead of him at Yale, and he was on a first-name basis with both Donaldson and Davidson, also Yale alumni. MacLeish looked like a promising choice. Like Percy, he had served in the previous world war. Like Percy and Benét both, he had been published by Yale University

Press. Unlike his predecessors, however, MacLeish was very much a public man. In fact, with the exception of Robert Frost, Archibald MacLeish was as close to being an American poet laureate as one could get in those years. He had won a Pulitzer Prize in 1932 (for his epic poem *Conquistador*) and had traveled around the country throughout the decade warning against the growing threat of fascism. President Roosevelt had taken to him, and he had been appointed Librarian of Congress in 1939. Four years later he still held that position, but he was also serving as director of the newly created Office of Facts and Figures. That meant he was essentially directing American propaganda during the war. (The new director may have created a Younger Poets connection at the Office of Facts and Figures: both Ted Olson and Jacques Le Clercq were among its operatives.) All this left MacLeish with little time to spare, a fact he made abundantly clear when his old friends in New Haven pressed him into service.

MacLeish was first urged to take the position of series editor in May 1943, but it was July before he could be persuaded to accept. When he did take the job, it was on a year-to-year basis, and he refused to see any more manuscripts than absolutely necessary. He told Davidson to send on only those submissions which he himself would be glad to see win the prize. "I should think that ought to have an astringent effect on the forwarding apparatus," he said. That it did. There were almost one hundred submissions in 1943 (about half had come from military camps), and only twelve went on to MacLeish's office at the Library of Congress. MacLeish wrote back complaining of the "millions of pages of manuscripts" he had received. He complained, too, that none of the material he had been sent was very good.

MacLeish offered up three possibilities (à la Percy), asking the press to choose one. The manuscript the press favored was a book-length poem in a style reminiscent of E. A. Robinson. Despite some grumbling about the "staleness" of the verse, hardly a compelling quality, on August 27 MacLeish gave his approval. The volume was already in the planning stages when MacLeish wrote again, hoping that things could be put on hold. He had just heard from a former winner of the Yale Younger Poets prize, Muriel Rukeyser, who recommended the work of a fellow aviator, a Navy pilot by the name of William Meredith. A letter went off to Meredith, who was on active duty on the West Coast. A couple of months went by. The press began to get nervous. Then, in early November, MacLeish sent in the new manuscript, asking for unanimous approval.

Meredith's manuscript was quite short, and all concerned felt that it was uneven. MacLeish summarized his reservations in one sentence: "There are traces of the sterilizing influence of Mr. Auden in some of the earlier poems which I deplore." But he wanted the book, and when a letter of endorsement came in from Allen Tate, the press was convinced. Meredith, stationed in Seattle at the time, was named the winner, and his *Love Letter from an Impossible Land* was published as MacLeish's first series selection in April 1944. It had to be cleared by Naval Intelligence beforehand, but the young pilot's poetry got by the censors.

Meredith's little book (its brevity prompted a return to the smaller format of the initial volumes in the series) sold out its first printing and went into a second before the year was out. All in all, the early indicators on MacLeish as an editor were not bad. If he did not have much time, it had been time enough, and he was warming to the work. He certainly knew the field, and he was ready to search out strong manuscripts. But then, as had happened with Percy, events intervened. MacLeish became distracted, and he soon ceased to function as editor almost entirely.

In Percy's case, the distraction had been the Mississippi River. In MacLeish's it was government service, for in 1944 he was appointed assistant secretary of state. MacLeish had had little time before—a guest lectureship at Cambridge University had strained his capacities even further—but now he had no time at all. He traveled incessantly, and he was incommunicado for weeks, even months at a time. When he did write, his letters were no more than notes, often consisting of one scrawled sentence initialed in place of a signature. The editors at the press did their best to adapt to the circumstances, but it wasn't much use. Mindful of his complaints the previous year, they sent MacLeish only six manuscripts in 1944, and Davidson assured him that there was no need to read them all "word for word." MacLeish favored Charles Butler's *Cut Is the Branch,* but once again he hesitated, asking the opinion of the press and deferring his decision. At last, with the fall catalog deadline all but gone by, MacLeish agreed that Butler's book might as well win.

Charles Butler had sent in his work many times to the series during the Benét years, but he had not submitted his book on this occasion. Instead, it had been submitted for him by friends, because he was serving as a staff sergeant in England. It was these friends who acquiesced when the press wished to shorten the book, and it was they who mentioned, a few weeks after the winner had been declared, that Charles Butler was not quite so young a Younger Poet as had been thought. He was thirty-six, and the age limit was thirty. Butler, informed by his friends of his selection and his apparent ineligibility, wrote a rueful letter to the press, assuming the worst. He was resigned to withdrawing his manuscript, but the press did not wish him to do so, as the winner had already been announced. Besides, it had been hard enough to get one decision out of MacLeish, and no one wished to repeat the process unnecessarily. Butler's volume, a collection of thoughtful and subdued antiwar poems, was published as scheduled, with no birth date given on the book jacket. The contest rules were evolving again, by accident, as usual.

The year 1944 had been a difficult one for the series, with much delay and indecision, but 1945 was impossible. MacLeish was on the road virtually without stop, and although he was sent only five entries that year, he simply could not get to them. Spring became summer, and the summer went by. So did autumn. As they had back in the flood year of 1927, contestants complained. After six months of no news, one exasperated finalist demanded his submission back, but MacLeish couldn't be reached to return it. At long last, in late November, MacLeish contacted the press, only to say that he hadn't yet gotten to the manuscripts but hoped to soon. Soon, however, was not until March of the following year, when he chose Eve Merriam. Long before then, the university had concluded that a change was in order. In the Council's Committee on Publications meeting of January 14, 1946, it was decided that as MacLeish "does not seem able to give the necessary attention to the Yale Series of Younger Poets, we should arrange to get a new editor."

This left MacLeish's friends at the press in a delicate position, faced with the duty of sacking the man they had begged to hire in the first place. Donaldson grasped the nettle on April 10, suggesting in a letter to "Arch" that with Merriam's book under way, it might perhaps be "the proper time for me to raise with you the question of whether you wish to continue as Editor of the Series. I feel I did something of a blackjacking job when I persuaded you to take over, and therefore I want to open the way for you to withdraw now if that is really what you feel you should do." It was a very graceful pink slip, and as a professional diplomat, MacLeish was not slow to take the point. He bowed out immediately, so that by the end of the month the series was once more without an outside editor.

MacLeish served as series editor for only three years, and he served haphazardly. His name in itself surely attracted continuing attention to the Yale series, but beyond that bare fact, it is difficult to assess his contribution. The three poets MacLeish chose appear to have shared little besides his approval, and they went on to very disparate careers. William Meredith has become one of the better-known poets of his generation, the winner of both a Pulitzer Prize and the National Book Award. Eve Merriam grew successful as an author of children's verse, was a vocal advocate of the international left, and wrote a landmark text in the field of women's studies, *Growing Up Female in America.* Charles Butler returned from the war to continue his work as a librarian in West Virginia, where he wrote one novel, *Follow Me Ever* (1950). What MacLeish might have done for the Younger Poets Series under ideal circumstances is a matter of conjecture, though one may suppose along with the press that he would have followed Benét's lead. As it was, circumstances were anything but ideal, and his tenure had little impact on the series other than to make the press wary of inattentive editors.

Once again, it was time to draw up a list of editorial candidates, and this time the scope of the search widened. The list of possible editors included the leading critics, publishers, and poets of the time: John Crowe Ransom, Edmund Wilson, and Cleanth Brooks; John Chipman Farrar; Louise Bogan, Marianne Moore, Robert Frost, and W. H. Auden. George Parmly Day was no longer director of the press, but he still put in his vote. Day's was a nostalgia candidate: Chauncey Tinker, a recently retired Yale professor from the era of Lewis, Pierce, and Dodd. There was no going back to those days, though. The series had outgrown the Yale campus, and the Council's Committee on Publications recognized it. The committee reached a decision quickly—by May 6—and the object seems to have been to engage the practicing poet with the most intellectual authority possible. That was Auden, and Davidson was given permission to contact him. He wrote the next day, offering the position on the same terms as those extended to Benét and MacLeish. Auden accepted at once, saying in a letter of May 10, "I am not at all sure that a poet is the best judge of his contemporaries, but I'm willing to have a shot at it if you are."

Born in Yorkshire, England, in 1907, Wystan Hugh Auden had been living in the United States for seven years and was just in the process of becoming an American citizen. Now based in New York City, he was in a period of midlife transition, not only of nationality, but also of creed and artistry. He had been educated at Oxford and was a prominent Marxist in the thirties, but he had abandoned that movement and had recently returned to the Christian church. He had written some of the most sophisticated verse ever to articulate political views, but lately he had begun to argue in favor of a private poetry of therapeutic frivolity. The author by now of eleven books (his first, entitled simply *Poems,* had been published by T. S. Eliot at Faber & Faber), he wrote essays, plays, and opera libretti as well as poetry. On the basis of that output, he had at age thirty-nine already established a reputation as one of the most important authors the century had so far produced. Of medium height, with lank hair and a horsy face, like Benét Auden was a chain smoker. His features had lately begun to show the smoker's wrinkles that would deepen dramatically as his series tenure progressed. A bon mot that circulated during these years described him memorably: an ant crawling over a face like that would break a leg.

Like most editors the Yale series has had, Auden had no sooner taken the job than he began to worry about the amount of work involved. He asked Davidson to send him no more than six manuscripts to consider, and he complained vigorously about the introduction requirement he had agreed to only a week before: "Personally, I am *very* much against the critical estimate business and would like to see the policy changed. These introductions always sound awful, and the whole idea that a new poet should be introduced by an older one as if he were a debutante or a new face cream, deplorable and false."

The press held its ground, though. If Benét and MacLeish could do it, so could the new editor. And so, over his objections, Auden was brought to do a task he would accomplish spectacularly well. Auden's forewords are in themselves some of the best writing to come out of the Yale series, and they are far more ambitious than those of his predecessors. The forewords written by Benét and MacLeish do contain their share of insight and apothegm, but for the most part the two were content to describe the poetry being offered for sale and provide some background information about its author. Not so Auden, who had been a schoolmaster in his youth, taught seminars for much of his life, and even in conversation tended to hold forth in a learned fashion. Auden preferred to lecture. Reading the forewords to his Yale volumes one can almost hear the ferule rapping the desk to bring the class to attention: "Every poem, be it big or small, simple or complex, is recognizably a world. What we call *the* world we infer to be a world, but no individual can perceive it as such; for each of us it is broken into fragments, some of which he knows quite well, some a little, some not at all, and even of those he knows best he can never truthfully say 'I know what it is' but only 'I know what it was.'"

Auden uses his Yale introductions to give a short course in poetry. One foreword treats of the pastoral genre in our technological age. Another outlines the attractions and dangers of surreali.

Others investigate the role of myth in art, the benefits of formal constraint, the relation of poetry to music. Anyone coming to verse for the first time (or even for the second time, as Auden might have said), would do well to prepare for the experience by reading through these little essays beforehand. There is, however, one Auden selection that does not carry an instructive foreword, and that is his first: *Poems,* by Joan Murray. Perhaps it took him a year to get over his irritation with the requirement and see the possibilities in it instead. Or maybe it was a case of due decorum, because the first poet he introduced was dead.

As happened regularly with editors newly appointed to the series, Auden was unimpressed with the poetry the press had waiting for him. He had not been on the job long enough to attract submissions in his own right, and the ten manuscripts he took with him to Fire Island that summer left him cold. Fortunately, he had an alternative. "I have just heard that the poems of Joan Murray which I told you about are available and, in my opinion, they are the best we have," he wrote Davidson. "May I have your permission to choose them? She died in 1942 at the age of 23."

Actually, she died at twenty-four. Such misinformation is typical concerning Murray, for she is a mysterious figure, one of the most accomplished and least known poets the Yale series has produced. She was born in London in 1917 during one of the dirigible air raids which left that city the wasted landscape of Eliot's poem. Via Paris and Canada she arrived in New York City, where she studied acting, dance, and poetry. There is an impression among her surviving contemporaries that she was in Auden's poetry class at the New School. In any case, when she died of complications from a rheumatic heart in January 1942, her papers were left in the possession of her mother, who, wishing to see them published but unable to bear the emotional distress of handling them, gave the papers to a middle-aged family friend named Grant Code. A poet himself, Code cut down Murray's bundle of poetry and prose to a manuscript of verse and contacted Auden. He thought Auden might want Murray's book for the Yale series, but he insisted that he be retained as titular editor. Admiring the work and having some affection for the memory of his dead compatriot, Auden did indeed want the book. He didn't mind having Code act as an intermediary, either, because he'd had a taste of Mrs. Murray. In fact, he recommended that the press avoid her, too: "From what I know of Mama, I would advise you confidentially to deal with her through Mr. Code."

It seemed a bit odd to print a posthumous Younger Poet—it could hardly be said to provide fair promise for the future—but the press let Auden have his way. Auden seemed bent on making a lot of changes. He wanted the series opened up to any poet writing in English, with no limitation on age or nationality. The Council's Committee on Publications eventually decided to extend the contest's age limitation to forty. Given Butler's publication, the change simply ratified existing facts, but it made sense regardless. American poets do not as a rule mature early, and any restriction that would have disqualified, say, Whitman (who first published at age thirty-six) could well be dispensed with. The committee also agreed that Auden could look for a book in England, if he wished, though nothing ever came of it. Beyond that, the committee drew the line. The contest would stay one for first books, and it would remain one for younger, or relatively younger, poets.

Meanwhile, the press discovered that Auden had been right about Mama Murray. She made difficulties, and she would not make up her mind. Now she couldn't bear the pain of her daughter's poems going into print; now she could bear it, and thought that the poems deserved lots of money; and now she was upset about just which poems were to be included. She also stood upon her dignity: the flap copy for the book describes Murray's mother as a "diseuse." Auden sympathized, but was not surprised. As he told Davidson, "Beautiful girls who die young can cause an awful lot of trouble. (Mrs. M. once wrote me a letter accusing me of having killed her.)"

The money question was solved by the usual fiction of a one-hundred-dollar award from the Barnes Fund, which was turned over to Mrs. Murray. (It was the last year the Yale Younger Poets prize carried a cash award, because the money was no longer coming out of the editor's fee.) Publication went forward, though not without complications. Grant Code, as he explains in a companion introduction to Auden's, had performed a good deal of surgery on Murray's sheaf. He provided titles, added punctuation, altered spelling, inserted a "colorless connective" when he thought necessary, added words where he discovered a "hiatus in meaning between lines," selected among variant words and versions of poems, and then arranged the whole. Code's own poetry demonstrates that the talent that makes Murray's work so compelling was all hers, but Code must have invested a lot of time in preparing the manuscript. Certainly he invested enough emotion in the project to take a proprietary interest, because he took exaggerated offense at Auden's suggested cuts. His letters became arias of injured self-importance, and eventually Auden withdrew from the squabble. He let Code have the poems he cried out for, but when it came to Code's notes and biographical essay, Auden simply refused.

Code had worked up something he called "A Faun Surmising," a biographical piece that combined his own commentary with material culled from Murray's letters and journals. Auden was no fan of author biography (see his introduction to the Signet edition of Shakespeare's *Sonnets*), believing that it derived from prurient interest and more often distorted than illuminated literary accomplishment. That went in spades for Code's notes. He told Davidson that the notes were not to appear in the book, "because—entre nous—they make me very sick."

Auden's first selection appeared in May 1947, and his reputation ensured that the book was reviewed. In fact, the books published during Auden's tenure were reviewed in all the best places: *Poetry*, the *New Yorker*, the *New York Times Book Review*, *Partisan Review*, the *Hudson Review*. In Murray's case, reviewers lamented the poet's early death, but the work mostly left them nonplussed. "Good taste and good sense are clearly indicated . . . still the poetry gives the impression of being unborn," wrote Milton Crane in the *New York Times*. The lukewarm reception might have been expected, because Murray's book is one of the most demanding in the entire series. The author of these poems is thinking all the time, and the reader must have patience and a penetrating mind to take much away from the work. The poems in it ask to be reread, but they can seem all the stranger the second time through. The transition from MacLeish's last choice (Merriam) to Auden's first is so abrupt that those following the series (the staff at Yale University Press included) may be pardoned if they were disoriented. Series editors have sometimes used the forewords to their initial selections to announce their intentions (Merrill and Dickey were to do so), but Auden did nothing of the kind. He didn't have to. Joan Murray's poetry, intellectual and uncompromising, served notice for him.

If Davidson and the rest of the press had found Murray's book and Auden himself difficult to get a handle on, things were not going to get any easier. In the summer of 1947, Auden was again vacationing on Fire Island, where the press sent him the manuscripts of twelve finalists. But as in the previous year, Auden was unmoved by the submissions. Davidson allowed that Auden was not obliged to choose a winner at all, and that as with editors past, he was free to hunt up a submission if he so desired. He did, and the manuscript he brought in was by Robert Horan, a young poet from Oakland who was now living in Mount Kisco, New York. Auden probably learned of Horan through his opera connections. Horan was a friend of Gian Carlo Menotti and Samuel Barber, sharing a house with them for awhile. Regardless of the provenance, though, Auden was quite enthusiastic about the work: "It seems to me to be quite a find," he wrote when he sent in the manuscript. Horan was a member of a group known as the Activists, to which Auden had taken a shine.

Activism was a tiny movement in American poetry, but it made its mark on the Yale series. The movement was an intimate affair, consisting of friends and family who had gathered around Lawrence Hart, a professor of poetry at Mills College and later at Berkeley. The group first met at night school, in a high-school extension course that Hart was teaching, and it was made up primarily of Hart's wife, Jeanne McGahey, their son John, Rosalie Moore (related to McGahey by marriage), and Robert Horan. Professor Hart believed in the poetry of intensity, to be achieved through formidable diction, and his model was Hart Crane. The Activists imitated Crane to differing degrees (Horan rather more, Moore rather less), but taken as a whole their movement represents one of Crane's principal legacies. Auden was impressed. He became acquainted with Lawrence Hart and would eventually visit the Bay Area to meet the Activists and give a lecture at Mills. In 1947 he went out of his way to select Horan's book, and the following year he choose Rosalie Moore's. Moore had submitted her manuscript through the regular channels, but surely she had been stimulated by Auden's interest and Horan's success.

Moore's book was, on the face of it, the most difficult that Auden had yet chosen. Even its title was puzzling: *The Grasshopper's Man.* Eugene Davidson was becoming impatient. The work Auden favored was flagrantly inaccessible, and the Yale volumes, which had sold in the thousands in the era of Benét and MacLeish, were now selling miserably again. Auden himself was not very accessible, for that matter. Benét had been willing to work with the press on a footing of friendship, but Auden was not so disposed. He resisted Davidson's effort to shift their correspondence to a casual tone, replying to such overtures with succinct formality. Auden's manner was chilly, and he was hard to get ahold of, too. It had been thought that, living as he did in New York, his proximity to New Haven would be advantageous. But he never seemed to be in residence when the contest needed to be judged. He had been off on Fire Island two years running, and now things had just gotten worse. As of 1948, Auden began to spend the spring and summer on Ischia, in the Bay of Naples, so that correspondence and manuscripts had to cross the Atlantic and navigate the Italian post to reach him. Worst of all, he didn't seem to be giving the Yale series much attention. The new editor threatened to be Archibald MacLeish all over again, but with a taste for impenetrable and unsalable work. Davidson began to think Auden was an experiment that had failed. By the end of 1948, it seemed time for a change.

The first thing Davidson did in preparing his putsch was to contact Louise Bogan, who edited poetry at both Scribner's and the *New Yorker.* She had been one of the candidates considered before Auden's appointment, and she was Davidson's choice to succeed him. He wrote to ask if she would meet him over lunch and discuss the Yale series. Bogan's reply is a classic, full of the dash and glamour one likes to attribute to the big town in that era: "Tuesday, December 28th at 12:30 under the Biltmore clock will be fine. — I wear black."

The luncheon took place, and Bogan behaved well. Rather than undermine Auden, she praised him as an "authentic genius" incapable of choosing a poor book, and she said she would take the job only if he had first voluntarily stepped down. Davidson returned to New Haven and reported on the meeting the next day. His memo not only describes events in progress but also gives an overview of the Yale series up to this time:

> We have had in the past three main types of editors: the lyric in William Alexander Percy, what might be called the popular in Steve Benét, and now this example of the experimental but well-established school of which Auden is undoubtedly the leading exponent among the younger people. My criticism of his choices, as I told Miss Bogan, is that they seem to stem from a relatively small proportion of his time and creative energy. His last choice, for example, was merely the best of the two or three manuscripts we weeded out of those submitted, and while both his earlier choices were manuscripts he himself brought in, we are under the impression that he is doing what for him is a perfunctory job. Miss Bogan saw that point, I believe, and would be willing, if matters could be amicably arranged with Auden, to take over the editorship.

With Bogan's provisional acceptance in hand, the game now was to convince Auden that he wished to resign. Davidson bided his time, waiting for the moment when Auden's distractions would be self-evident. In March 1949, with the contest due to get under way again and Auden about to head overseas for another extended stay, he asked for a meeting in New York. Auden said he had five days free at the end of the month before leaving for Ischia, and Davidson made his appointment.

After lunch, they ended up in Auden's apartment, at 7 Cornelia Street in lower Manhattan. The confrontation that ensued seems to have been a comic affair. Auden's living habits were famously filthy.

Friends of the time (Harold Norse and Howard Griffin) describe his bed as "an unmade army cot" and the apartment itself as "small and squalid, boxlike, lit by garish overhead lightbulbs in a tacky chandelier at the center of the dusty ceiling." Auden once said that if young people could be trained to keep an orderly desk, "everything else would follow." The avuncular advice becomes cause for amusement when given a peek at his own: "a smallish worktable, overflowing in monumental disarray; books, magazines, manuscripts, cigarette cartons and packs, ashtrays choked with butts, a portable typewriter." Dishes piled up in the sink, books lay scattered on the floor, and dirty laundry was strewn about. Compounding the usual mess was the fact that Auden was in the middle of packing for a six months' absence. There were boxes of books. Boxes of recordings. *All* his clothes were spread out. Those were the days of ocean liners and steamer trunks. The scene begins to resemble something out of the Marx Brothers.

MacLeish had been ready to step down, but Auden was not, and Davidson couldn't say what he wanted straight out without in effect firing Auden and losing Bogan in the process. He appears to have tacked toward the mark, saying that the series must maintain high standards and that all involved must be careful that those standards not suffer. Auden was too many for Davidson, though. He agreed that every effort must be made to ensure the highest standards, but if it occurred to him that those standards could be achieved with anyone else as editor, he did not say so. Davidson got nowhere, and left with his plot unhatched. A few days later Auden left for Ischia, and Davidson wrote to Bogan: "I had a chance to see Mr. Auden before his departure for Italy, and we had a somewhat inconclusive talk. With all the packing boxes and signs of sailing, there wasn't much room for a basic discussion about the Series and its future, so it looks as though we'll have to defer getting his approval for a change in editorship until his return."

The deferred approval never came. Bogan reemphasized that her actions depended on Auden's, and Auden made a point of his willingness to continue. Perhaps he had heard something of what was up from Bogan. In any case, he fended off Davidson several times, saying he would withdraw if the press wanted to replace him but that he was otherwise ready to stay on. "I'm quite willing to read the manuscripts," he wrote from Ischia, "but, of course, I shall understand if you would rather get someone nearer home and save all the bother of shipping." That wasn't quite what Davidson needed, and he tried for an explicit resignation: "It is essential that we have your decision within the next week or two. If for any reason it is not convenient for the manuscripts to go forward to you, please let me know and we'll try to get someone else to act as editor of the Series in your absence." Auden refused to take the hint, writing in return: "Parcels are apt to take some time. If you are therefore in a great hurry, you had better get someone on the spot to judge. If not, send them and I will read them immediately."

By now it was mid-July, and Davidson decided to let the matter rest for the time being. Fourteen manuscripts were sent to Auden on Ischia, who read them promptly, as promised. Within a week of receiving them he announced his decision, which was that none of them would do. He used Davidson's own words to guarantee agreement: "After our conversation last March, I have assumed that you want me to set the standards high and not accept anything in which I don't wholeheartedly believe." Put that way, Davidson could hardly object. No Yale Younger Poet was named in 1949, and hence no volume was published in the series in 1950.

As time passed, Davidson ceased trying to obtain Auden's resignation. Instead, he set about making the best of things, and Auden set about selecting many of the poets who would define American poetry in the second half of the twentieth century. In 1950, he read twenty-one manuscripts (including May Swenson's) and picked one by an undergraduate at Radcliffe, Adrienne Rich. In 1951, he read eighteen and chose a young man living on Majorca, W. S. Merwin. In 1952, Auden chose Edgar Bogardus, who would die at age thirty and so be one of the few Auden selections who did not go on to gain prominence. In 1953, it was Daniel Hoffman. Hoffman's collection of thirty poems was called *An Armada of Thirty Whales,* and Auden appreciated the metaphor: "One of the reasons I picked out your volume from the rest that were sent me was that it was the only one which showed any real joy in life, a genuine contact with things and creatures." Auden had compiled an impressive string of selections, but it came to a halt in 1954. He felt that none of the manuscripts that year would do, and again the series did not declare a winner. What's more, 1955 looked to be no better. The series might have to skip publication for the second year in a row.

As usual, Auden was on Ischia that spring, where he had been sent twelve manuscripts. After he went through them, he wrote Davidson an unhappy letter. Not only had he not found anything he liked, he had not found what he was looking for:

> I am very worried because, for the second year in succession, I do not find among the mss. submitted to me one that I feel merits publication. It so happens that there is another poet staying here, and I have asked him to read them also as a check on my own judgement. He came, however, to the same conclusion.
>
> What bothers me particularly is that a young poet (John Ashbery) whom I know personally told me he was submitting a manuscript this year. I have reservations about such of his poems as I have seen, but they are certainly better than any of the manuscripts which have reached me. I don't know how or by whom the preliminary sieving is done at the press, but I cannot help wondering whether I am receiving the best.

The other poet reading manuscripts with Auden was Anthony Hecht, who had been traveling in Italy and had met Auden by chance. As for John Ashbery, his manuscript had indeed been weeded out, along with that of another New York poet, Frank O'Hara. Auden contacted them both and asked that they resubmit their work directly to him. He received the manuscripts in little more than a week and made up his mind within days. The winner was Ashbery, salvaged from the slush pile to become in time one of the best-known poets the Yale series has ever published.

Auden made a few changes in the winning manuscript (among other things, he took the name of a poem, "Some Trees," and made it the title of the book) and then sent it off to the press. Back in New Haven, reaction ranged from confusion to outrage. The in-house reader, understandably embarrassed, threw a fit in the form of a memorandum, at the end of which he announced: "Needless to say, I bow out of future work on the Y.S.Y.P." Other press personnel were equally unenthusiastic, and a couple of staff members refused their complimentary copies when the book appeared the following year. It's not hard to sympathize with such consternation, because this time Auden had managed to select not only one of the most difficult books of poetry ever to be printed by the press, but one of the most difficult poets ever to publish in English. Ashbery was a Stevensian (ironically, Stevens' influence reached the Yale series in the very year he died, 1955), and he was quick to imitate Stevens' ornate language and relentless philosophical inquiry. Stevens is not the most accessible poet, but Ashbery's work compounds the difficulty by wholeheartedly embracing Eliot's notion of cultural fragmentation. As a result, while a meditative intellect directs a good half of an Ashbery poem, the other half is unashamedly open to random information. *Some Trees* remains a challenging book today. Forty years ago, come upon cold in a mass of mediocre work, it must have seemed sheer gobbledygook.

The press personnel didn't like Ashbery's book, and the remarkable thing is that neither did Auden, really. As his letter to Davidson says, he had reservations. What those reservations were can be gathered from the letter of rejection he wrote to O'Hara: "I think you (and John too, for that matter) must watch what is always the great danger with any 'surrealistic' style, namely of confusing authentic non-logical relations which arouse wonder with accidental ones which arouse mere surprise and in the end fatigue." Ashbery's aesthetic—at ease with aleatory content, at play in the rubble of the Western literary tradition—is virtually the opposite of Auden's, as Auden knew very well. That Auden would go out of his way to choose a book so at odds with his own art testifies to his capacity for detached evaluation. Emerson had been presented with Whitman's *Leaves of Grass* and recognized it as the great work for which he had long been eager. In *Some Trees*, Auden recognized and endorsed powerful work with which he was not in sympathy at all. He deserves enormous credit.

Some Trees

John Ashbery

YALE SERIES OF YOUNGER POETS

FOREWORD BY W. H. AUDEN

After Ashbery's book, Auden selected those of James Wright, John Hollander, and William Dickey. He decided to make Dickey's book his final choice, but the press did not know that until Auden's foreword came in, a little essay offering advice on what to look for in a replacement. Auden warned of the danger of engaging anyone like himself: "A practicing poet is never a perfect editor: if he is young he will be intolerant of any kind of poetry other than the kind he is trying to write himself; if he is middle aged, the greater tolerance of his judgment is offset by the decline of his interest in contemporary poetry." The weariness implied in that caveat is confirmed in his brief letter of resignation, dated August 13, 1958, which he sent in with his valedictory introduction. "I have decided that it is time you got a younger and fresher editor for the Yale Younger Poets," Auden wrote. "Twelve years is a long time."

It had actually been thirteen years, and it had been a very long time. Auden's remains the longest tenure to date in the series, and the longest we are likely to see. It had been a remarkably sustained effort, as early and late he identified authors destined for major careers. The Yale Younger Poets chosen by Auden are still the ones on which the series' reputation rests, and they include some of the most adroit poets America has ever produced. One or two of them enjoy international reputations, and not a few have by now acquired so many adherents as to constitute schools in their own right. Even the lesser-knowns in Auden's group are well worth reading. By any measure, it was a virtuoso performance.

Well, perhaps not by every measure. It is impossible to have any position of individual responsibility without coming under attack, and the rule holds true for the Yale series editorship. Easy as it seems in retrospect to praise Auden's acumen and foresight, the situation was not cut and dried at the time. His resignation elicited a vituperative reaction from Kenneth Rexroth, who wrote the press to say that under Auden the Yale prize had come "very close to being a kiss of death":

> For many years I have advised young poets under *no* circumstances to submit mss to the Series if they valued their future.

Auden has been the worst offender of all and with few ex-
ceptions his choices have been ridiculous. Even more absurd
have been his prefaces—each designed apparently quite uncon-
sciously to show that the poor little poetaster in question wrote
exactly like WHA. Since this series could be of inestimable cul-
tural value and persists (unfortunately) in being a target of hope
of young poets, I think the press or the YYP's committee or
whatever runs the thing should convoke a solemn meeting and
try to do something about it. This is NOT part of my general war
on 'the Reactionary Generation'; most YYPs are dismal by any
and all standards.

What this letter reflects is the emergence and divergence of
San Francisco's Beat movement, of which Rexroth was by then an
elder statesman. The Beats had not been represented in the Yale
series, though their radical energies would be felt indirectly in
the decade to follow. Eventually the West Coast, in the person of
Robert Hass and the poetry of conscience, would have a great im-
pact on the series, but that development would have to wait until
the mid-1970s. In the meantime, Rexroth attempted to shout the
series down, making the sort of sweeping judgments that incline
one's head upon the chopping block of posterity.

Those not convinced that Auden was "the worst offender of
all" may look for a principle underlying his choices beyond that of
self-replication. Auden's Yale Younger Poets have often been called
academic poets, and it is true that he appears to have favored tech-
nique over content and intellect over feeling. This is not to say that
these poets have remained formalist and undemonstrative, for they
have matured in different directions, and several of them have since
found ways to admit a great deal of emotion into their work. Their
first books, however, do share an emphasis on formal acquirements.
(Even Ashbery, who is not thought of as a formalist, included poems
in his first book which flaunt technique.) Auden chose the poets
with the highest skill level and greatest control he could find, and he
left it to life to provide powerful content with the passage of time.

With Auden's resignation, the series had come to a turning
point. In the autumn of 1958 Yale University Press was about to

become officially part of the Yale Corporation, and in 1960 the University Council's Committee on Publications, which had supervised the press, would be replaced by a Publications Committee that reviewed literary decisions and was responsible to a Board of Governors. In another change, the press ceased to print its own books, becoming strictly a publishing house and farming out manufacture. A transition of press personnel was under way, as well. Norman Donaldson, who had become the press's director in 1950, was preparing to step down. He would be replaced in January 1959 by Chester Kerr. Eugene Davidson, who was passed over for the job, would soon be leaving, too. And in October 1959, George Parmly Day would die at the age of eighty-three. The men who had founded and furthered both the press and the Younger Poets Series were disappearing, leaving Kerr and a succession of new subordinates the freedom and the burden of adapting to profound changes in the publishing industry. Some of those changes were conducive to the publication of verse. The rise of high-quality paperback editions, the introduction of photo-offset printing, the arrival of the baby-boom generation at the age of college education and book buying, and the general robustness of the American economy in the 1950s and 1960s all meant that publishing poetry was no longer the sure money-loser it had been. If there was no great financial opportunity in poetry, still the market forces no longer militated quite so heavily against it. As a result, the way was open for other presses, particularly university presses, to enter the field. Moreover, the conspicuous success of the Yale series—success in terms of prestige rather than profitability—inspired imitation.

The series has, of course, always had some sort of competition. Although the large trade presses have never been enthusiastic about publishing unknown poets, they have until recently felt the responsibility to publish a few of them pro bono. Books printed by the trade presses have long competed with the Younger Poets volumes in the marketplace, and certain houses have sought to distinguish themselves by taking a special interest in poetry. Other competition has come from the small-press series that have operated from time to time, such as Black Sparrow, Tibor di Nagy, and

City Lights. As early as the 1930s, Yale Younger Poet Harold Vinal had published a few books by other young poets. And in 1949, Alan Swallow instituted his New Poetry Series, open to "anyone who has not previously published a book-length collection of poems." Swallow printed one to four volumes a year, and his list included such talented authors as Harvey Shapiro and Edgar Bowers.

Swallow's new poets represented direct competition, but the field remained uncrowded in 1949, and the Yale series did not feel the effect. At about the time Auden resigned, however, that ceased to be the case. In 1958, Wesleyan University Press founded its own poetry series, which would soon become one of the major venues for poetry in this country. Over the course of the next two decades, university press after university press started series of their own: Louisiana State University Press in 1964, Massachusetts in 1965, Pittsburgh in 1968, Illinois in 1971, Princeton in 1975, and Johns Hopkins in 1979 were only the more prominent among them. To this may be added the National Poetry Series, begun in 1978 and publishing four books per year. The series these various presses undertook have not confined themselves to printing first books, but neither have they avoided them. And soon there were others that did specialize in first books: in 1975, the Academy of American Poets instituted its Walt Whitman Award, which combines first book publication with a $5,000 prize. All in all, the Yale series began to find itself competing for talent, as well as for publicity and sales, with the poetry series its own achievements had in large part brought into existence. The series editor the press appointed in the winter of 1958–59 would, then, have to accommodate changes in the publishing business. As it happened, the new editor would face changes in the landscape of American poetry as well. The sixties were at hand, and the social upheavals of that decade would soon be evident in the series submissions.

The man asked to cope with these developments was Dudley Fitts, a secondary-school teacher of donnish sensibility who specialized in the classics. The choice was unexpected, but it was not a choice made in haste. Whether by accident or intention, Auden had resigned at an opportune moment, with the 1958 contest just completed, and the press had plenty of time in which to find a replacement. As usual, several Yale English professors (Louis Martz, Cleanth Brooks, Norman Holmes Pearson) were solicited for their suggestions, and a list of candidates was drawn up. Several of the names on the list were by now standard—Louise Bogan, Marianne Moore, Randall Jarrell—but there were a few surprises, including Fitts, Richard Eberhart, and Winfield Scott, a Rhode Island poet and journalist well liked in the New England literary world. The appointment now required the approval of the press's Publications Committee, and the person whose input was decisive was Norman Holmes Pearson, who was then an influential academic in poetry circles. Together with William Rose Benét, he had edited the Oxford Anthology of American Literature in 1938, and in 1950 he had collaborated with Auden on a five-volume anthology, *Poets of the English Language*. As of 1958 he was taking part in the founding of the Wesleyan Poetry Program for Wesleyan University Press.

In late September, Pearson responded to Eugene Davidson's call for candidates by saying that one name came instantly to mind, that of Dudley Fitts. Oddly, Pearson cited Fitts's physical disabilities (the result of Charcot-Marie-Tooth disease) as an advantage, saying that Fitts's difficulty in moving about would leave him lots of time to devote to the series. Ill health is not usually a selling point in a series editor, but Davidson still had a point to make. Almost his last act regarding the Younger Poets Series (he would soon take a permanent leave of absence from the press) was to promote a candidate likely to give more attention to the series than had ever been extracted from Auden. His efforts were not in vain, and the Publications Committee agreed that Fitts should be offered the job. Later Norman Pearson described the decision this way:

> What the Yale Press looked for was of course a man with a sufficiently recognized name so a certain dignity could be derived from that. He ought also to be able to write well enough so that an introduction by him would have some weight on its own. He ought also to be reasonably independent, by which I mean he ought not to be allied to any particular group of poets so that

his choices would not seem to be influenced by the politics of poetry. For example, one would not have chosen an Allen Tate for this post even though on the first two counts he would be immensely suitable. I suggested Dudley Fitts who is the present editor taking into consideration the fact that he was a poet and critic himself but independent in every way.

As a result of Pearson's suggestion, Fitts was formally invited to take the position on December 1, 1958. He accepted quickly, and as the new year opened, the series had a new editor.

Dudley Fitts walked with crutches, and it required a lengthy struggle for him to cross a room. In repose, his bespectacled face was drawn by his physical distress, but his expression became animated in conversation. He was fifty-five years old, and his dark hair was thinning a bit, but he remained trim, as neat in appearance as Auden was slovenly. Fitts was respected as a poet, but his real reputation was based on his translations from Ancient Greek. He translated plays by Sophocles, Aristophanes, and Euripides into a line at once metrical and colloquial, and his versions of the *Lysistrata* and *Oedipus Rex* (the latter accomplished with the collaboration of his friend and former student, Robert Fitzgerald) are still read. A Boston native, Fitts had gone to Harvard and had lived in Massachusetts for most of his life, teaching at Phillips Academy in Andover for almost twenty years. In manner, Fitts was lively and learned, much given to bawdy puns and classical allusions. His typical letter is more of the same, an elaborate pastiche of nonce words, baby talk, double entendre (even single entendre), scraps of foreign language, and pith. "After all the hullaballoo has boo'd itself to hull," begins a characteristic sentence. Or, "I've writ this danois meláncolique that the litterprise or ¡IBM! idea is acceptable, and that his traductions from the gk are acceptable, too." Peter Davison, whom Fitts selected for the Yale series in 1963, remembers him as a "grave, learned, witty, gossipy, and pungent presence." And he recalls that Fitts was anxious to distinguish his choices from Auden's: "Dudley was cagey, furtive, judgmental, and desperate to be fair: he once said something to me about how badly he wanted to choose a woman poet after a run of males."

The editor might well be desperate, because no woman had received the prize since 1950. Auden, though not resolutely hostile to female poets (he had, after all, selected Murray, Moore, and Rich), was removed from such considerations, quite content to choose seven men in a row if he felt them the best qualified. It would take Fitts until 1962 to find a woman poet to endorse (Sandra Hochman), and he did so with palpable relief. Sylvia Plath might have been chosen instead—Fitts considered her the runner-up in both 1959 and 1960—but she had decided to publish her first book overseas rather than submit to the series a third time. Plath, always alert to her own ambitions, had been particularly chagrined to lose out in 1959 because the winner was George Starbuck, an acquaintance of hers. Starbuck, Plath, and Anne Sexton were all in Robert Lowell's writing class at Boston University that year, and Plath's journals show her to be rankled by Starbuck's success : "the grim news Starbuck got the Yale, to which I am now resigned, if disappointed in Fitts's judgment." What was grim news to one was, of course, welcome news to another, and the winner received it over the phone direct from Dudley Fitts. Starbuck was an editor at Houghton-Mifflin at the time, though he had specialized in mathematics in what had been a picaresque career as a student. (He had attended Berkeley —where he studied with Lawrence Hart—as well as Cal Tech, the University of Chicago, and Harvard, all without obtaining a degree.)

Starbuck's poised verse does not differ greatly from the poetry chosen in the Auden years (though it is perhaps less formally accomplished; Auden had in fact passed over the manuscript in 1958), but from the standpoint of the series' publishing practice, his book was a landmark. Chester Kerr, whom Davison calls "that great impresario," had hold of the series now, and he planned to make some noise with it. Kerr determined to bring out a paperback edition along with the cloth, with the result that the number of books printed instantly tripled. The response was so good that the advance orders threatened to exhaust the paperback run prior to the publication date, and the book was in a second printing before it ever appeared in the bookstores. Kerr made other changes, too. He gradually increased the series' advertising budget, he authorized an increase in production costs in order to print the covers on glossy stock, and he paid the poets an advance. Kerr, who enjoyed the social side of the business, also instituted annual fêtes, starting in 1961, on the occasion of each Yale Younger Poet publication. For years, the poets and editors associated with the Yale series had pleaded for money to be spent on publicity. With Kerr as press director, it finally happened, and the series thrived. The Yale series received great public attention during these years, and no poet in the series drew more of it than the one Fitts picked in 1960: Alan Dugan, a thirty-seven-year-old World War II veteran who was born in Brooklyn and had grown up combatively intellectual.

"I've found a terrific unpublished poet, whose ms probably won't go through here, and who has agreed to let me give it to Fitts." Dugan's manuscript had crossed Starbuck's desk at Houghton-Mifflin before it arrived in New Haven, and Starbuck alerted the in-house editor to look for the book while screening submissions. There were 146 entrants that year, many of whom would go on to distinguished careers, but Fitts agreed with Starbuck, and Dugan was the winner. Fitts's judgment was confirmed by critical acclaim as few editorial decisions ever are, for Dugan's book was positively reviewed in almost all the major newspapers and magazines — even in Vinal's *Voices*, still being published these many years later. But the praise didn't stop there. Dugan's *Poems* received both the Pulitzer Prize and the National Book Award, and Dugan was awarded the Prix de Rome soon after. It was the writer's version of the triple crown. *Poems* is a disgruntled and rigorous book and not at all the light material one might expect to prove popular. Given the tremendous publicity, however, it did very well, eventually selling some thirteen thousand copies.

Dugan's spectacular success made his selection a hard act to follow, and Fitts opted for balance rather than trying to find more of the same. The next choice after Dugan's fierce ratiocinations was a quixotic and amused book, Jack Gilbert's *Views of Jeopardy*. Written in reaction to the counterculture of San Francisco and New York's Greenwich Village, Gilbert's is one of the Yale volumes that reflect the cross currents of the sixties. Several other books that

Fitts chose would do so as well, particularly those of Helen Chasin and Judith Johnson Sherwin. It is a long way from the studied technique and careful content of Auden's final selections (Wright, Hollander, William Dickey) to the wild orthography of Sherwin's book or the unorthodox behavior chronicled in Chasin's. American poetry, and the Yale series with it, was moving very quickly.

Gilbert's book was the winner of the 1961 contest, which was unusual in that the press paid for a reader, Ted Stein, to screen the manuscripts off premises. In spite of this, Fitts asked to be sent almost all of the 157 entries that year. He was concerned that the screening process not exclude anything deserving, and he was particularly concerned that it not deprive him of a prurient chortle. Fitts wanted to see any manuscripts with erotic content, and the more "eccentrick" the better. In a letter to Judy Jenkins, Stein's replacement at the press, Fitts explained: "I shall want to see all but the worst of the entries, and the funniest of the worst, as I did last year; the job is not so onerous as to make me despair of life, although I must confess that at times it makes one despair of art."

All but the worst meant that Fitts wound up reading far more manuscripts than any series editor had before him. Submissions climbed steadily during his tenure, until the contest was averaging upwards of three hundred entries per year. Unlike Auden, Fitts read all comers; but also unlike Auden, he drew the line at the dead. A New York author known to be interested in young writers (it was Stanley Kunitz) wished to send in the work of a deceased poet named Bove, but Fitts refused to accept the submission. He objected that such publication could not possibly fulfill the series' purpose of launching a career: "alas, not even Yale encouragement can give much impetus to a corpse."

Gilbert's book was followed by Sandra Hochman's, Peter Davison's, and Jean Valentine's. A small flap arose when word of Valentine's winning the prize made its way into the papers before the Publications Committee had approved the choice. Fitts offered to step down as a result. (Unwilling to overstay his welcome, he offered to resign almost on an annual basis, but Kerr never took him seriously.) When Valentine's manuscript was finally proposed to the committee, it became apparent that it had benefited from two extra readers whose opinion Fitts valued. The proposal included the recommendations of John Frederick Nims and Robert Fitzgerald, both of whom had helped Fitts read through the finalists that year.

Valentine's book was published in February 1965 (*"not* February 14," insisted the author.) It was reviewed in *Newsweek,* as well as in many newspapers and the usual quarterlies. The Yale Younger Poets volumes could be counted on to sell well, and in their literary way their publication was national news. The best young poets of the day were submitting to the contest (recognizable names from many different camps turn up regularly among the contestants by this point), and their numbers were climbing. The 1965 contest would be another bumper crop. There were 280 entrants, L. E. Sissman and Audre Lourde among them, but Fitts found nothing to his taste. For the fourth time in the history of the series, no Yale Younger Poets prize was awarded, and Fitts prepared a statement for public consumption:

> The Editor of the Yale Series of Younger Poets announces with regret that he has been unable to make a selection this year. The technical competence of the better manuscripts submitted was generally high, perhaps higher than in most previous years; but it was the editor's feeling that none of them was decisive enough in pushing beyond facility into poetry. What was lacking was, primarily, daring. The editor is not necessarily in love with audacity, certainly not in the too frequent mistaking of eccentricity for force; but he does believe that technical skill is not enough in itself to justify the publication of a new poet.

Things improved again the next year. There were 336 manuscripts submitted, and all but thirty of them were sent on to Fitts. More than one of the 1965 manuscripts came from the University of Iowa, where George Starbuck was now teaching and where Paul Engle still survived as an eminence grise. Starbuck made his recommendation, but the winning poet in 1966 was James Tate, who was a protégé of another instructor at the workshop, Donald Justice. The Iowa Writer's Workshop and the Yale Series of Younger Poets have been no strangers to each other over the years, and the connection was particularly close in the late sixties and early seventies. No fewer than fifteen Yale Younger Poets have passed through Iowa City, either as students, instructors, or spouses, and seven of the ten poets chosen between 1964 and 1974 would be associated with the workshop in some way. These were the years when workshop instruction first became a dominant presence in American poetry.

Poetry workshops have been accused of enforcing conformity, but Tate's volume is pleasantly distinct. *The Lost Pilot* is titled in reference to Tate's father, who disappeared on a mission during World War II, yet the book is not elegiac. Rather, it is gently existential, providing restrained observation of the unrestrained scene of mid-sixties America. It is very much a work of the baby boom, hearkening back to the war that gave rise to that generation and investigating the new confusions and possibilities the World War II infants had created with their majority.

Tate's book echoes the tenor of the day quietly, but not so the two books that followed it. Helen Chasin's volume, the winner of the 1967 contest and thus selected at the height of the flower-power, tie-dyed, war-protesting counterculture, contains plenty of references to sex and drugs. Judith Johnson Sherwin's (she now publishes as Judith Johnson) is a wildly experimental book, wacky on its surface and expressive of the anxieties unleashed by the cold war and the atomic age. Ecologically passionate, it looks forward in subject matter if not appearance to the poetry of the environmentally conscious 1970s. Dudley Fitts's choices as editor, then, were often unexpected, and he was clearly interested in and open to the ongoing experiments in American culture and verse. Given his background in pedagogy and his great competence in classical literature, the press perhaps thought it was getting a more conservative judge than Fitts proved to be. Fitts did not eschew so-called academic poets. One can imagine Auden selecting Jean Valentine, say, and possibly Dugan or Davison. But it seems unlikely that Auden, though he had been willing to print Ashbery, would have gone so far as to select Sherwin's *Uranium Poems*. Auden was willing to be surprised if need be; Fitts sought surprise out.

One must identify the principles underlying Fitts's judgment for oneself, because his forewords provide little help. They do not greatly illuminate the books they introduce, and they are unified only by his perpetual complaint about being obliged to produce them. What, then, is the common denominator of Fitts's selections? They often contain the unexpected, but simply to note their unorthodox aspects is to miss their essence. Fitts liked unusual work; he liked work with erotic tension; and he liked work that felt au courant. But at the same time, he looked for manuscripts that showed intellectual poise and demonstrated an acquaintance with classical texts. Jack Gilbert's poetry, concerned "for whales and love, / For elephants and Alcibiades," illustrates the case. It was the poets who could combine contemporary and ancient passions who most often won Fitts's approval. He wanted up-to-the-minute content in the poetry he picked, but he wanted long perspective, too. Unlike the poets that had appealed to Benét and would appeal to Stanley Kunitz, the authors Fitts picked only appear to be caught up in the world they portray. Norman Pearson saw as much, writing to a colleague: "My own impression of Dudley Fitts is that he responds most quickly to manuscripts with a decided ironic tinge to them." Fitts's poets brandish their involvement, but they are at heart detached.

Nine such poets had been selected by the summer of 1968, and the series was flourishing as never before. The average sales during Fitts's tenure were far and away the best the series had seen. The poets Fitts picked had won major awards and been widely reviewed. Furthermore, with the passage of time, Auden's achievement as judge was beginning to come into focus, and the Yale series enjoyed a central position in American poetry. Fitts had done as well following in Auden's wake as anyone had a right to expect, and the press was enthusiastic about the books it was publishing. "Who's next? I can't wait to see what you have up your sleeve," Kerr wrote his editor late in the decade.

Fitts, too, was flourishing. His brilliant work as a translator, his deep knowledge of the classics, and perhaps also his reputation as editor of the Yale series were bringing him the kind of academic acclaim few secondary-school teachers ever receive. Columbia University awarded him an honorary degree in 1968. (Columbia was the site of radical student protests that year. "I'm going down next Tuesday," wrote Fitts to the press, "ostensibly to collect a Litt.D. degree, but probably to get involved in an insurrection.") Other and more concrete honors awaited him, too. He had been engaged to teach at Harvard come fall, and he was moving off the Andover campus. The move, made July 7, 1968, was strenuous for a man in Fitts's chronically ill condition. He inhaled a good deal of incidental dust during it and died of a heart attack four days later.

"I won't accept it, damn it. It's just not fair," wrote Kerr to Cornelia Fitts. However unfair it felt, though, the series needed a new editor. Again, the interregnum came at a convenient time of the year, and the press had time in which to plan its next move. The usual letters soliciting advice went out to professors and critics and Yale Younger Poets, but the advice that counted came from those close at hand, particularly the members of the Publications Committee who would have to approve the choice. Dudley Fitts had been chosen for his status as an independent mind outside the literary mainstream. This time, consensus settled on a member of the Northeast literary establishment, Stanley Kunitz.

In 1969 Kunitz was sixty-four years old. His appearance today, at ninety-two, remains much as it was then: thin and erect, with a ruff of white hair, a trim moustache, and large dark eyes. Born the son of Lithuanian immigrants in Worcester, Massachusetts, he is a Harvard graduate and a veteran of World War II. Kunitz is married to Elise Asher, an accomplished painter, and they then lived in an elegant townhouse on West Twelfth Street in New York City, where they threw glittering parties that put them at the center of Manhattan's art and literary circles. Summers still find them at Provincetown on Cape Cod, and there Kunitz (like William Alexander Percy) cultivates a garden that has been been one of the great pleasures of his life. Though never a prolific writer, Kunitz has had staying power, and by 1969 he had emerged as a poet of some reputation. The editor of several biographical dictionaries, he has also published translations from Russian, and he won the Pulitzer in 1958 for a volume of his selected poems. Kunitz began teaching at Columbia University in 1967, but he had taught previously at many other institutions (Bennington College, the New School, Brandeis University, the University of Washington), and he had become known as a generous friend of young talent.

Early in February 1969, Kunitz accepted the invitation to take on the series. (For the first time since the pro tem service of Reed and Pierce in the early twenties, the series editor was appointed to a specific term: three years, renewable by mutual consent for another five. Also for the first time, the press publicity material began to refer to the series "editor" as "judge"; the terms have since been used interchangeably.) It soon became apparent that he would go about his duties differently from Fitts. More mobile, he went to the mountain of mail rather than having the mountain come to him. Early each summer he would travel to New Haven and stay as long as a week, looking over manuscripts and chatting. One person at the press remembers him this way: "Stanley Kunitz was a twinkly-eyed man, very easy to approach, and he liked to talk with the young people around the office. He dressed casually, and he wore a little yachting cap with a short brim. What did we talk about? Well, poetry sometimes. But mostly we just talked." While he was chatting, though, Kunitz attended to business. The press personnel screened manuscripts, necessarily so as the number of entries continued to climb steeply, but Kunitz liked to look for himself. He monitored the screening process, picking up and glancing through each and every manuscript at least once.

These were new methods, but they did not immediately yield new results. Kunitz's first selection, a manuscript of obsessively lovelorn poems by Hugh Seidman, did not reveal any departure in taste. Neither did the next year's choice: Peter Klappert was a wildly funny and ironic poet (so much so that Kunitz was uneasy with his work, writing in his foreword that Klappert "is such a recklessly clever poet that one's first inclination is to mistrust his seriousness"), and he would have fit Fitts's criteria quite comfortably. For his third contest winner, however, Kunitz picked a poet one feels Fitts would never have chosen, and it became clear that the series was again shifting course.

The Yale Younger Poet for 1971 was Michael Casey, twenty-four years old and recently returned from Vietnam. Casey had been drafted into the war and had served a two-year hitch as a military policeman. (He carried a volume of verse in his pack: it was *Poems*, by Alan Dugan.) Casey's book, *Obscenities*, has nothing of the intellectual detachment favored by Auden and Fitts. Instead, it consists of short and good-humored descriptions of a ghastly and morally unaccountable bloodletting. *Obscenities* is as much journalism as it is poetry, and the author evidently intended it that way. He had a story to tell, and he only wished he could have gotten more of his devastating experience into his brief accounts. Asked in a press questionnaire to describe his work, Casey responded: "The book's language is real but the book's subject is very incomplete. Part of it attempts to deal with the military police in Vietnam and that part ignores drugs and corruption. The MP's in Nam do not ignore drugs or corruption. The enmity between black and white American soldiers is not touched. The racial prejudice against the oriental people is not mentioned to anywhere near its reality."

Casey felt that his book was incomplete, but it is still a far more immediate account of war than any of the other books in the Yale series. If it does not aspire to the literary context and painstaking artistry of, say, Meredith's war poetry, it nonetheless packs a wallop Meredith's verse (much less that of the World War I veterans who comprise the series' earliest poets) makes no attempt to deliver. Casey's straightforward and high-impact verse addresses a much wider audience than poetry usually reaches, and as its publication date approached in 1972, that audience was ready to listen. It was an election year, and the Vietnam War was the central topic of public debate. The press tried to make the most of the situation, aiming to publish the book on May 1 (the day of mass antiwar demonstrations in Washington, D.C.), though that target was missed, and the volume appeared two weeks late. Even so, by the end of the summer *Obscenities* was already in a third printing. Moreover, Warner Paperback Library negotiated to pick up the book, eventually purchasing the right to publish a simultaneous edition that included photographs. The mass-market paperback came out on election day of 1972, and the run dwarfed anything a Yale Younger Poet had known before: 117,500 copies.

Casey's book created a stir, and one result was a surge in submissions. During the Fitts years, annual entries had doubled to an average of three hundred plus, but now, just a couple of years later, they had doubled again. Submissions during Kunitz's tenure ran between six hundred and seven hundred per year, which has been roughly the average ever since, although in 1975 the number spiked to an all-time high of 902 manuscripts.

In its grisly description and powerful impact, *Obscenities* was unprecedented in the series, and it soon became apparent that therein lay an editorial bent. Fitts had liked to surprise with his choices. Kunitz liked to stun. He selected books of deliberate daring, and his taste resembled Benét's in that he was more interested in poetry that comes to grips with human problems than he was in the art of intellectual distance. The Kunitz years reprised the Benét era, with the difference that the great topics of the day had changed. The issues in the thirties had been public and international: economic crisis, communism and fascism, the prospect of world war. Casey addresses similar public issues in his Vietnam poems. So does Robert Hass in *Field Guide* (1973), though his poems of protest are domesticated, often taking place over a good meal. (Hass's book takes the logical step from a neo-Romantic rendering of the divinity immanent in nature to the condemnation of environmental irresponsibility as a sort of blasphemy.) But many of the issues in the seventies were private, or rather private issues brought forth for public inspection, and it was in the Kunitz years that such by now familiar subjects as lifestyle, ancestral identity, and gender preference first made their appearance in the series.

Kunitz's forewords emphasize the controversial aspects of his selections. Thus, in introducing Carolyn Forché's *Gathering the Tribes* (1975), a book written in praise of so-called primitive societies, Kunitz singles out a poem in which a retreat from civilization culminates in two women engaging in sex, thrashing wildly on a beach ("there is sand in the anus of dancing") and copulating in the foam, the brine and with it the natural surround literally entering them. Similarly, he opens his foreword to Olga Broumas's *Beginning with O* by announcing, "This is a book of letting go, of wild avowals, unabashed eroticism." Broumas's book (published in 1977, it was the editor's "valedictory choice for the Yale Series") is all of that. The celebration of lesbian sex in the volume had rarely been seen in mainstream publishing circles, and once again the Yale series benefited by the attention that comes with controversy. *Beginning with O* went on to sell over eighteen thousand copies, and as with Casey's book, it brought the series an audience that it could not otherwise expect. Broumas's unabashed poems occasioned controversy at Yale, too, particularly after her reading at the press, and there were people on campus who considered the book the worst ever published in the series. No volume printed after the Lewis/Percy years could possibly qualify for such honors, but regardless such a judgment ignores the talent for metaphor exhibited in Broumas's poetry, as well as the contagion of its sheer enthusiasm. Yet extreme reaction, pro and con, is what the book and its selection actively sought. Kunitz had fired a parting shot that reverberated.

Following the 1976 contest Kunitz retired as scheduled upon mailing in his foreword to Broumas's volume. He left a series that had reached new peaks in sales and reached a new audience, one that had opened itself to new aspects of American poetry and new currents in American society. He also left a series that had become substantially more organized internally. The Younger Poets Series had reached a crisis in the 1975 contest, due to the flood of submissions. As envelopes piled up at the press, things got out of hand. The manuscripts wandered around various offices, in and out of knapsacks, back and forth to readers' homes. In the end, thirty manuscripts were lost. Chester Kerr was appalled, and he made changes. Over the objections of his staff, he insisted that a fee be charged for submissions, in the hope of discouraging less serious contestants. Kerr also required an overhaul of the screening process, and a meticulous system for tracking and handling manuscripts was developed.

Kunitz's departure was foreseen, and Kerr had been making plans to find a successor. After Kunitz's run of provocative selections, the press director would have drawn little criticism around New Haven if he had pulled in the reins, but he did nothing of the sort. Instead, he had an idea he might shake things up. It had been fifty-five years since the series had had an editor from outside the Northeast, and it had never had one whose tastes had not been formed at Oxford, Harvard, or Yale. Kerr was looking for an editor who could provide what he called "a little ventilation." As usual, the press had collected nominations from members of the Yale faculty and former Yale Younger Poets, and among those whose input was decisive was Professor Louis Martz. "I felt the Series had become too insulated," says Martz, "and I told Chester we ought to find someone who wasn't East Coast, someone not beholden to the usual publications or associated with any particular school of poetry." The unbeholden poet Martz recommended to fill that bill was Richard Hugo.

Whether the series had become insulated is a matter of debate, for Kunitz's selections had been anything but one-dimensional, and they certainly were not confined to poets of the Northeast. Quite the opposite: it was during Kunitz's tenure that the attitudes we now think of as characteristic of the West Coast (a distrust of all institutions, particularly those ultimately derived from Europe; a corresponding openness to Asian philosophy and art; a rejection of puritan attitudes regarding food, the body, and vocation) first made an impact on the series. It was true, of course, that Kunitz himself was highly connected in the New York literary world, though his circumstances do not seem to have defined his judgment. Still, if Kunitz was the consummate insider, Richard Hugo was not. He was the consummate outsider, and he knew it.

Hugo was born in Seattle in 1923 and educated at the University of Washington. In 1977 he was living in Missoula, Montana, where he was director of creative writing at the state university. A big, burly, balding man, he had lived hard, and it showed. This would be another series editor plagued by ill health. Hugo's poetry was nothing like Kunitz's or Fitts's, much less Auden's. His literary antecedents had little to do with Eastern Europe or neoclassicism and everything to do with the line of Theodore Roethke. Set in his native Northwest, his poems combine an enthusiasm for the great outdoors with a fascination for the blight that has so often accompanied human intrusion into the wilderness. Because he lived far from the centers of publishing, it had taken Hugo quite some time to establish his reputation, but the publication in 1975 of *What Thou Lovest Well Remains American,* together with the magazine appearance of the poems that would soon be collected under the title *31 Letters and 13 Dreams,* had recently made him well known. It would be a mistake to think of Hugo as a quirky choice for editor. In 1977, his volumes were in every bookstore, and his name was one to be reckoned with.

In January of that year, Hugo was invited to New Haven, and he came on the understanding that he would be appointed editor unless the visit was a disaster. He turned out to be a warm and likable man, and even those Yale professors who had viewed him with suspicion found themselves disarmed. The academics ceased to be wary of him, but he remained wary of them. Hugo's letters to Kerr and the rest of the press personnel are bluff and amusing, but they are often facetious in tone and are consistently self-deprecatory. He seems to have felt some anxiety regarding the Northeastern intellectuals, attributing to them a degree of literary sophistication no one could possibly match. In any case, this was an editor who cultivated the press as much as it did him. He and Chester Kerr became quite close, with Hugo sending the director his new poems in typescript and Kerr going out of his way to socialize with the poet. Hugo came by the press offices, too, whenever his reading tours took him near New Haven. He lived far away in Montana, but he was far less distant than Auden or Fitts had been (the one due to disposition, the other to immobility). Hugo made his presence felt. He wanted to belong.

The trial visit to New Haven went swimmingly, and Hugo was duly appointed. With the editorship decided, the screening process proceeded, and forty-two manuscripts were sent off to Missoula. After some deliberation, Hugo decided on a book set in the Big Sky country of Wyoming and Colorado. It was called *Border Crossings* and was by Greg Pape, who did not become the seventy-third Yale Younger Poet. The competition had caught up with the Yale series: notified of his victory, Pape revealed that he had just signed a contract with the University of Pittsburgh Press. Kerr was furious and fired off an angry letter to the offender, but there was nothing to be done. Hugo went back to the manuscripts and found a new winner. So it was that Bin Ramke became Hugo's first selection for the series.

Aside from the Pape affair, 1977 was a banner year for Richard Hugo. He was named series editor, he published his *31 Letters and 13 Dreams* to excellent reviews, and he won a Guggenheim Fellowship. Taking a leave of absence from the University of Montana, he took the award money and departed for the Isle of Skye, off the west coast of Scotland, for a stay of several months. Chester Kerr joined him in Edinburgh for a few days in October. Kerr soon returned to New Haven, but Hugo did not make it home so easily. He ran short of funds and had to beg the Press for an advance on his fee in order to get out of Scotland. According to Hugo, the trouble involved bank errors and a disagreement with the Internal Revenue Service; but whatever the cause, it was an unusual request. Poetry is not a moneymaker at any publishing house, and poetry editors do not often receive large cash advances. Still, Hugo had become a friend, and Kerr had the press fly him home. He was not so rash as to give Hugo a check, however; he sent him the tickets instead.

Hugo got back in time for the 1978 contest, and his choice was Leslie Ullman. The selection made for contrast. Where Ramke's book is surreal and guilt-ridden, Ullman's is languorous and plain-spoken. The contrast continued, as Ullman was followed by William Virgil Davis, John Bensko, David Wojahn, and Cathy Song, none of whom writes much in the manner of the others, or of Richard Hugo for that matter. (Wojahn, writing about border towns and blue-collar desperation, is probably the least removed from Hugo in style and subject.) There is a thread of low-key domesticity running through many of these selections, but beyond that they do not have much in common. Hugo's taste does not show any unifying principle, but that disunity is a principle in itself. The editor knew he had been hired in order to bring new blood to the series, and he quite consciously tried to stretch the Yale list as much as possible. The fact that Hugo's poets were stylistically disparate was the point, as was the provenance of the poets themselves. By way of illustration, Hugo's Younger Poets may be compared to those of Fitts. Eight out of the nine Fitts poets were based in Manhattan or Cambridge (this need not surprise: for two hundred years Harvard has produced the lion's share of America's great poets, and the sixties — the acme of Robert Lowell's influence — were a particularly fertile time there). Not one of Hugo's poets came from those nexuses, or even from the Northeast. They came from New Mexico and Kansas City, from Texas and Alabama. As one Yale Younger Poet from a previous era wrote the press to say, Hugo's list constituted "affirmative action for western poets." Hugo's last selection came all the way from Hawaii. Cathy Song, whose reticent poems delicately explore the conflicts inherent in growing up Asian-American, is situated both aesthetically and geographically as far from the Northeast as one can get and still be writing in America.

Song's volume, *Picture Bride,* was published in May 1983, but the editor did not live to see the book into print. Hugo had been diagnosed with cancer, and he died of complications, succumbing in October 1982. His editorship was cut short, but he had held on bravely against his disease and had managed to select six poets before it caught up with him. Hugo's tenure was a difficult time for the press and for the series, a period of retrenchment and belt-tightening. The late 1970s were high-inflation years, and projecting expenses became a ticklish business. Pricing books was correspondingly difficult and subject to revision, and in 1978 (Ullman's year) the list price of the series volumes ceased to be printed on the jacket. Readership declined as the baby boomers passed beyond their college years and as generations raised entirely on television took their place. The decline would accelerate throughout the 1980s, and press runs of the Younger Poets books would shrink in consequence. It became less and less justifiable to spend excess money on the series, and the publicity budget was reduced.

During the sixties, volumes had been advertised in fourteen or fifteen magazines, some of them mainstream publications. Midway through the Hugo years, that figure was cut in half. The dinner parties Kerr had organized around the series publication dates became a thing of the past, too. They were too expensive, and they were spottily attended. Even the readings by Yale Younger Poets ceased to be annual and became hit or miss. There wasn't always money available to fly in those who lived far away (and many of Hugo's selections lived quite far away), and when there was, the poets weren't always available. William Virgil Davis was receiving a Fulbright for 1980, and when Kerr called in the summer of 1979 to tell him he had won the Yale prize, he had to say that he would be in Vienna when the book was published. "That's never happened before," Kerr protested. "No one's not been here. . . . Well," he added after a moment's reflection, "that will be my successor's problem."

Chester Kerr had reached the age of retirement by the end of 1979, and the Great Impresario stepped down. "We'll miss you," wrote Hugo fondly. "*We*. That's your doing, O wisest of Press Directors." Kerr had been an energetic executive, and his instinct for promotion, together with that of the editors he appointed, had brought the series the greatest attention it has ever enjoyed. If Auden was the series editor most singly responsible for the high literary reputation of the Yale Series of Younger Poets, Kerr was the press director who did the most to aid and abet the cause.

Kerr was succeeded by John Ryden in January 1980, and when Hugo died two years later, that was his problem, too. He asked a number of people active in the field of poetry who their candidates for a new editor might be. With each change of editorship the press was casting a wider net in soliciting advice, and Ryden sent letters of inquiry not only to several of the Yale faculty and some of the former Yale Younger Poets, but also to critics, magazine editors, and prominent authors. In response to a great many letters came a great many opinions, but the majority recommended a poet based in nearby Stonington, Connecticut: James Merrill. Merrill's supporters included the former Yale Younger Poet and current Yale professor John Hollander, and Ryden engaged Hollander's help in urging Merrill to accept. (Like Percy six decades earlier and other editors since, Merrill was worried that the series would take too much of his time.) By early January 1983, Merrill had been talked into it.

James Merrill was born in 1926, and he was born rich. His father had been a founder of the securities firm Merrill Lynch, and the child grew up both protected and isolated by astonishing wealth. He had received a gentleman's education at Amherst, sandwiched around a year in the army, and had gone on to further refine himself in Europe, where he developed a lifelong affection for Greece. If Richard Hugo's background had left him an eternal outsider, so Merrill's privileged status left him with a lingering sense of not having earned his position. Perhaps in consequence, he was an exceptionally generous man, a generosity that extended to all the arts and to needy authors in particular. The Ingram Merrill Foundation, which he started, gave cash awards of several thousand dollars to fifteen or twenty writers and artists each year. In theory, Merrill did not influence those awards, though the foundation happened to meet in the living room of one of his several residences, a New York City apartment. Just the same, he knew where the money went, so that the foundation helped to keep him abreast of the work of young poets.

Merrill was a thin, almost elfin man, with a bony face and a boyish smile. A nervous person who did not seem quite comfortable in his own skin, he did not make others uncomfortable. On the contrary, he was so tactful and well mannered (though not at all stuffy) as to make one believe in the value of breeding. If charm may be defined as the use of one's intelligence to make people feel good about themselves, James Merrill was the most charming man who ever lived. Not being a teacher, he was not accustomed to hold forth on literary matters, and he did not like to talk shop. When asked, though, he provided excellent critiques: gentle, useful, never less than honest. Pamela Alexander, whose first volume would be Merrill's second selection for the series, recalls this exchange on the occasion of a subsequent book: "JM asked me about my work. 'A new manuscript,' he said, 'tell me the title.' I did. There was a pause during which he must have marshalled his famous generosity and tact. 'Sometimes the title is the last to come.'"

Merrill's own work is deeply cultured and highly formal. His verse is very inclined to puns (as was the poet himself), and it rhymes as well as any in the English language, a trick accomplished in part by the importation of foreign words whenever necessary. Merrill's poems combine intimacy with grandeur, so that a single stanza may speak of lover, home, family, the dog, and, say, Wagner's *Ring* cycle. At the time he was appointed series editor he had just published *The Changing Light at Sandover*, a genuinely epic poem that purports to extract an understanding of three thousand years of history and art, as well as supernatural instruction in the meaning of life, from a Ouija board. Asked once what sort of poetry he wrote, Merrill didn't hesitate. "Mandarin," he replied, on the mark as always.

Merrill brought as much literary acclaim to the job as any editor could—he had won a Pulitzer, the Bollingen, and two National Book Awards, among many other prizes—and he brought a distinct point of view. He made his own poetry out of a dizzying range of personal references and literary allusions, and he was not interested in simplicity. "Why is our poetry so wary of things 'the reader' might not know?" begins his foreword to his first series selection (Richard Kenney). He goes on to ask whether it solves anything to "sing purely of tree and stone, body and breath? For in so doing we reduce the self's prodigious cross-index to at best a heartfelt small talk." Of Kenney and his work, he says: "He is not out to disguise the liveliness of his mind or the breadth of his learning. . . . With its agreeable eddies of temperament, reflections that braid and shatter only to recompose downstream, this book moves like a river in a country of ponds." The recomposing river describes Merrill's own art at least as well as Kenney's, but the argument is plain enough. The new series editor did not care for the poetry of "stones and bones." The new editor favored the poetry of wit.

The poetry he favored and the poetry he could find were two different things. None of the Yale Younger Poets selected by Merrill approaches the "prodigious cross-index" of Merrill's own poetry

(Kenney probably comes closest), for even the most talented among them are still in the learning stages. But Merrill recognized parts of himself in all his Yale poets (or at least he said as much to some of them), and we may look to the different volumes Merrill chose for individual qualities analogous to aspects of his work. If Kenney's is most like Merrill's in its bewildering quantity of information, Daniel Hall's is most like Merrill's in its Cavafyesque approach to the heart's education. Julie Agoos has some of Merrill's finely tuned sensibility, Thomas Bolt shares Merrill's debt to Dante, Pamela Alexander writes with some of Merrill's whimsy and good humor, and Brigit Pegeen Kelly shows something of Merrill's insight into family matters.

Just as Kunitz's selections reprised Benét's in the way that the age demanded, Merrill's might be seen as a reprise of Auden's to the extent that the era allowed. In returning to the values Auden articulated in his forewords, that is, in seeking abstract perspective and technical ability, Merrill was constrained by the state of the art. Twentieth-century American verse has conducted several variations on the age-old dispute between Apollonian and Dionysian notions of inspiration, between the poetry of intellect and the poetry of emotion. (The debate finally presents a false choice, but it has been prosecuted with vigor nonetheless). During the period when Auden and Fitts were Yale editors, both credos were well represented among the nation's poets. The argument is pretty much over now, at least for the time being, and a balance has been lost. With the triumph of unmediated emotion in the latter half of the century, formalism has suffered neglect. The lack of instruction, approval, and practice has had a cumulative effect, and if it is deemed worthwhile to recover the skill level of a Merrill or an Auden, it is going to take a sustained movement to effect the recuperation. In the meantime, a resource has gone out of our art.

Like Auden, Merrill considered acquired technique the foundation of poetic accomplishment. Compositional skill is not the only virtue that Merrill (or Auden, either) sought in young poets, however. He was also looking for authors capable of both emotion and emotional control, and for the most part he found them.

Throughout his tenure, Merrill selected manuscripts that showed an Audenesque combination of intimate voice and intellectual detachment. The Apollonian art of perspective and complexity was what Merrill believed in, but he liked those chilly virtues to be tempered by human warmth. For seven years he consistently chose manuscripts that answer this description. He made his final choice (Daniel Hall) in 1989, and by then his term was up. It was time to listen to other ideas. The next editor would be James Dickey, and he wanted dithyrambs.

As with Kunitz, Merrill's departure was expected, and the press had plenty of time to consider his successor. More people than ever were asked for their suggestions, but within the press the question boiled down to whether the next editor ought to represent a continuity of taste or a new direction. The press opted for a change, true to the principle first enunciated by Edward Bliss Reed, that the point of bringing in a new editor is to avoid staleness. With the editorial direction resolved, there was no need to wait. The new editor would not need to judge any manuscripts until May 1990, but he was offered the job long before. James Dickey's letter of acceptance is dated July 26, 1989.

James Dickey was about as different from James Merrill as a poet could be. There was nothing elfin about him. Born in Atlanta, Georgia, in 1923, he played football in high school, graduated from Vanderbilt, and served in the air force during both World War II and the Korean War. A large and physical presence, with blond hair combed across the bald patches, Dickey cultivated robust pastimes to the point of ostentation. Helen Chasin, who heard him read in Cambridge in 1967, wrote the press that Dickey was "quite flamboyant and recently clawed by a bear while hunting with a bow and arrow. Really." Dickey's readings were famous, not to say notorious, and they could be chaotic affairs. Like Hugo, he lived hard, and that included drinking hard. But beneath the affectation and naughtiness, there was a serious artist. Dickey had published twelve books of poems (many of them with Wesleyan, where Norman Holmes Pearson and John Hollander were advisers), and one of them had won the National Book Award. He had also published two books of criticism and two novels. The first novel, *Deliverance* (1970), was made into a successful movie in which Dickey himself had appeared, with the result that Dickey had become a recognizable figure outside the world of poetry. Like MacLeish, he had served as Consultant in Poetry to the Library of Congress. Like MacLeish, James Dickey was a public man.

By 1989, Dickey had settled in Columbia, South Carolina, where he taught at the state university. His punishing lifestyle was catching up with him, and his health had begun to fail. To see him in those years—barrel-chested, thin-legged, and laboring on a cane— was to be reminded of Hemingway's observation that when a big man's body goes, it goes completely. Like Fitts, poor health made it impossible for Dickey to spend time at the press (toward the end of his life he was on doctor's orders not to leave his house, advice that often went disregarded), and while he was editor the contest was handled entirely by mail. He and the press agreed that the yearly submissions could be culled rigorously, leaving about twenty finalists to be sent on to the editor. (Merrill generally read about fifty manuscripts, which he picked up en route between his homes in Key West and Stonington.) The notes Dickey made while reading some of these submissions remind one of a man watching a sports event: "I think I'm gonna like this one . . . I'm really pulling for this poet . . . come on now . . . yeah!" He was a fan of poetry, but he could be a harsh judge when the work was not to his taste. Thus, a contestant he felt lacked intelligence and deep commitment "might develop these qualities in another life. Or maybe in another cosmos."

The kind of verse Dickey enthused about was no secret. As far back as the early 1960s his criticism had been unapologetic, even polemical, in calling for a poetry of deep and untrammeled feeling. He wanted visionary fever, he wanted lines that inspired awe, he believed poetry that did not resemble mystical transport was mere trifling and no poetry at all. Here he is reviewing George Starbuck's Yale volume: "For the almost trance-like or instinctive quality of authentic poetry, Starbuck's work is content to substitute a knowledgeable chattiness." And here he is on Dugan's first book: "There are clever parable-poems about dancing mice, and others with the tough-talking cynicism of the literary rather than the authentic tough."

Trance and the authentic tough. Thirty years later, the battle cry had not changed. Dickey's foreword to his first Yale series selection, Christiane Jacox Kyle's *Bears Dancing in the Northern Air,* is a veritable manifesto: "When one speaks seriously and committedly of poetry—when one truly levels—one speaks in the end of something difficult to define, but which must in some way be acknowledged: of the natural wildness from which poetry comes: the unpredictable and untamable part of the human psyche: pell-mell, throng-like and compulsive, an onrushing self-proclaiming force, asserting its own order." Merrill's first foreword had proclaimed an aesthetic, too, calling for art unafraid to be learned and puzzling. Now Dickey was ready with the rebuttal, praising Kyle as "neither a dry predictable wit nor a professional maker of tiny surprises."

Dickey's selections, then, bid fair to be extravagant; yet the poetry he picked was curiously at odds with his pronouncements. Where one might have expected fireworks, Dickey's poets have been restrained. Kyle's book, despite its Dickeyensian title, is made up of quiet anxieties, of feelings partially hidden rather than wild. It is true that there has been a mystical element to a few of the books Dickey chose: Jody Gladding's volume has a Zen-like stillness to it, and the books of both Nicholas Samaras and Tony Crunk show strong religious impulses. None of these poets is a witch doctor, though, or wishes to be. They are hushed far more often than they howl. Samaras's sad and loving poems about Greece might well have struck a chord with Merrill, grecophile that he was. Merrill might even have found a couple of Dickey's selections—Valerie Wohlfeld and Ellen Hinsey—unafraid of things the reader does not know, though their wit is not always dry and their surprises are not necessarily tiny. Talvikki Ansel, whose *My Shining Archipelago* was published, like Cathy Song's volume, after its editor was dead, is the poet whose work to date most resembles Dickey's ideal. Her lengthy excursion into the Amazonian rain forest entails a departure from civilized behavior and a fascination with nature at its most elemental. Still, no one gets shot or goes berserk in Ansel's book, and her language shows more in the way of hard work than madness.

The virtues of Dickey's Yale Younger Poets are other than the ones he pretended to affirm. It may be that this is another case of an editor hampered by prevailing artistic practice, i.e., that trance and the authentic tough are not easy to find in the manuscripts of young poets these days. More likely, Dickey recognized the subtler strengths of his Younger Poets, for one suspects in reading through their work that his was a personality divided against itself. Reynolds Price, in a memoir of Dickey that ran in the *New York Times Book Review*, says that the poet resembled Hemingway most in that both men possessed sensibilities "as delicate as an eggshell." Perhaps Price is right to suggest that Dickey was an aesthete trapped in the role of a Viking. His performance as series editor reveals a like dichotomy.

James Dickey did not live to see his successor appointed, but he did complete his work as editor. In spite of serious illness, he concentrated his energies on the Younger Poets series, partly out of duty, but also partly out of pleasure. As his career drew to a close, Dickey found purpose in encouraging a new generation of writers. He greatly enjoyed his tenure with Yale, and he was convinced the series' mission remained important. It is fitting, then, that this vigorous poet and enthusiastic editor has been commemorated by the publication of verse: the James Dickey Contemporary Poetry Series, whereby the University of South Carolina Press publishes four volumes of verse per year, began publication in 1996.

Even reduced by sickness, Dickey was a figure larger than life, full of bravado and gregarious good humor regardless of his isolation and personal distress. "Who do you want to hear from more than anybody in the world," were the first words Jody Gladding heard when she picked up the phone one day in the summer of 1992. Somewhat prepared by an earlier call from John Ryden, she answered: "Uh, James Dickey?" "You got it," the big voice boomed back. The big voice fell silent in January 1997, and the series was orphaned again.

The person chosen as Dickey's replacement was W. S. Merwin, the current series editor. Merwin is the first Yale Younger Poet to fill the position, and in many ways he combines the attributes and interests that have alternately held sway in the series. He makes his home in Hawaii, every bit as far from New Haven as any of Richard Hugo's poets, although he was born in New York, educated at Princeton, and still spends part of every year in Europe. He knows European literature as thoroughly as any poet now writing in English, yet he is a passionate advocate of Polynesian culture and is quick to express outrage at the depredations of European colonialism. A cosmopolitan man who has lived in many countries and translated from many languages, he is (like Percy and Kunitz) most at home following Voltaire's advice, tending a garden that contains hundreds of specimen palms. Though he became famous for his minimalist style and vatic voice, his work is at the same time deeply neoclassical. As the Yale Series of Younger Poets approaches the end of this turbulent century, as tumultuous in its artistic movements as it has been violent in its political ones, Merwin seems an ideal candidate to reconcile the series' contradictory impulses. His appointment in itself shows fair promise for the future.

Regarding a series that has come so far from its origins on Yale University's old campus in February 1919, come all the way from Howard Buck to Talvikki Ansel, from the trenches of Verdun to the depths of the Amazonian jungle; a series that has registered the impact of two world wars, two conflicts in Asia, one cold war and its centrifugal aftermath, that has responded to political fevers and artistic movements, to modernism and confessionalism and the deep image, to socialism and communism and student revolutions, that has traveled from the time of Jim Crow and share-cropped plantations through the era of civil rights marches to the age of identity politics and multiculturalism; a series that has grown from the harmless indulgence of undergraduate verse to become a major national award identifying early promise and forecasting significant accomplishment; regarding a series that has covered nearly as much ground as American poetry itself during its seventy-eight years of existence, and that has covered much of the same ground as American society in that interval, what can be said today?

It can be said that on balance, considering its long survival and adaptive ability, the Yale Series of Younger Poets has been the leading poetry series in English in this century, whether for first books or no. Other series have had significant successes for brief periods, for a decade, even two or three. Yet, as all lovers and most series editors learn, it is easier to begin well than to sustain high standards. Many series have flourished and faded even as the Yale series has continued. The series has maintained a high level of performance for over six decades, ever since Stephen Vincent Benét first conceived the ambition of making publication in the Yale Series of Younger Poets the coveted honor it is. No one notion of poetry has predominated in the series, and no single point of view will find it entirely satisfactory. Those who complain about the series usually do so because it has not been given over in its entirety to their ideas of art. Nevertheless, the greater part of the varieties of verse practiced by American poets in the twentieth century are represented in the Yale list, albeit sometimes indirectly and often by only one or two books. Most critics will find selections in the series to approve; most will also find cause for irritation. Through it all, the Yale series has set an example. It has shown others what professionalism in a literary competition might be, and its long-term success has inspired other presses to initiate similar programs. Thus, the Yale Series of Younger Poets has occasioned young poetry series even as it has fostered young poets. Finally, the Yale series contains most of the ambitions and many of the achievements of twentieth-century American poetry, one of the nation's significant contributions to world culture. Where else in the field can one look for a record of similar length and breadth? Resilient and various, year after year, the Yale Series of Younger Poets has been the ledger upon which American poetry has been writ.

The Early Years

JUDGES

CHARLTON M. LEWIS, 1919–1923

FREDERICK E. PIERCE, 1923

EDWARD BLISS REED, 1923–1924

WILLIAM ALEXANDER PERCY, 1925–1932

Howard Swazey Buck was born in Chicago in 1884 and received his under-graduate and graduate education at Yale University (Ph.D. 1925). An ambulance driver for the French army during World War I, he later taught at both Yale and the University of Chicago, publishing some poetry as well as criticism (on Tobias Smollett). He died in 1947.

Le Mort

Here on this stretcher now he coldly lies,
    A burlap sack hiding his beaten head.
    The idle hands seem heedless lumps of lead,
And the stiff fingers of abnormal size.
I almost stooped to brush away the flies,
    Musing if yet she knew that he was dead.

Gayly laughing they brought him
    Up the dusty road,
Chatting as if they thought him
    But a luckless load,
And laid him here beside this scarred old tree,
Till some death-wain should chance by luckily:
Those wagons carry back the honored dead.
    But, necessarily,
On the return trip they will carry bread.

All day he lay there, and all night,
    Wrapped in the shining mists that swim
Along the ground. The sullen might
    Of thunder shaking the earth shook not him.
And strangely lightening through the mist that crept,
    Moving like some slow, luminous, foaming sea,
    Washing black shores of twisted tarn and tree,
      The flaring star-shells here
      Over his lonely bier,
White meteor-tapers, his pale vigil kept.

John Farrar was born in Burlington, Vermont, in 1896. He was an aviation inspector in World War I and graduated from Yale in 1919. The author of many books, Farrar was best known as a publisher: he was a founding partner of both Farrar and Rinehart and Farrar, Straus & Giroux. Farrar, who also helped start the Breadloaf Writer's Conference, died in New York City in 1974.

Song for a Forgotten Shrine to Pan

Come to me, Pan, with your wind-wild laughter,
  Where have you hidden your golden reed?
Pipe me a torrent of tune-caught madness,
  Come to me, Pan, in my lonely need.

Where are the white-footed youths and the maidens,
  Garlanded, rosy-lipped, lyric with spring?
They tossed me poppies, tall lilies and roses
  And now but the winds their soft blown petals bring.

Where are the fauns and the nymphs and the satyrs?
  Where are the voices that sang in the trees?
Beauty has fled like a wind-startled nestling,
  Beauty, O Pan, and your sweet melodies.

Come to me! Come to me! God of mad music,
  Come to me, child of the whispering night.
Bring to all silences, torrents of music,
  People all shadows with garlands of light.

Born in Detroit in 1893, David Hamilton was a Yale graduate and served in the medical corps in France in World War I. The president of a textiles firm, he did publish two novels (*Pale Warriors,* 1924, and *Picaresque,* 1930), as well as another volume of verse (*Hoofs and Haloes,* 1941). Hamilton died in 1953.

Ajax

Ajax, the bull-dog, on his cushioned place
   In the new Packard sits with chin held high.
Like some great withered pansy is the face
   He turns upon the people passing by;
And, as life goes unseen beneath his eyes,
   Viola bends and with his soft ear plays.
How close her cheek upon his broad head lies!
   And still unaltered is his pompous gaze!
My indignation he ignores each day:
   But once I saw him in the pantry stand,
With eyes agleam, while James arranged a tray
   And let a morsel slip from his deft hand;
And Ajax stooped and ate it from the floor!
With dripping mouth he plead for one piece more!

ALFRED RAYMOND BELLINGER   *Spires and Poplars,* 1920

Alfred Bellinger was born in 1893 and was both a Yale graduate and a World War I veteran. He became a noted numismatist, publishing many books about ancient and classical coinage (*Essays on the Coinage of Alexander the Great,* 1963). Bellinger was a professor of classics at Yale and for a time dean of Yale College. He died in 1978.

Bright as a single poppy in a field
   This perfect afternoon has been to me,
   Breaking the long days of monotony
As with a flash of scarlet. It shall yield
Full many a song whose music lay concealed
   Until this magic moment set it free.

Bright as a single poppy in a field
   This perfect afternoon has been to me,
For where the summer woodland made a shield
   Against the jargon of humanity
   I looked beneath the veil of tragedy
And saw immortal gaiety revealed
Bright as a single poppy in a field.

THOMAS CALDECOT CHUBB   *The White God and Other Poems,* 1920

Thomas Chubb, who was born in 1899, was a grandson of the founder of the insurance company Chubb & Son, of which he wrote a history (1957). A Yale graduate, Chubb translated from Italian (*The Letters of Pietro Aretino*), wrote history and criticism, and continued to publish poetry (*Cornucopia, 1919–1953,* 1953). He died in 1972.

Merlin

A lonely man, his head among the stars
Walks on the clean sand white beside the sea, —
Merlin, the lonely man of Camelot,
Who left King Arthur and the tournaments
And decorous garlands and the sight of man
Dear to him, yea! the knights and pageantry
To walk beside the waves that curl in foam
And sparkling splendor round him.

                       This because
His vague mysterious power—alchemy
Of mind, by which to purest testable gold
The baser man he strove to elevate
Through curious kabala, muttered words
And formulae, and fiery distillation

Of the elixirs red and white (for this
The allegorists hold to be the sum
And substance of the prime materia,—
Soul-purifier, leaving earth to rest
As 't was)—him lifted flaming far and far
Through unimagined distances of thought
And dream, by pathways metaphysical
To God's own face. And he had seen the face
Of glorious God. And God had looked upon
His eyes.

       So now he walks beside the sea
Alone. And nightly chants he: "I have seen
The Moon, and far beyond her. I have seen
The ringèd planets curve around the Sun,
And the great Sun himself, and far beyond
Strewn stars and stars and filmy nebulae.
Past them across the night, too, have I seen
And known that unapproachable face of God
And now I walk alone lest man should see
Divinity reflected from mine eyes
Which I am granted only to behold."

Thus Merlin. And the waves around his feet
Break in a fiery phosphorescence, while
The stars above are flaked in fire around,
And the moon floats among them like a barge
Of whitest silver on the unrippled mere.

DARL MACLEOD BOYLE   *Where Lilith Dances,* 1920

The first Yale Younger Poet not to have attended Yale University, Darl
Boyle was a graduate of Stanford University. He was a World War I vet-
eran and taught at the University of California, Los Angeles, where he sold
remaindered copies of his Yale Younger Poets volume to his students.

The Curtain

Like some seraglio of an Eastern king,
Secret and screened from gaze of prying eyes,
So is the soul of many a friend we know.
And as some gazer hidden 'mong the palms,
In some fair garden by the water, sees
A dark Sultana for a moment stand,
Dreaming, behind the casement curtain-folds,
The red gold gleaming on her dusky brow:
The hidden beauty for a moment stands,
And gazes, dreaming, from some well-known eyes.

THEODORE H. BANKS, JR.   *Wild Geese,* 1921

Born in 1895, Theodore H. Banks, Jr., was a senior at Yale when he enlisted in the navy to serve on a gunboat in China during World War I. He returned to earn his B.A. from Yale, his M.A. from Harvard, and his Ph.D. from Yale. He then became an English professor, teaching at both Yale and Wesleyan University. The author of several academic texts (*Milton's Imagery,* 1950), Banks also translated Sophocles. He died in 1969.

Tempest

Savage the sea leaped high; on the rocks plunged ponderous breakers,
Hoary with streaking of spray; and the surges with foam swift flying
Moaned by the bases of sheer cliffs, smitten and shaken with tumult,
Furious sprang at the land, and rebounded in wildest confusion,
Twisted and tossed in their clutches the sinuous ribbons of sea-weed
Torn from the still, dark bed of the sea by the might of the tempest.
There in the deeps and the hollows of white crests curling and
        combing
Darted on flickering pinions a petrel, intrepidly flying.
Hurled from the heart of the east, huge thunder-clouds swept o'er the
        ocean,

Trailing their fringes of rain with its low hiss lost in the clamor.
Loud was the voice of the wind; and the sunlight in fugitive flashes
Glorious shot through the clouds with their clefts and their terrible
    caverns,
Gleamed for a time and was gone, as the clouds came sullen together.
Trees in the stream-filled gorges dividing precipitous headlands
Bent with their boughs that were wrenched by the wind as it
    swooped through the valleys,
Bent to the banks of the brooks as they rushed in their mad haste
    seaward.
Full in the sting of the rain and the fury of wind I was standing;
There by the ruinous waste of the ocean I stood in amazement;
Wondered and worshipped in sight of the grandeur of God the
    All-mighty.

VIOLA C. WHITE   *Horizons,* 1921

Viola Chittenden White was born in 1889 in Hancock, New York, grew up
in Brooklyn, and was educated at Wellesley, Columbia, and the University
of North Carolina. A librarian at Middlebury College in Vermont, her publi-
cations include *Reveries* (1925, written with Diana Hunt), *Not Faster Than a
Walk* (1939), and *A Vermont Diary* (1956). She died in 1977.

Child of Adam

I was the rock
Warm or cold as sun came or went,
I was the oak
And boughs grew out of me,
I was the lake, reflecting early light,
Ages ago. The event came between,—
Dark, estranging, mighty, ineffable,—
Between me and my brothers so innocent and sure.
No sign of it dwells in the caverns of ocean,

No mark of it on hills unscalably divine.
What was it that could isolate a race,
That, all the source grown mythic, yet can drive
Me through rejoicing May, a bowed and contrite man?

HERVEY ALLEN   *Wampum and Old Gold,* 1921

B orn in Pittsburgh in 1889, William Hervey Allen was a World War I veteran
and a graduate of the University of Pittsburgh. He became a best-selling
novelist (*Anthony Adverse,* 1933), and his success helped launch the publish-
ing career of his editor and fellow Yale Younger Poet, John Chipman Farrar.
Allen wrote a biography of Edgar Allen Poe (*Israfel,* 1926), several volumes of
verse (*Carolina Chansons,* 1922), and many historical novels (*Action at Aquila,*
1938; *It Was Like This,* 1940). He died in 1949.

The Wingless Victory

Nike of Samothrace,
Thy godlike wings
Cleft windy space
Above the ships of kings,
Fain of thy lips,
By hope made glorious,
Time kissed thy grand, Greek face
Away from us.

Our Nike has no wings;
She has not known
Clean heights, and from her lips
Comes starvèd moan.
Mints lie that coin her grace,
And Time will hate her face,
For it has turned the world's hope
Into stone.

Dragon's Breath

We held the last stone wall—when day was red—
They crept like morning shadows through the dead,
The *flammenwerfer* with their dragon's breath
Compressed in nippled bottle-tanks of death.

They puffed along the wall and one long cry
Withered away into the morning sky,
And some made crablike gestures where they lay
And all our faces turned oil gray,
Before the smoke rolled by.

It is beyond belief
How men can live
All curled up like a leaf.

I saw a man bloom in a flower of flame,
Roaring with fire,
Three times he called a name;
Three times he whirled within a white-hot pod
With busy hands and cried, "Oh, God! Oh, God!"

Now when the trumpets lie with blusterous joy
And the silk, wind-tweaked colors virgin fresh,
Borne by the blithe, boy bodies glitter past,
As the old gladiators throw their mesh;
The dragon's breath leaps from the bugle blast
And Azrael comes pounding with his drum—
Fe, fe, . . . fi, fo, fum—
I smell the roasting flesh!

Oscar Williams was born near the turn of the twentieth century, claiming variously to have been born in Brooklyn in 1900 and in Odessa, Russia, in 1899. He worked in advertising for sixteen years before turning exclusively to poetry. Williams wrote several books of verse (*Selected Poems*, 1947) but was better known as an anthologist, editing the Little Treasury series for Scribner's. He died in 1964.

With Me

When I was born a million stars
    Flamed out of dead eternity,
And heaved the hills into the sky
    As moonlight heaves the shaggy sea.

Out of dead silence wild birds sang,
    As out of shade, emerged their grace;
When I was born a million flowers,
    A million trees sprang into place.

Out of dead darkness rivers roared,
    Out of dead darkness, wind and sea,
Out of dead darkness, dawn and spring, —
    All time and space were born with me!

But when I die, some monstrous hand
    Out of a night that is not night,
Will draw a silence down the wind,
    A darkness down life's pane of light.

And all will vanish, birds and trees,
    And dawn and spring and shaggy sea; —
The weary hills will settle back,
    And all the stars will die with me!

H arold Vinal was born at Vinalhaven in Maine in 1891. Largely self-educated, he did have some musical training. Vinal's subsequent books of poetry include *Hurricane* (1936) and *The Compass Eye* (1940). He founded a magazine of verse called *Voices* in 1921 and continued to edit it throughout his life. Vinal also ran bookstores in Boston and New York. He died, at Vinalhaven, in 1965.

To Persephone

No more you weave, Persephone,
Gowns the colors of the sea.

Your ivory fingers now are still
And your grave a grassy hill.

But everywhere songs are sung
They sing of you who died so young.

And lads and lassies passing by
Place bergamot where you lie.

No more you weave, Persephone,
Gowns the colors of the sea,

Emerald, chrysoprase and blue
That looked beautiful on you.

But everywhere songs are sung
They sing of you who died so young.

MEDORA C. ADDISON *Dreams and a Sword,* 1922

Born in Fitchburg, Massachusetts, in 1890, Medora C. Addison was edu-
cated at the Low-Heywood School of Stamford, Connecticut. Living in
Cambridge, Massachusetts, under her married name of Medora Nutter, she
continued to contribute to literary publications throughout the thirties and
served for a time as associate editor of *House Beautiful Magazine.*

Names

These are names to haunt our dreams—
   Babylon, Samarkand,
Valparaiso, Singapore,
   Khartoum and Somaliland.

These are names to shatter dreams—
   Chattanooga, Yonkers, Rye,
Walla Walla, Steubenville,
   Noank, and Schenectady.

BERNARD RAYMUND *Hidden Waters,* 1922

Born in 1891, Bernard Raymund taught at Ohio State University and lived in
Dublin, Ohio. He died in 1977.

The Well

There are all things reflected here, yet all
Subdued to quieter, smaller worlds than ours;
From hidden crevices the slow drop's fall
Measures with ring on ring the pace of hours.
So deep the mirror shines, so far below
This lichen-covered ledge the cool springs lie,

That none who looks down the dark shaft may know
Where air and water meet. Against that sky
Faces loom dimly, are they ours that peer?
Or yours and yours, who now draw up to drink
A shining pail, as cool as ours and clear,
And lean it dripping on that nether brink?
Surely in your small world you feel the spell
That's lying at the bottom of your well!

PAUL TANAQUIL *Attitudes,* 1922

Paul Tanaquil was the *nom de plume* of Jacques Georges Clemenceau Le
Clercq, who was born in Austria in 1898, the godson of his namesake,
Premiere Clemenceau of France. Le Clercq became an American citizen and
graduated from the University of California, Berkeley, in 1921. He served in
the Office of War Information during World War II. As Paul Tanaquil (Tana-
quil is a clairvoyant Etruscan queen in Livy) he continued to write poetry, and
as Le Clercq he translated Balzac, La Fontaine, Sforza, and Giono. He worked
as a journalist in San Francisco, taught in New York at Columbia University
and City College, and sat on the editorial board of Brentano's. Le Clercq, who
was the father of the prima ballerina Tanaquil LeClercq, died in 1972.

A Very Young Man Speaks . . .

The stars are old and wise. Tonight they look
With such cold pity at us that I know
They see a million lovers that forsook
Vows by their light, made centuries ago;
Yet by the still and skeptic stars above
I swear I will be faithful in my love.

Dean Belden Lyman, Jr., was born in 1896 and educated at New York University (M.A. 1929). He became treasurer of the Union and New Haven Trust Company, and he wrote a history of that firm. An amateur historian of New Haven, Lyman's master's thesis was titled "The Blue Laws of the New Haven Colony," and he compiled an *Atlas of Old New Haven* (1929).

The Eternal Controversy

To youth alone the mad, impassioned measure,
The crashing climaxes, the gorgeous chords
And colorous clamor, florid, fraught with pleasure,
And fretted with the cruelty of swords.

Love is a paradise, crimsonly resplendent;
Life is an ecstasy, soaring in the ascendant;
The past is of rose-leaves and rapiers compounded;
The future is a vista full of happiness unbounded.
Laughter lifts a cup to drain, rapture is the draining;
Not a goblet save of gold; not a song but golden;
Not a mouth but sweet to kiss—everywhere the olden,
Oft-recurring dream, of roses round about them raining.

But what of age, when roses die neglected,
When hopes have ceased to shine so bright and starry,
When death is daily—momently—expected?
Lilia decrescere et rosas expirare!

No, there is hope in age, when hopes are banished
And passions, in their fieriness, are vanished;
When striving is remote, and all unthought-for,
Beauty comes of itself, unsought, unfought-for.

The music must come from afar, in suffusion of fragrance—
"Deferred resolutions," and dissonances untroubled—
To a slowly changeful rhythm.

Age is the dim and glimmering
Close-casemented and silent place—
Sheath'd swords and quiet courts.
Peace is on every face:
And quietude, impervious to gloom,
Pervades the coolness of the darkened room.

AMOS NIVEN WILDER *Battle-Retrospect,* 1923

Amos Wilder was the elder brother of Thorton and Charlotte. Born in 1895,
he served in World War I, attended Oxford and the University of Belgium,
played at Wimbledon (1922), graduated from Yale Divinity School (1924),
was secretary to Albert Schweitzer, was a Congregationalist minister, held the
oldest professorship at Harvard, was president of the Society of Biblical Litera-
ture, edited the *Journal of Religion,* and published numerous books, some of
them about the relation of religion to poetry. His World War I journal, *Arma-
geddon Revisited,* appeared shortly after his death in 1993.

from Battle-Retrospect

Those sultry nights we used to pass outdoors
And through the cherry orchards to the fields
That stretched down to the floor of the Champagne,
And there that steady thunder in the west
That nightly rolled and echoed without rest
Broke on our ears with new intensity.
As those who come out suddenly upon
The sea, whose murmur reached them in the woods,
Are stunned by the loud-crashing surf that runs
In surging thunder all along the coast,

17

So the great breakers of this sea of sound
Broke over us when we had reached the fields,
And through the starry silences was borne
That fluctuating roar, its rise and fall
And climaxes that filled the soul with dread.

We saw the febrile flashes, hour by hour,
Incessant, over many miles of front,
Succeeding each the other instantly
As though in some fantastical pursuit,
In ever madder race. They shot their light
To the last stars; the empyrean throbbed
With man's device, — or were they men, or gods?

We saw the soaring signals flare and float,
Likewise incessant, multitudinous,
As though some city of the Vulcans lay
Across the land with flaming forges bright,
And panting furnaces that scorched the night,
Hammering out the ribs of a new earth
Or some new instrument of destiny.

A perturbation deeper far than fear
Took hold on us,
Never did man behold or hear
A thing more ominous;
So regular, so fierce, fatality
Was in its voice; no power on earth
Could halt that tempest for the briefest space,
Nor cool that mighty furnace, nor reach down
To guard the myriad souls within its blast.

Gazing upon that scene, it seemed there boiled
Red lava from the ground, some mouth of hell
Gaping, and smoking horror to the skies;
Or that some molten tide of death swept down

Beating relentlessly against the fields,
The summer fields that would not be submerged.

And I have seen, or thought I saw, the gods
(Mayhap the saints and devils of our faith)
Gather like planing eagles in the dusk
Above the battle and direct its course,
Clashing in mid-air, sweeping in great troops
To new reliefs and warring in the sky,
Whose immanence translated the dark hour
And sublimized the drama till it seemed
A war of genii and a spectre strife,
Enveloped in an Æschylean shade.

MARION M. BOYD *Silver Wands,* 1923

Born in Marietta, Ohio, in 1894, Marion Boyd was educated at Smith College and Yale University (M.A. 1926). The author of *Murder in the Stacks* (1934), she married the novelist and historian Walter Havighurst and lived in Oxford, Ohio, until her death in 1974.

Sea Spray

Endlessly, endlessly the blue waves break
Here at my feet.
And starfish strew the sand, and make
Patterns in purple, pink and gold.
And tiny silver fish with glassy eyes
Stiffen their tails
Like futile sails
Here at my feet.
And little shells that never knew a sunset
Open their sunset colors in the wet

And mingle in the slippery strips of seaweed.
And blue, as if the deepened skies of years
Had dropped their colors in long storms of tears
Into the sea,
The waves leap up in foam
And fade out at my feet.

Seaweed and shells and little colored fish,
You are as nothing to me,
Though the sea
May wash you on the shore
Forevermore.
I stand and stretch my hands to the white foam
That tops each breaking wave,
As silver dreams leap high and brave
Across the surge of life.
I reach my hands to catch the spray
But it falls, colorless and gray,
Into the sand
Here at my feet.

BEATRICE E. HARMON *Mosaics,* 1923

Next to nothing exists in the public record or the press archives about Beatrice E. Harmon. She lived for a time on Bestwick Street in Los Angeles, California.

Chanson Délice

Old wines for those who will—
    Sauterne and Burgundy,
Clos from a golden hill,
        Rare, red, sweet Lipari.

Old wines for those who will—
    But old books for me!

Honors for those who must,
    Glory for those who dare.
For me a book with dust,
    And a deep fireside chair.
Honors for those who must—
    For me, old books and rare!

Riches for those who can
    Fortune's caprices brook—
But I care for mint nor man
    In a warm inglenook.
Riches for those who can—
    For me, an ancient book!

Love for the fortunate,
    Fame for a chosen few.
For me a wide Georgian grate
    With neither bay nor rue.
Love for the fortunate—
    For me, old books and true!

Old wines for those who will—
    Sauterne and Burgundy,
Clos from a golden hill,
    Rare, red, sweet Lipari.
Old wines for those who will—
    But old books for me!

Elizabeth Jessup was born in Alieh, Lebanon, in 1894. She came to America in 1911, graduated from Smith College, married Kingsley Blake, and raised three children in Scarsdale, New York. A privately printed volume of her poems, *Through the Years,* appeared shortly after her death in 1973.

"Within and Without"

It took Without to make Within a heaven,
For though Within held all men's treasures safe,
Without, at first, was tantalizing, mild;
All blue, with clear far reaches spaced with clouds
Or interrupted by a mountain screen
That tempted—"Up and climb and look beyond!"
With such a rival four straight walls seemed gloom
And it was then Within was but a room.

And then Without grew restless, sighing, wild;
Dark banks of grey shut in from mountain's crown
To low surrounding hills a strange new world;
The air was filled with war songs; rain like whips
Wielded by fury winds, relentlessly
Lashed down on trees and fields and homes of men
Who hurried in, made fast against the storm,
Then looked about them slowly, till they saw
Their lamplight shining on the driven rain—
And heaven was bounded by a window pane.

Dorothy Ellen Reid was born in 1900 and graduated from Ohio State University in 1925. She worked for the *American Insurance Union Magazine* and published some verse for children. Reid lived in Worthington, Ohio.

Between Aphorisms

Come then, my dear—although I warn you now
That consummation is an empty cup
Stainless of liquor; if you take it up
Your tongue will tangle in the why and how.
But never mind, and come. The slender hand
Is shifting nothingness in artful guise,
And to our keen and philosophic eyes,
A vision in a non-existent land.
The little hand, the little slender knee,
The little this and that, are shreds and patches
Of immaterial energy—confess
The what-is-really-you can surely see
All we may know (take care, that ribbon catches!
Let me—there!), all is nothing, more or less.

ELEANOR SLATER *Quest,* 1926

Eleanor Slater was born in 1903 and lived in Rochester, New York. She is the author of a biography, *Charles Henry Brent: Everybody's Bishop* (1932).

Search

I took the road from Brighton-town
    Early in the spring
To find a scarlet tanager
    With a black wing.

I went to Irondequoit
    Down by the Bay
To find the hepaticas
    That bloom in the May.

But I found only sparrows
And I found only crows,
And if there were hepaticas
Nobody knows.

THOMAS HORNSBY FERRIL   *High Passage,* 1926

B orn in Denver, Colorado, in 1896, Thomas Ferril received his bachelor's degree from Colorado College in 1918. Ferril served in the Signal Corps in World War I and afterwards worked as a journalist. He and his wife edited and published the weekly *Rocky Mountain Herald* from 1939 to 1972. Ferril, who earned his living as a press agent for the Great Western Sugar Company, published a collection of prose sketches (*I Hate Thursday,* 1946) and continued to write verse all his life (*New and Selected Poems,* 1952). Named poet laureate of Colorado in 1979, Ferril died in 1988.

Jupiter at Beer Springs

"The night was very still and cloudless, and I sat up for an observation of the
first satellite of Jupiter . . . but fell asleep at the telescope."
—*Fremont's Journal,* 1843

John Charles Fremont waited for Jupiter,
But fell asleep before the first bright limb
Shone down his glass, while stars in feather and fur,
Instead of Jupiter, rolled over him.

Over this white sage Idaho would be,
Wagons would trail the dreamer's telescope,
The stars of old Chaldean prophecy
Would warn the crane to warn the antelope.

But here no Jupiter . . . Sky Women talked,
With crows for chins and blue stripes on their heads,
They circled round the Star-That-Never-Walked,
And stroked the lizards in the lava beds.

No Jupiter . . . but Coyote in the sky
Limped like a squaw and sprinkled river spray
To feed young stars, and letting ashes fly
From Walking Stick, renewed the Milky Way.

Blowing their wingbone whistles at the moon,
These holy stars marched over lodge and hill,
They flaunted fur and feathers while he slept,
And sang of wars, and he was very still.

Needless his Jupiter in Idaho,
For young stars in the aged pageantry
Wear peacock plumes and garish calico,
Stolen from men who came across the sea

LINDLEY WILLIAMS HUBBELL *Dark Pavilion,* 1927

L indley Hubbell was born in Hartford, Connecticut, in 1901. Tutored in seven languages by a polyglot aunt, he was a reference librarian at the New York Public Library for twenty-two years before returning to Hartford to head the literature department at the Randall School. In 1954 he moved to Japan to teach English and Greek drama at Doshisha University in Kyoto. Hubbell became a Japanese citizen in 1960, taking the name Hayashi Shuseki. He published seventeen books of poetry (*Seventy Poems,* 1965) and wrote several studies of English literature, particularly Shakespeare's plays, for the Japanese audience. He died in Kyoto in 1994.

Birth-Hour

There was rain falling as I walked through the quiet streets;
    It was still coming down, later, as I lay on the bed
Listening in the dark to the great drops striking the window;
    And I knew that something was born and something was dead.

My heart spoke to me out of the voices of the raindrops,
    Saying, "From this night onward, until you are dead,
You will lie alone, you will lie without your desire;
    Not even in the grave will you find a colder bed."

MILDRED BOWERS   *Twist o' Smoke*, 1928

Mildred Bowers was born in 1901 and educated at Mount Holyoke College, Northwestern University (B.A. 1923), the University of Chicago, and the University of Wisconsin. While in college, she contributed poems to a Chicago newspaper under the by-line Twist o' Smoke, whence the title of her book. Bowers married John Armstrong, and she continued to publish verse in magazines under her married name before moving to Great Neck, New York, and raising two children. She died in 1984.

Answer

You must answer softly
Or not at all.
Night is too gentle
For a loud call.

That would raise the wren's head
From his brown wing
Or rouse the blinking white owl
From his pondering.

Let the katydid or the cricket call.
Answer quietly, or not at all.

Born in Laramie, Wyoming, in 1899, Theodore B. Olson graduated from the University of Wyoming in 1920. He served in the Office of War Information during World War II and later worked for the State Department, stationed in Olso, Athens, and Reykjavik. Olson was also a journalist, writing for the *New York Herald-Tribune,* the *Denver Post,* the *San Francisco Journal,* and the *Oakland Enquirer,* as well as editing the *Republican-Boomerang* of Laramie. He published a second book of poetry in 1941 (*Hawk's Way*) and wrote a childhood memoir, *Ranch on the Laramie* (1973). He died in Washington, D.C., in 1981.

Hypothesis

A long time ago, I think,
God scribbled this universe
Across a random scrap of infinity;
Paused midway for lack of ink,
And, in the slovenly way of Divinity,
Let it go for better or worse.

Now and then
God picks it up again.
(Earth, I think, is a period
Or a semicolon's half, or the dot
On an *i.* Not that it matters.)
                                    And God
Pores for a minute or two at best
Over the dog-eared palimpsest,
And muses: "I wrote this, I know, but what
I meant it to be I've quite forgot.

"I'll have to get rid of this rubbish soon.
It will make a bonfire some afternoon."

Francis Mason was born in 1900. He received an M.A. from Harvard University and a Ph.D. from the University of Virginia. In 1931 he was an assistant professor of English at Gettysburg College in Pennsylvania.

Sunken Sailor

The tarred rope's end of life burnt through his hands
And suddenly there was an empty deck
And a spent wave hissing leeward. Seas and sands
Too long had coiled their cables about his neck;
And he whose body is salt no sun can dry,
Who is warp and woof of the sea, can never drown
Except as every ship must come to lie
On her beams' ends, clean scuttled and gone down.

His bones are like a vessel perched for flight
In tropic calm; the slantwise fishes wheel
Above his seaweed sails like gulls; the white
Sea-sand lies ballast-like along his keel;
And a curious anchor, hollow at the core,
Bites bony flukes into the hard sea-floor.

FRANCES M. FROST   *Hemlock Wall,* 1929

Frances Frost was born in Saint Albans, Vermont, in 1905 and was educated at Middlebury College and the University of Vermont (B.A. 1931). The author of six books of poetry, five novels, and some children's literature, Frost lived for many years in lower Manhattan, where she died in 1959.

Deserted Orchard

They have given the orchard back to itself again,
And left it to huddle, untended
Under the hill, companioned by only a fence
That never was mended.

The dead boughs twist and slant in the bloom of the year.
White petals drift and scatter
With no one to measure the coming yield or to think
That apples matter

In a year or a life. But the orchard puts forth its fruit,
And in time the apples tumble,
Slice open and crush on a stone or smother in grass.
A man might stumble

On meanings here, as well as on orchard hummocks.
With even the fence uncaring,
The trees will blossom and yield until petals are ended
And ended the bearing.

HENRI FAUST   *Half-Light and Overture*, 1929

Henri Faust is the pen-name of William E. Spencer, who lived in Los Altos, California, and worked in a "quasi-judicial capacity" for the federal government. He later disavowed his Yale book, hoping to make a fresh start as an author, but he does not seem to have published anything else.

After the Storm

The morning after the storm, townsmen found
At the base of the courthouse tower
An amazing morgue of birds,

Warblers and orioles and yellow-throats,
Pawns of the wind's moron power
That broke them on stone and strewed the ground
With their dead, a motley company.
One still alive made querulous notes,
Pecking the beak of a stiff cold comrade
And trailing its wings most pitifully.

Here is fate in a bleak parade
Shorn of its vaunted, austere majesty!
Towers projected in midair—a driving force—
Wings all pitiful, all powerless to veer—
Dashing on doom in the furious course
Of wind that has overtaken their flight!

What orchard dreams of the everglades
Drowsing in auras of green sunlight
Wither at the chill smile of death!
What delirious dawn-symphonies fade
As the stone takes its toll of breath!
Townsmen brought up a truck and carted away
The feathered dead, silencing the cheep
Of the wounded one whose loud dismay
For many nights troubled their sleep.

Six Cranes at Dusk

I came to the lake and six cranes were there
And twilight was there and a thin mist fell;
The cranes were like blooms that subsist on air,
Amazingly white and spirituelle.

The cranes were frail loiterers at the edge
Of twilight, deep plunged in a silver sleep,
Or lovers transfixed in the motionless sedge,
Or tenuous pale ghosts that the shadows keep.

The twilight blew thin and the moon came up
And wove the mists in tapestries of gleam;
The mallow rose lifted a silver cup,
Immaculate white cranes stirred from their dream:

Tranquil and radiant as saints' avatars,
Or like moon-moths, they ascended the light—
Their long legs latticed the sprays of stars
That clung to the high oriels of night!

Like snowflakes that melt as they skim through air
They were lost, like the throb of an ancient tune;
They had crossed the marshlands of stars and there,
I think, had found refuge, on lakes of the moon.

LOUISE OWEN   *Virtuosa,* 1930

L ouise Owen was born Louise Guyol in 1901. She graduated from Smith College in 1923 and a year later married the architect Harold Holmes Owen. While raising a family and working as an editor and proofreader, she continued to write poetry (*Song Without Words*). Owen died in Hopkinton, New Hampshire, in 1995.

"Chart Showing Rain, Winds, Isothermal Lines and Ocean Currents"

So, here, tied in that crooked line,
that is the North Wind,
trapped—and mapped!
And here,
raging, spitting, lashing its dragon-tail,
the furious East gale!
There, limed, caught in sticky color,
Zephyr and struggling South crouch together.

And see, writhing silver,
all the rains of heaven hiss and rear
here.
Look! Coiled and wild,
a hundred green flashing currents,
all the ways and waves of the Atlantic
are meshed and bound.
And wound
in sinuous red lines
an isothermal pattern
holds the Sun!

DOROTHY BELLE FLANAGAN   *Dark Certainty,* 1931

Dorothy Belle Flanagan was born in Kansas City, Missouri, in 1904. She
earned a bachelor's degree from the University of Missouri and also
studied at Columbia University and the University of New Mexico. She worked
as a journalist for newspapers in Albuquerque and Los Angeles. As Dorothy
B. F. Hughes she wrote ten mystery novels, including *The Cross-Eyed Bear*
(1940) and *The So-Blue Marble* (also 1940), and published a biography of Earl
Stanley Gardiner (1978). She received two Edgar Allen Poe Awards, for criti-
cism in 1951 and for lifetime achievement in 1978. She died in 1993 in Ashland,
Oregon.

Three Years from Sorrento

The little boats were patchwork on the bay,
And there were children singing on a distant hill,
One wore blue, the color of the sky;
One waved her flowers; one did not turn our way,
Continuing her song, a fragile thread,
Strung with the rocking waters, the slim boats moving by
In bright-sailed arrogance, the flowers spread
In spendthrift glory on the hillside's stubble, the cries

Of amber and coral hawkers. Do not hark
To those who say I have forgotten everything
That made us one; I recall the skies
Of Italy too blindingly; over in dark
That should spell sleep, I remember still
The heartbreak song we heard Sorrento daughters sing.

PAUL ENGLE   *Worn Earth,* 1932

Paul Engle was born in Iowa in 1908 and educated at Coe College, the University of Iowa, Columbia University, and Oxford University, where he was a Rhodes scholar. He taught for many years at the University of Iowa and was the founder of the Iowa Writers' Workshop. Engle wrote ten volumes of poetry, two novels, an opera libretto (for Philip Bezanson's *The Golden Child*), and a number of plays. With his second wife, Hua-ling Nieh Engle, he translated a collection of Mao Zedong's verse. He died in 1991.

Hart Crane

1932

Not these tall towers of no song,
Stone piled on stone, nor these singing
Streets where the quick life gropes for its little
Uncertain self-significance,
Where in the dark a white hand fluttering
Under a street lamp (O white hurt moth!) speaks more
Pain than a last racked cry,
Will mourn your going, or its strange
Wild-flinging way.

Not the black rush of the sub nor the loud
Stutter of rivet hammers hard leaping
Over blue steel (O nervous

Laughter of building hands!), the silent
Stifle of sea mist crawling cold
Over the town;

But the vast
General grief of the world, repetitive
In the body of no more breath, the first green
Thrust of the split seed out of the earth, the burning
Fingers against wet eyes (O sad
Ache of the bitter heart!) will be
Desolate mourning for you, driven
To the place of the rifle-winged bird, the crushed
Rat by the rail, the slow
Waste of the rotting lung, the twisted
Leaf in the lurching wind.

In the never-ending end of time
When our lips have told their sorrow to our hearts
For as long, and in no greatly different way,
As they have held gossip or a whistled tune,
There will be no deeper cry of grief
Than that wailing of the dim foam (O song
Of the life-caught ghost!) over the black
Breathless surge of the falling wave,
In that shuddering pause between
The last gulp of the lungs and the heart's splitting.

(O joining of the great
Hands of the sea above you.
O last wash of the pale foam!)

The Modern Series

JUDGES

STEPHEN VINCENT BENÉT, 1933–1942

ARCHIBALD MACLEISH, 1942–1945

W. H. AUDEN, 1946–1958

DUDLEY FITTS, 1959–1968

STANLEY KUNITZ, 1969–1976

RICHARD HUGO, 1977–1982

JAMES MERRILL, 1983–1989

JAMES DICKEY, 1990–1996

SHIRLEY BARKER   *The Dark Hills Under,* 1933

B arker's book was Stephen Vincent Benét's first selection for the Yale
Younger Poets prize, but it does not differ appreciably from the previous volumes in the series. The poems in it are set mostly in the ungenerous landscape of New England. Barker's persistent subject is sexual restlessness constrained by Puritan mores, and the frozen, stony earth seen in her verse is felt only as repression. She was still an undergraduate when this book appeared, and Benét devotes most of his introduction to excusing the immaturity of the work.

Shirley Barker was born in Farmington, New Hampshire, in 1911. She was educated at the University of New Hampshire, Radcliffe College, and the Pratt Institute Library School, and she went on to a career at the New York Public Library. She also wrote ten novels (*Peace My Daughters,* 1949; *Swear by Apollo,* 1958). Barker returned to live in Farmington and committed suicide in 1965.

There was not loveliness nor fortune there
In that gnarled countryside, austere and plain;
For there was always autumn in the air,
The twilights settled early and with rain;
A land of trim-kept homes and tidy folk
With spirits sterner than the hillside stone,
Who mocked at things less tangible than smoke
And taught that man can live by bread alone.
But I shall go to look for my heart's kin,
Back from rich cities to these towns forlorn,
And choose a comrade who was born within
The same gray ring of hills where I was born —
Whose laughter is like mine, but forced and thin;
Whose speech is silences, whose wit a thorn.

JAMES AGEE   *Permit Me Voyage,* 1934

Agee's publication marks a turning point in the series, for his work embodies aspirations the earlier volumes do not possess. This book includes an extended verse narrative in the mode of Frost, a prose poem dedicating his work to most everyone who ever lived, an epithalamium preoccupied with the instant of lost virginity, a sonnet sequence conflating the love of God with the love of women, and more. Agee's poetry attempts a lot, then, though it achieves somewhat less. His early verse is often overwritten, but it reveals the large ambition that drove this author.

Born in Knoxville, Tennessee, in 1909, James Agee graduated from Harvard in 1932. He worked as a journalist for *Fortune* and *Time* magazines, and he wrote the text for Walker Evans' acclaimed book of documentary photographs *Now Let Us Praise Famous Men* (1941). The screenwriter for several well-known movies (*The African Queen, Night of the Hunter*), Agee also wrote film reviews. He died in 1955, but a novel, *A Death in the Family,* appeared posthumously in 1957 and received the Pulitzer Prize in 1958. Agee's *Collected Poems* came out in 1966.

Description of Elysium

There: far, friends: ours: dear dominion:

Whole health resides with peace,
Gladness and never harm,
There not time turning,
Nor fear of flower of snow

Where marbling water slides
No charm may halt of chill,
Air aisling the open acres,
And all the gracious trees

Spout up their standing fountains
Of wind-beloved green
And the blue conclaved mountains
Are grave guards

Stone and springing field
Wide one tenderness,
The unalterable hour
Smiles deathlessness:

No thing is there thinks:
Mind the witherer
Withers on the outward air:
We can not come there.

Permit Me Voyage

From the Third Voyage of Hart Crane.

Take these who will as may be: I
Am careless now of what they fail:
My heart and mind discharted lie
And surely as the nervèd nail

Appoints all quarters on the north
So now it designates him forth
My sovereign God my princely soul
Whereon my flesh is priestly stole:

Whence forth shall my heart and mind
To God through soul entirely bow,
Therein such strong increase to find
In truth as is my fate to know:

Small though that be great God I know
I know in this gigantic day
What God is ruined and I know
How labors with Godhead this day:

How from the porches of our sky
The crested glory is declined:
And hear with what translated cry
The stridden soul is overshined:

And how this world of wildness through
True poets shall walk who herald you:
Of whom God grant me of your grace
To be, that shall preserve this race.

Permit me voyage, Love, into your hands.

MURIEL RUKEYSER   *Theory of Flight,* 1935

Aggressive, impatient, and unafraid to be difficult, this book is plainly that of a considerable poetic talent. Rukeyser is a modernist—she chooses to imitate Pound and Eliot rather than Frost or Whitman, much less Rupert Brooke—and her poems are up-to-the-minute in style: irregular on the page, idiosyncratically punctuated, immodestly long. Anything but a nature poet, she is politically committed and embraces technology, showing particular enthusiasm for the movies and the fledgling industry of flight. There is nothing remotely like Rukeyser's book before it in the Yale series. She enters kicking down the door.

Born in New York City in 1913, Muriel Rukeyser was educated at Vassar College (where she knew Elizabeth Bishop, Mary McCarthy, and Eleanor Clark) and Columbia University. She published fifteen books of poetry (*Collected Poems,* 1978), along with biographies, children's literature, and translations (Octavio Paz). Rukeyser, who taught at Sarah Lawrence College, was a lifelong advocate of left-wing causes and an agitator for civil rights. She died in 1980.

The Gyroscope

But this is our desire, and of its worth. . . .
Power electric-clean, gravitating outward at all points,
moving in savage fire, fusing all durable stuff
but never itself being fused with any force
homing in no hand nor breast nor sex
for buried in these lips we rise again,
bent over these plans, our faces raise to see.
Direct spears are shot outward from the conscience
fulfilling what far circuits?   Orbit of thought
what axis do you lean on, what strictnesses evade
impelled to the long curves of the will's ambition?
Centrifugal power, expanding universe
within expanding universe, what stillnesses
lie at your center resting among motion?
Study communications, looking inward, find what traffic
you may have with your silences   :   looking outward, survey
what you have seen of places   :

41

many times this week I seemed
to hear you speak my name
how you turn the flatnesses
of your cheek and will not hear my words
then reaching the given latitude
and longitude, we searched for the ship and found nothing
and, gentlemen, shall we define desire
including every impulse toward psychic progress?
Roads are cut into the earth leading away from our place
at the inevitable hub.   All directions are **out,**
all desire turns outward   :   we, introspective,
continuing to find in ourselves the microcosm
imaging continents, powers, relations, reflecting
all history in a bifurcated Engine.
Here is the gyroscope whirling out pulsing in tides illimitably
widening, live force contained
in a sphere of rigid boundary   ;   concentrate
at the locus of all forces, spinning with black speed
revolving outward perpetually, turning with its torque
all the developments of the secret will.
Flaming origins were our fathers in the heat of the earth,
pushing to the crust, water and sea-flesh,
undulant tentacles ingrown on the ocean's floor,
frondy anemones and scales' armor gave us birth.
Bring us to air, ancestors! and we breathed
the young flesh wincing against naked December.
Masters of fire, fire gave us riches, gave us life.
Masters of water, water gave us riches, gave us life,
masters of earth, earth gave us riches, gave us life.
Air mocks, and desire whirls outward in strict frenzy, leaping,
elastic circles widening from the mind,
turning constricted to the mind again.
The dynamics of desire are explained
in terms of action outward and reaction to a core
obscured and undefined, except, perhaps, as "God in Heaven," "God
in Man,"

Elohim intermittent with the soul, recurrent

as Father and Holy Ghost, Word and responsive Word,
merging with contact in continual sunbursts,
the promise, the response, the hands laid on,
the hammer swung to the anvil, mouth fallen on mouth,
the plane nose up into an open sky.
Roads are cut, purchase is gained on our wish,
the turbines gather momentum, tools are given   :
whirl in desire, hurry to ambition, return,
maintaining the soul's polarity   ;   be   :   fly.

from Night Flight : New York

Believe that we bloom upon this stalk of time   ;
and in this expansion, time too grows for us
richer and richer towards infinity.
They promised us the gold and harps and seraphs.
Our rising and going to sleep is better than future pinions.
We surrender that hope, drawing our own days in,
covering space and time draped in tornadoes,
lightning invention, speed crushing the stars upon us,
stretching the accordion of our lives, sounding the same chord
longer and savoring it until the echo fails.
Believe that your presences are strong,
O be convinced without formula or rhyme
or any dogma   ;   use yourselves   :   be   :   fly.
Believe that we bloom upon this stalk of time.

The Blood Is Justified

Beat out continuance in the choking veins
before emotion betrays us, and we find
staring behind our faces, accomplices of death.
Not to die, but slowly to validate our lives   :
simply to move, lightly burdened, alone,

43

carrying in this brain survival, carrying
within these ribs, history,
the past deep in the bone.

Unthread time till its empty needle prick your flesh
sewing your scars with air, treating the wounds
only by laceration   and the blood is fresh
blood on our skin on our lips over our eyes.

Living they move on a canvas of centuries
restored from death in artful poses, found
once more by us, descendants, foraging,
ravelling time back over American ground.
How did they wish, grandparents of these wars,
what cataracts of ambition fell across their brains?   :

The heavy boots kicked stones down Wisconsin roads,
Augusta Coller danced her début at Oshkosh   :
they spoke these names   :   Milwaukee, Waukesha,
the crackle and drawl of Indian strange words.

Jungle-savage the south
raw green and shining branches, the crying
of parakeets, the pointed stone,
the altars stained with oil   :
Mexico   :   and Canada wheaten and polar with
snow halfway up the sky   :
all these unknown.

:   What treason to their race has fathered us?
They walked in the towns, the men selling clothing etc.
the women tatting and boiling down grape jelly.
:   If they were asked this, surely they did not answer.

Over the country, Wisconsin, Chicago, Yonkers,
I was begotten, American branch no less because
I call on the great names of other countries.

44

I do not say   :   Forgive, to my kindred dead,
only   :   Understand my treason, See I betray you kissing,
I overthrow your milestones weeping among your tombs.

From out your knowing eyes I sprang, child of your distant wombs,
of your full lips.   Speaking allegiance, I turn,
steadfastly to destroy your hope.   Your cargo in me
swings to ports hostile to your old intent.

In us recurrences.   :   My generation feeds
the wise assault on your anticipation,
repeating historic sunderings, betraying our fathers,
all parricidal in our destinies.

How much are we American?   Not knowing
those other lands, being
blood wrung from your bone, our pioneers,
we call kindred to you, we claim links, speaking
your tongue, although we pass, shaking
your dream with revolution since we must,
By these roads shall we come upon our country.
Pillowed upon this birthright, we may wake
strong for such treason, brave with your fallen dust.

O, we are afflicted with these present evils,
they press between the mirror and our eyes,
obscuring your loaned mouths and borrowed hair.
We focus on our times, destroying you, fathers
in the long ground   :   you have given strange birth
to us who turn against you in our blood
needing to move in our integrity, accomplices
of life in revolution, though the past
be sweet with your tall shadows, and although
we turn from treasons, we shall accomplish these.

In contrast to his immediate predecessor in the series, Weismiller views urban life and the technological age as threats to nature and hence to poetic vision. This poet is consciously working in the Frostean line, but his poems are something more than imitations. He is independent minded, he can find the apposite phrase, and his renderings of the New England landscape are freshly observed. Weismiller's is a reticent art, and he does not possess Rukeyser's moxie. Aside from her, however, Weismiller achieves more in his book than had any of the Yale Younger Poets before him.

Edward Weismiller was born near Oshkosh, Wisconsin, in 1915. He spent time on a farm in Vermont and attended Swarthmore College before transferring to Cornell College in Iowa. He later attended both Oxford (as a Rhodes Scholar, Ph.D. 1950) and Harvard. Weismiller has published two more volumes of verse (*The Faultless Shore,* 1946; *The Branch of Fire,* 1980), as well as an espionage novel based on his experience in the O.S.S. (*The Serpent Sleeping,* 1962). Weismiller has been a Fulbright fellow and a Guggenheim fellow (twice) and is a professor emeritus at George Washington University. He lives in Washington, D.C.

Vermont: Spring Rains

Along this road where tiny frost-crabs edged
clawing the iron ground, the water walks
with windy footsteps softly; and not over
this road only, but through cloudy hollows
darkened with mist it paces, over ledges,
on meagre grass and twisted cedar, stalking
the germ of this paralysis, ice-clothed
and spawning winter. The cold hills are walls
that cup a frozen broth: but the cup is offered
over the flame of season now, the world
brews over flame, a pale unlovely fire
of no man and of no Prometheus sought.

Yet from this brew of laden wind and soft
ravelling bark of birches; the numbed earth
prodded with rain and chapped with the dark sky's

endless assault; the spidery step of water
on old grass, and the damp warm smell of leaves
rotting, with wood rotting, in black stumps
and sodden logs beside the careful ways
that deer have, and that the earth dissolving
must show at last, although it be but briefly:
out of this muddy brew of air rumpled
with sooty thunder, and ground beaten and stained
with rain and yellow freshet, will resolve
in one sharp breathless hour, past belief
and yet somehow recalled, the distillate
of this dark ferment, green and young, and foaming
up through the rusty branches.

                          Let it lie
softly, tainting the air with spring, and leaving
only a few dregs: a soiled crystal
sheath cracked and sprung, a crust of loam
high on the ledges, and a broken sky. . . .

Hemlocks in Autumn

All day the wood is open, with the maples
Stripped wind-bare and gray as the racing cloud.
The air, turned sharp with autumn, swings the branches
Upward in the wind: they are unbowed

By weight of summer now; only the hemlocks
Stand cold and heavy, waiting in the numb
Frosty air for the passage of deer, and waiting
For all the secret things that dare not come.

But after dark the hemlocks crowd around
Softly, trailing their long dark gusty sleeves;
And two by two the wary eyes come out
Above a thin cold rustling in the leaves.

Frog

Between the marsh and air he lies
With close-set bubbles for his eyes,
And contemplates with solemn gaze
The slow perfection of his days.

Along his trim green-varnished flank
The water lies unmoved and blank;
His legs are drawn like coiled springs
Against his heart's cold measurings.

His tiny bodice moves with breath
So slight it seems entire death,
Yet he will tread from night to night
As timeless as a water-sprite;

And while thin shadows lengthen down
The alleys of his level town
He will for hours linger on,
A lean, precise phenomenon.

Yet if the sharp discerning coon,
Fishing by glow of this night's moon,
Should sieve the dark cold under-spring
And come upon this perfect thing,

He would know only that he stands
With food in his two naked hands,
And ponder only on the bright
Intricacies of appetite.

Crystal Moment

There the deer stands with morning on the hilltop,
The sun behind him like a thin gold wall

That he may never touch, though sharp light fall
Brittle against his body. Let him crop
Whatever moss is here: the day will rise
Swiftly enough from rock and the clinging mist.
Here is the grass he touched, the stone he kissed—
This is the world he guards with lonely eyes.

Let no bird sound, though frosty barberry sprays
Hang red at dawn, and apples crack from the bough—
This is the crystal moment: now—oh now
Let fall no lightest step on the flinty ways
Lest the deer leap back for the night, and day own
A thicket of withered grass; a heap of stone.

Skull

The mind, and some thin longing that ensnared it,
Were outraged here. In one brief sullen thrust
The bullet tapped the skull, and so prepared it
For occupancy of dust:

And that was long ago, before this season
Wrote its precarious legend on the leaf.
Here flesh was forfeit. Simply, with adequate reason,
Waiving consent or grief,

The mind forsook its trim elaborate tower,
Its windowed room, so artfully contrived.
All beauty it controlled before that hour
The stinging lead was hived—

The vision, all the intricate ways of seeing,
The pallid flesh bemused by its own doom—
Gave over then. But the bullet remains, there being
At length, sufficient room.

Characterized by biblical verb forms and archaic diction, Haley's poetry is a throwback to earlier volumes in the series. She is fond of horticultural metaphors and is occasionally willing merely to observe.

Born in 1906, Margaret Haley graduated from Bryn Mawr College in 1928. Shortly after her manuscript won the Yale prize, she married a man named Storms and moved to Caracas, Venezuela, where she reported to the press that she was writing suspense fiction.

Tropicalia

A grasshopper
With a body
Like a lozenge of amber
And dark green
Beads for eyes:

A frog
With a back
Of alabaster
And belly the peel
Of half a ripe orange:

And beetles seeming
Rusted iron,
And moths that only
The mad could imagine,
With platinum-speckled
Basalt wings,
And wings of fur
And cracked brown crystal
And winter twilight
And dimity
Sere and old
And thin pink glass:

And lizards turquoise
And peridot,
Freckled yellow
And quick as trout:

And the black vulture,
A spread fan
Split through the middle . . .

As the title implies, *Letter to a Comrade* contains a good deal of political verse, poems about international communism and the Spanish Civil War. The book also includes a number of Whitmanian imitations that extol the virtues of New York City in contrast to the vast outback of, say, New Jersey. Davidman's best work, however, constitutes an intelligent examination of sex, about which she writes with both skepticism and zeal.

Joy Davidman was born in New York City in 1915 and was educated at Hunter College and Columbia University. A Jew by birth, she declared herself an atheist and joined the Communist party. Later, she converted to Christianity and moved to England, where she married the Oxford don and Christian apologist C. S. Lewis. Davidman continued to write poetry (*Weeping Bay,* 1950), as well as novels and screenplays, and she edited an anthology called *War Poems of the United Nations* (1943). She died of cancer in 1960. Davidman's marriage to Lewis was the subject of his memoir, *Surprised by Joy* (1956), as well as of a successful movie, *Shadowlands* (1993).

Night-Piece

I shall make rings around you. Fortresses
In a close architecture of wall upon wall,
Rib, jointed rock, and hard surrounding steel
Compel you into the narrow compass of my blood
Where you may beat forever and be perfect,
Keep warm. The blood will keep you warm, the body
Will curl upon you not to let the air
Sting you with ice. And you shall never be wounded
By your bright hostile business of living, while
I and my charitable flesh survive.

Interminably
I shall come with windings and evasions, I shall bar
My lover from the aggression of a star
Cold, unperturbed, and meaning death. Nor shall you
Suffer one touch of pain or recollection of evil
While you are in my bed; nor shall you suffer

The old iniquities of the universe
If I will have you safe.

Now the first ring
Is the devious course of my blood going all around you
And you with a blind mouth growing in my flesh
In the likeness of a child. You cannot break free,
For I have locked a little of your life
Into my life; and the second ring to enclose you
My breast and arms; then a smooth round of light
And a wall winking with sleek and brittle windows
With darkness cowering at them; the cold starry endless enemy
Crowding you in, crushing my arms around you
To keep off black terrors. For one more magic circle
I have the world.

Now in a ring of ocean
Far away, there is a hollow island holding
A flat blue pool, holding a bird. They kill the bird
To find a round egg covering one round nutshell
That hides the smallest yellow oval grain
Of wheat that ever had a life for kernel;
They shall not find your life. Lie and keep warm
In your own rolling planetary shell; keep warm,
My lover. Lie down lover. If there is peace
Arrested in any memorable fragment of time
I have shut you in with it and drawn a circle.

Lament for Evolution

Apollo, having been given my desire,
my ancient passion, my desire, my lover,
I find my answer is no more than emptiness
and a bitter taste; yet praising Apollo, craving
only the soft and friendly unconsciousness of the beasts

outdistanced, I give thanks; I return thanks for the admirable
    delusion,
the bright and soundless explosion of my world
which might have meant fires, instead collapsing
flaccid into the shape of bitterness.

Never the intrinsic sun spawned in a body
so tight and perfect a serpent, Apollo;
never your sunlight on your lover's lip
stung with so cruel, so salt and beautiful a virtue;
never before so nakedly pain
struck the eyes sculptural. Bitter crusts of salt
freeze my eyes white and cold. Apollo,
never your sunlight, never your lean marble
stretched shuddering like my body like a wire. Pure, narrow,
the mind extends itself against the winds,
barren as its own smiling tooth.

Bitterness in the tooth
devours and poisons; whose flesh envenomed
yields blood to the cannibal maceration of self
feeding on self. Bitterness on the lips
tastes more profound than kisses. Bitterness
seeps down the throat into hollows, pits of destruction, laboring
    channels
where my fine pain creates itself to remain alive
with a sweet functional music, while bitterness
mews at my ear like a cat.

Bright, acrid blood upon a bitten tongue,
the fine, ultimate, perfect taste of blood
completes desire. I, feeding upon myself,
lecherous in the satisfaction of myself, pure as a circle
in the round whole of myself, taste my blood;
my mouth, thick and strangling, eats divinity
54   repugnant to the guts;

these guts being sweet and wholesome,
untroubled by realization, smirking profoundly,
discreetly making flesh, and if at times
confused and bubbling with odd stresses of emotion
they belch and sleep again. They are not I
myself, the nodding, grinning, thinking sack, the impossible
laughter of self against self, created in jelly
to hate and make conjectures.

Topped with brain
the whole blind and happy edifice of guts
tumbles into despair. Besieged with sweet sounds,
environed by odors, ambushed by delectations,
the brain grows sweetly drunk on itself; thereafter
sits in sour vomit and chews on bitterness.

It is bitterness to know that I am alive;
it is bitterness to find no reason for life, Apollo,
except the subterfuge and apology of dying,
and to fear death, knowing the flesh will crawl,
nerves, bubbling glands, voracious guts, crawl screaming
away from dying. It is bitterness
in knowing life, anticipating death, playing softly with emotions,
to feel the blind slug brain recoil, turn inward,
and love its own contemplating lunatic eyes
sick with disgust; it is I, Apollo.

And Pilate Said

(For Basil Rathbone)

Pontius Pilate, remembered as a Roman
leaving the shape of a cold hawk on the mind,
is perished. There is no more to find
now than greyness, in starlight

the webby feathers of hawks on chilly wind,
cold crying out of a bird's throat, thin as air, and no man
but is supplanted by nebulous angels. Nor sunlight
cutting and white comes sharp against the dead,
but the throat perishes and the tongue is broken
beyond a whisper forever; nor overtaken
by the slight wings of anything said
in voices, remainders of ashes are shaken
along a thin watery running twilight.

Once in a doubtful year between age and youth
the hawk cried questions in barbarian
lands of confusion, and his answers ran
thick painted noise out of a barbarous mouth,
whereat the hawk disdaining: What is truth?
clamored like starfire from the leaning sky
all shrill with only one sweet murderous cry
tearing fine air;
cry like a talon, like a question, tear
the lying heart, tear loving, tear the heart,
let bravery out, let the clear spirit go fly,
tear nestling bones from anchorage, tear apart
the tender lips, the soft flesh of a lie.

REUEL DENNEY   *The Connecticut River and Other Poems*, 1939

Denney's book is set in a New England from which the farms and factories and much of the intellectual energy have moved on. Despite such landscape, this poet is anything but a Frostean. His poems are not folksy, and his lines are never simple, deceptively or otherwise. Denney's language is sometimes hard-pressed to keep pace with his imagination, but his is an interesting volume: offbeat and brooding, darkened with the shadow of impending war.

Reuel Denney was born in New York City in 1913 and graduated from Dartmouth. After working as a journalist, he became a professor of sociology, teaching at the University of Chicago and the University of Hawaii. A Guggenheim fellow in 1941, Denney published a study of Conrad Aiken, as well as three more volumes of poetry, but he is best known for his collaboration with David Riesman and Nathan Glazer on the sociological study *The Lonely Crowd* (1950). He died in 1996. A miscellany of Denney's work, *A Feast of Strangers,* was published in 1997.

The Mathematician's Dream

(For Robert Colburn)

If, flying south, gas, cylinders, and wings uphold you
On the flockless airs your level course is through
And on the cumulus that buttresses the blue,
You will at last outpass the greener ground
That charts the world with hills and surfs around
Into an eddied fog, muffling the motors' sound.
Your frosted ailerons that sink and gyre there
With idle, noiseless engines will descend the vacant air
To that white continent that ends the hemisphere.

There you will breathe where few brought lung before,
On a pale space where neither house nor store
Is found—or if was once, is here no more.
You'll find that the endless dry wind there is known
As a quick tourniquet turned on the skeleton,
But broad as the horizons are, and solid as a stone.

And to conserve your breath you will not speak or sigh
Or, waste of brawn, wipe crystals from your eye,
Or look up much into the snowy sky.
But, in remembering, old images may pass
Of morning streets in cities clear as glass
That seemed, like this, empty of men and grass.

The still, surrounding, circular perfection
Of no more south, of north in each direction
Will ring you where the longitudes vanish in an intersection.
That will be the bottom, and you cannot stay there,
But lift a cairn, that ancient shape, familiar,
Over the day you came and that day's fear.

Building the Dam

Shadowy as a blueprint is,
And just as weak against the years,
Fade out the payrolls of the tombs
They scooped in valleys for the kings;
And few find name of architect
Or signets of the engineers
Under Egyptian river-gods
Built of some sandy stone that sings.

The dust in every drafting room
Falls sad as drifts the finer sand
Over the curving Syrian sill
The older builders planned upon;
And archways that the knowing men
Would measure by a shadow's length
Some sacred day of Mexico
Record on no found cornerstone
The names of any journeymen.
And the strength of many slaves is there,
But not their pictogram.

The curse of monumental things
Is that they lose in them the name
Of most the men who lent a hand,
Although a thousand came.
And travelers find anonymous
The stones of pyramid and dam,
Except for a reigning emperor's
Repeated and repeated sign.

Song

No use to aim that sextant now.
All homeward stars have drifted by.
These are outlandish beasts that coil
And perforate deceptive sky.

The lead will never fetch a weed,
Nor bowsprit swing, nor topsail flap.
Flat, still, rock in a dream,
She lies beyond the map.

from Elegy on the Pilot

I.
Death in an ancient country was a simple passport
To heights so Himalaya-like the ghost itself was frozen
Like a god's breath, blown out in winter sleeping,
Contracted on death's hill so small a pin could pierce a million.
Yet some in an uncorporeal fire as fierce as oil's and whiter,
Were bathed so softly that they sang as bones were turned to snow.
Death in some countries was a fine felucca, freighted,
And a man with a dog face at the helm, who knew the way to go.
On various tongues life veered to various ends;
Some misers ended spiders, and spiders ended kings;

And whether all flowed or stayed, each to the scheme sank back
As molecules, majestic in the wave, serve springs.

Skies that they saw in death, this pilot saw awake:
Unsmoky stars in animals that, pricked on the tented spaces,
Swung the great circus of the year not with platonic music
But the silence of machinery too far to hear or guess.
Above eight thousand feet his prow's blunt sucking silver
Burst through the veil of fog like a whale through silver schools,
And, plumed with corkscrew ribbons of that mist,
Drifted such lunar distances as Arctic breathes and cools.
His hands moved with the dials: his polished power fled
Through the vast court of midnight like a prayer's wan word
Whose syllable, in the shrine, flies whispering down the floor
Toward the carved ear, unseen, of an unawakened god.

NORMAN ROSTEN *Return Again, Traveler,* 1940

Norman Rosten's strengths as a poet are his ear for the spoken word and his ability to draw character quickly. Traveling widely through American geography and history, his verse imitates that of Whitman and Hart Crane (the Crane of "Tintex—Japalac—Certain-teed Overalls"), but Rosten has little of Crane's intensity and even less of Whitman's teasing ambiguity. This book reflects the impact of the Great Depression and the closing of the frontier, for one senses a natural exuberance muted by diminished possibilities.

Born in New York City in 1914, Norman Rosten was educated at Brooklyn College, New York University, and the University of Michigan. He first received attention as a playwright, but he was better known as a radio writer, working with Archie Oboler. Rosten was a Guggenheim fellow and was poet laureate of Brooklyn. He published three novels, three collections of essays, seven volumes of poetry (*Selected Poems,* 1979), and a memoir of Marilyn Monroe. He died in 1995.

We came during those years
when the land was free for conquerors:
remembering that dawn with the great moon
still on our sails and the gulls wailing,
the green wind coming out to us over water,
and to the shore line of birches and pines
we rode with the lift of the sea into shining harbor.

Out of an East ancient with ikons
from countries of the legendary wheat
with many winds and the speech of many peoples,
from Northern boundaries facing the Arctic
where men broke their violent horses on the plains:
from the South, southward to the islands,
from every climate we came with a new century in our eyes.

Dreaming of peace and sunlight forever
we spanned a sea by the strange rumor,

across the long horizon with the late sun burning
into its curved sky, holding our prow against the star:
Believing in a free place, believing the earth
was still free for us if we believed it!
(The rumor said: Here is your land,
come and get it, march over it,
come and take the valleys in your hands!)

Our blood was clean and we had hope;
we let fall into the water our simple clothes:
it was our wish to arrive beautiful.

I am immortal in Cheyenne!
My signature listed for the ages;
on the white sheet my fingerprints
are filed away in century ledgers.

(Charge was vagrancy; the jail was cold;
Eli, a hitchhiker, sat on the iron bed
and we swapped tall stories until dawn.)
And on the morning I checked out
I put my fingerprints with great care
on the offered record, talking about
the time when I first came through
when a man had to cut his way through . . .

Never mind the tall story;
keep goin' West, buddy, stay out
of Wyoming
            and Utah
                and Oregon
                    and California.

In the space for religion I wrote
American. And the jailer told me:
That ain't no religion,
what are you and how do you spell it?

I said, I'm sort of a mixture . . .

Listen, he said, stay out of Wyoming.

I shall be found among ancient statistics:
my signature next to Balboa, shellacked,
preserved in City Hall, encased in glass.

Ingalls writes Christian poetry for the twentieth century, a difficult task which she manages surprisingly well. Although her faith can occasionally seem complacent in the context of the late 1930s, she was aware of the catastrophe that loomed, and she writes well enough to convey something of the terror of the times. Her best work is inspired by apocalyptic scripture, and she sustains tone sufficiently to participate in the power of that genre.

Mildred Dodge Ingalls, born in Gloucester, Massachusetts, in 1911, was renamed Jeremy in childhood to commemorate an ancestor. Educated at Tufts and the University of Chicago, she became a professor of Asian studies at Rockford College in Illinois. A translator from Chinese and Japanese, Ingalls is also the author of scholarly essays, short stories, a verse play, and four subsequent volumes of poetry (*Tahl,* 1945; *This Stubborn Quantum,* 1983). She has been a Guggenheim fellow, a Ford Foundation fellow in Asian studies, and a Fulbright professor in Japan. She lives in Tucson, Arizona.

The Vision of St. Michael and St. John

The fire-blade split the known roof and the white ceiling,
Glass in windows crumpled to slag glaring the carpeted floor.
Under my shoulders the strong, assured, and lifting arms.
Then solid rush, lungs struggling in hollow ellipse
Of passage angelic through dense planetary air.
My head hidden against the pulse and throb
Of the mighty breast, my hand thrust in the near, delicate plumes
Of the unimagined wings, we rose
Above columnar storms in the first dark
Of the falling season's wind,
In the season of Michael, the time of the smoke-blue asters
Now far below and lost, the stars too dim
To light as much as slanted half-heard drift of leaves
Into the winter weather.

Lighter than leaf blown the great wings glide
Down again till naked feet
Glance upon wide water.
The massed nations, lorn and hungering bone.

Crouch silent by the last slow-ceasing river.
In limitless silence, eddy nor ripple's sound,
Unseen we hover. The huddled ones with countless eyes
Follow retreating lines of ultimate moisture
Departing with autumn to the fruitless ground.

Shall silence fall
Blinding their eyes, closing their ears
Forever?

A blaze, a comet's flight, we pass them by.
Muted mouth, Michael magnificent among the higher stars,
Speak.

But now only the tall form, the closed wings
Against the fallen roof, the wind-clear frame
Of the room I lie in. Once upon me turned
Compulsion of fierce eyes.

Who shall rouse
The lost crept in hunger and thirst to the savorless ridge
Of earth? Who shall save them
Driven to blindness, tongueless with terror?

Shall I lie night-long in this dark more dread
For the sharp glare of the sword driven
Into my own timber
Locking me to a desperate endeavor?

Johannes, give me your hand or surely never
Can I endure this inconceivable silence
More than the ear seeking the small sounds
Of life stirring can for long survive.

Now trees stand bare on the blunt hills,
We walk in the long glare of the late moon
On the thin last stream iced hard.

The nations wait
Huddled against the sea, a rigid mountain.

What of the wonder-working Word, fair-haired and faithful?
Speak, Johannes, the beloved.
Leave me not alone between the silence and the Word.
Time of your feast, Johannes, now with no
Pilgrim nor banner.

Shall I believe again in the sprout of grass and tides rising?
I am lost utterly before the new spring
With no bud greening.

I cannot hold your sword, tall Michael,
The blade left thrust in the thick beam
And waiting.
Shall I endure that Word
You bore on the rigid sea, Johannes,
The night of our winter walking?
Last dank mist of the last live brook drying
And now no sun. Did I ever think the stars
Were consolation?
Only this sword can strike the new fire,
Out of this icicle silence command a lingering Easter.
How shall I dare, knowing I might ask
And knowing I might receive
The valiance once to rend these shallow walls,
With one word strive against stark fear,
Summon life again by the dark river?

Apprehension

So slight a ritual can still remind
The wary eye, the sleepless, not yet blind.
The egg prepared, the lettuce crisped and clean
Rouse microcosm. Specters here convene.

You will disdain alarm, you sitting there
Warm, fed, and having an upholstered chair.
Though wrath of fire rise on the farther beach,
You say the house will stand; though terror reach
The nameless neighbor, never find the door
You closed upon the wakeful night. Before
I set the supper out, good friend, I saw
Blood on the egg. While I heard you draw
The curtains to deceive the too-red sky,
Holding the dripping leaf, most thoughtful, I
Removed the naked worm. Look. Blood is here
And sound of gnawing. Listen. Coming near.

Gun Emplacement: Sundown

There is a scud of cloud;
Birds are eveningward.

Long and lean and black
And up in the air.

Trees show strangely hued
With afterglow across the wood.

Long lean cannon
Up in the air.

Surely light will fail,
Will fall.

Hollow elliptical open mouth,
One ring of light will fall

And leave you last
Of all.

For the Intellectuals

I have put upon my wall
A picture of exiles.
I have by heart the poems of Tu Fu,
The man of exiles.
I have read the most recent documents.
I am accustoming my mind.
I advise
The exercise.

MARGARET WALKER *For My People,* 1942

T his volume stands as testimony. Walker writes knowing and skillful poems
detailing the miserable circumstances of rural blacks in the Deep South
during the Depression. Walker's book includes some short formal verse con-
cerning her personal past, along with a number of dialect poems drawn from
folklore. Her most powerful work, though, is long-lined and oratorical, putting
one in mind of both the Hebrew prophets and Walt Whitman.

Born in Birmingham, Alabama, in 1915, Margaret Walker was educated at
Northwestern University and the University of Iowa. The author of four sub-
sequent books of verse, Walker has also published a novel (*Jubilee,* 1966). She
taught for many years at Jackson State College in Mississippi, where she was
director of the Institute for the Study of the History, Life and Culture of Black
People. Margaret Walker still lives in Jackson, on a street that has been re-
named in her honor.

Delta

I

I am a child of the valley.
Mud and muck and misery of lowlands
are on thin tracks of my feet.
Damp draughts of mist and fog hovering over valleys
are on my feverish breath.
Red clay from feet of beasts colors my mouth
and there is blood on my tongue.

I go up and down and through this valley
and my heart bleeds with my blood here in the valley.
My heart bleeds for our fate.
I turn to each stick and stone, marking them for my own;
here where muddy water flows at our shanty door
and levees stand like a swollen bump on our backyard.

I watch rivulets flow
trickling into one great river
running through little towns

through swampy thickets and smoky cities
through fields of rice and marshes
where the marsh hen comes to stand
and buzzards draw thin blue streaks against evening sky.
I listen to crooning of familiar lullabies;
the honky-tonks are open and the blues are ringing far.
In cities a thousand red lamps glow,
but the lights fail to stir me
and the music cannot lift me
and my despair only deepens with the wailing
of a million voices strong.

O valley of my moaning brothers!
Valley of my sorrowing sisters!
Valley of lost forgotten men.
O hunted desperate people
stricken and silently submissive
seeking yet sullen ones!
If only from this valley we might rise with song!
With singing that is ours.

II

Here in this valley of cotton and cane and banana wharves
we labor.
Our mothers and fathers labored before us
here in this low valley.

High above us and round about us stand high mountains
rise the towering snow-capped mountains
while we are beaten and broken and bowed
here in this dark valley.

The river passes us by.
Boats slip by on the edge of horizons.
Daily we fill boats with cargoes of our need
and send them out to sea.

Orange and plantain and cotton grow
here in this wide valley.
Wood fern and sour grass and wild onion grow
here in this sweet valley.

We tend the crop and gather the harvest
but not for ourselves do we labor,
not for ourselves do we sweat and starve and spend
under these mountains we dare not claim,
here on this earth we dare not claim,
here by this river we dare not claim.
Yet we are an age of years in this valley;
yet we are bound till death to this valley.

Nights in the valley are full of haunting murmurings
of our musical prayers
of our rhythmical loving
of our fumbling thinking aloud.
Nights in the houses of our miserable poor
are wakeful and tormenting,
for out of a deep slumber we are 'roused
to our brother who is ill
and our sister who is ravished
and our mother who is starving.
Out of a deep slumber truth rides upon us
and we wonder why we are helpless
and we wonder why we are dumb.
Out of a deep slumber truth rides upon us
and makes us restless and wakeful
and full of a hundred unfulfilled dreams of today;
our blood eats through our veins with the terrible destruction
of radium in our bones and rebellion in our brains
and we wish no longer to rest.

III

Now burst the dams of years
and winter snows melt with an onrush of a turbulent spring.
Now rises sap in slumbering elms
and floods overwhelm us
here in this low valley.
Here there is a thundering sound in our ears.
All the day we are disturbed;
nothing ever moved our valley more.
The cannons boom in our brains
and there is a dawning understanding
in the valleys of our spirits;
there is a crystalline hope
there is a new way to be worn and a path to be broken
from the past.

Into our troubled living flows the valley
flooding our lives with a passion for freedom.
Our silence is broken in twain
even as brush is broken before terrible rain
even as pines rush in paths of hurricanes.
Our blood rises and bursts in great heart spasms
hungering down through valleys in pain
and the storm begins.
We are dazed in wonder and caught in the downpour.
Danger and death stalk the valley.
Robbers and murderers rape the valley
taking cabins and children from us
killing wives and sweethearts before us
seeking to threaten us out of this valley.

Then with a longing dearer than breathing
love for the valley arises within us
love to possess and thrive in this valley
love to possess our vineyards and pastures
our orchards and cattle
our harvest of cotton, tobacco, and cane.

Love overwhelms our living with longing
strengthening flesh and blood within us
banding the iron of our muscles with anger
making us men in the fields we have tended
standing defending the land we have rendered
rich and abiding and heavy with plenty.

We with our blood have watered these fields
and they belong to us.
Valleys and dust of our bodies are blood brothers
and they belong to us:
the long golden grain for bread
and the ripe purple fruit for wine
the hills beyond for peace
and the grass beneath for rest
the music in the wind for us
the nights for loving
the days for living
and the circling lines in the sky
for dreams.

We are like the sensitive Spring
walking valleys like a slim young girl
full breasted and precious limbed
and carrying on our lips the kiss of the world.
Only the naked arm of Time
can measure the ground we know
and thresh the air we breathe.
Neither earth nor star nor water's host
can sever us from our life to be
for we are beyond your reach O mighty winnowing flail!
infinite and free!

Love Letter from an Impossible Land, 1944

Meredith was a naval pilot in the Aleutian Islands during the period in which much of this book was written, and many of his poems present a bird's-eye view of subarctic scenery. In spite of the extreme circumstances of time and place, however, this is a curiously mild volume of war poetry, thoughtful but not provocative, troubled but untroubling. Meredith's style is distinctly literary, incorporating many allusions and combining old-fashioned inversions of word order with a modicum of modernist elision.

William Meredith was born in New York City in 1919 and graduated from Princeton in 1940. After serving in World War II, Meredith wrote eight more volumes of verse, winning a Pulitzer Prize (1988) and the National Book Award (*Effort at Speech,* 1997). He has been Consultant in Poetry to the Library of Congress, and he taught for many years at Connecticut College, in New London. Meredith lives in Uncasville, Connecticut.

Myself, Rousseau, a Few Others

From the boy's identification
The playground difference functions,
And hesitancy here
Marks surely as tow hair
Or unnatural height from glands,
Sets the peculiar bonds.

The earliest comparing
Disclosed the need for choosing,
Where the rest played and fought;
Even the collective sport
Became only imitation
Of others' spontaneous action.

Choosing is the full-grown gland
Yet to tell it to most were unkind
(Like the off-color joke
Told to a hunchback),

Provoking a desire
For what they cannot share.

This is the daily luxury
Which alone can rouse us early
And kisses us off to work;
And to this at night
We return with promises
Until the last choice passes.

Traveling Boy

Hurtled under the lover-sundering river,
He feels at a sea-green end the journey's tension
Between the longed-for and the doubtful place;
He is interested in the river floor above him
And in its dropped people and its sea-changed coins.
The white bellies of fish provide a weird excitement
For his concentration, and he watches squinting
The red hulls and the upward bubbling of the screws.
This dimension is comfortable, and he settles back
Beside the careless bones of a Dutch cabin boy
Whose centuries are cool and green to watch.
Riding beneath the love-dividing river,
He waits for the new commitments to be made.

June: Dutch Harbor

In June, which is still June here, but once removed
From other Junes, chill beardless high-voiced cousin season,
The turf slides grow to an emerald green.
There between the white-and-black of the snow and ash,
Between the weak blue of the rare sky
Or the milkwhite languid gestures of the fog,
And the all-the-time wicked terminal sea,

There, there, like patches of green neon,
See it is June with the turf slides.

Where the snow streams crease the fields darkly
The rite of flowers is observed, and because it is a new land
There is no great regard to precedent:
Violets the size of pansies, the huge anemone,
Sea-wishing lupine that totters to the brink;
Others are: wild geranium, flag, cranberry, a kind of buttercup.
In the morning sandpipers stumble on the steel mats,
Sparrows sing on the gun, faraway eagles are like eagles.
On the map it says, The Entire Aleutian Chain Is a Bird Sanctuary,
And below, Military Reservation: This Airspace To Be Flown Over
Only by Authority of the Secretary of the Navy.

Fly just above the always-griping sea
That bitches at the bitter rock the mountains throw to it,
Fly there with the permission—subject always to revoke—
Of the proper authorities,
Under the milkwhite weaving limbs of the fog,
Past the hurriedly erected monuments to you,
Past the black and past the very green.
But for your car, jeweled and appointed all for no delight,
But for the strips that scar the islands that you need,
But for your business, you could make a myth.
Though you are drawn by a thousand remarkable horses
On fat silver wings with a factor of safety of four,
And are sutured with steel below and behind and before,
And can know with your fingers the slightest unbalance of forces,
Your mission is smaller than Siegfried's, lighter than Tristan's,
And there is about it a certain undignified haste.
Even with flaps there is a safe minimum;
Below that the bottom is likely to drop out.

Some of the soldiers pressed flowers in June, indicating faith;
The one who knew all about birds spun in that month.
It is hard to keep your mind on war, with all that green.

CHARLES E. BUTLER *Cut Is the Branch*, 1945

This book consists largely of war poetry, or rather antiwar poetry. Accustomed as we are to thinking of World War II as the "good" war, it comes as something of a surprise to find a soldier writing and publishing pacifist verse during the wartime itself. This is yet another poet who owes much to Walt Whitman, and although Butler's poems are generally brief, he does succeed in capturing something of Whitman's manner line by line.

Born in Denver in 1909, Charles Butler was educated at the University of Colorado and the University of Chicago Library School. He served as a staff sergeant in England during World War II and returned to work for the Longwood College Library in Farmville, Virginia. Butler is the author of one novel, *Follow Me Ever* (1950). He died in 1981.

Letter to the Survivors

Men gave it different names: there were many words
Filling the living rooms: the radios
Were loud with the voices, pleading, exhorting, threatening·
And the books came thick as an autumn wind with leaves
Warning, exhorting, pleading. You will have the records
Of what the voices said, perhaps, and some
Of the books, but it was this way: listen:

In the early days it was as though a great
Tree rooted itself in the world, and we did not see it:
Some great malignant growth, and it flowered at last,
Pervasive and unseen, the tree of the time.
This thing I speak of in our time, this thing
Men called by different names, came from the bloom
Of the tree, the fragrance deep and pervading.
And the deep perfume seeped into each man's heart:
And the thing was this: with each it was a fragrance
Of hate or power or greed or weariness,
Or some despair . . . Do you see? We breathed it in,
And for some it was despair or weariness,
And we said: "But it does not matter: man is blind. . . ."

For some it was a greed of power, who said:
"But we shall rule them, conquer them and rule. . . ."
For some it was a hatred, and we said:
"Kill them, destroy them and their works. . . ." For some
It was a passion to remake the world,
To shape it in the image of some dream
Spun from a wound or from a loneliness.
Do you see? The words came from the radios
Into our evening lives shaped by despair
Or hate or greed or lust or weariness,
And we became these things, or were persuaded. . . .

You will know from the histories or from the mouths
Of the old men how it went with us. The books
Will tell you the names men called this sickness by,
But you can think of it as the tree and the fragrance,
And how we listened and breathed it and became
The action of the odor. You will know.

The Other Places

"I think heroic deeds were all conceived in the open air,
   and all free poems also . . ."
           —WHITMAN: *Song of the Open Road.*

But they have been dreamed too, in quiet rooms,
By the lost, by those whose voices
Did not rise above the clamor.
There are the quiet voices—
Strength, loudness, are not all—
That spoke of the dream, of the vision,
Seen in the shuttered place,
The key turned, locked in the door,
The curtains drawn, the room alone
And removed from the streets, from the sound
Of the loud easy voices crying the current dreams. . . .

You were right in many ways, Walt Whitman—
You were right—but there are as many poems
Conceived in the other places, as many deeds:
I know a shuttered room where Roland's horn
Was blown in silence, and I know a room
Where one man faced a Marathon of foes
And smiled, at last, fighting, heedless of doom.

The Darkness

I have lain awake in the darkness many nights
Thinking of poems, going to sleep on poems,
Finally, with the darkness closing on
The bright remembered words. I have thought of the darkness
Closing on the world, the words of the poems forgotten,
All the great beautiful words of the poems
Fading from the mind of the world, let go
Slowly, unknowingly, as from the mind
Of one diseased the light of man's endeavor
Fades to the idiot darkness and is lost.
Part of the darkness, I have lain awake
Watching the poems of the world fade out like stars.

EVE MERRIAM   *Family Circle,* 1946

M erriam's first book offers pointed vignettes drawn from the Bible and from domestic life. It also contains verse in forgiveness of the human failings of soldiers and poems encouraging the socialist cause. Later in her career she became a well-known author of children's verse, and the characteristics that brought her success in that vein are apparent in her first book: brevity, sprightly metrics, rapidly arriving rhymes, the ability to underscore a moral.

Eve Merriam was born in Philadelphia in 1916 and was educated at Cornell University and the University of Pennsylvania. A prolific author, she published over fifty titles, much of it poetry for children. She also wrote books on the sociology of sex, including *The Double Bed, from the Feminine Side* (1958) and *Growing Up Female in America* (1971). Merriam, who won an Obie for her play *The Club* (1977), died in 1992.

The Wonderful Whale

Too immense for imagination, just big enough for boredom,
Like lecturer marathoning on about the stars,
Folding chair creaking and cold,
You suddenly feeling old.

Or staggering Grand Canyon, dwarfing the circus fat lady,
Mind like your tired feet balking, reducing to razor-blade jokes;
Or at elephantiasis Sphinx
Longing for green iced drinks.

It was dark down there, he couldn't pass the time by reading,
And warm like a holiday dinner, leaving him drowsy and dull;
Ought to muse with immortal soul
Inside the infinite hole,

But only felt querulous, like a cranky convalescent
(Too glib for silent pain, throat still too tight for talking),
Delicious indulgent state
Of pitying ͵personal fate.

Some might have penned an epic, or belittled Beethoven,
But Jonah—like you and me—just trivially sat
Not even tossing about
Or fretting to be out.

Murray was remarkably wise for her age—indeed, for any age—and her book is one of the high points of the series. She writes epistemological poetry meditating upon cultural evolution, the relation of knowledge to instinct, and the philosophical implications of sex. These are challenging subjects, and her style, which stretches the limits of grammar and is inclined to odd word choice, does not make them less so. The result is a volume compelling on its surface and profound in its implications, one which offers rewards few first books are mature enough to afford.

Born in London in 1917, Joan Murray lived in France and Canada before moving to New York City. She studied acting and dance, as well as writing, and she wrote prose as well as poetry. She may have been a student of Auden's at the New School for Social Research. Murray suffered from rheumatic fever as a child and had a weak heart. She died at Saranac Lake, New York, in January 1942, a month short of her twenty-fifth birthday.

Lullaby

Sleep, little architect. It is your mother's wish
That you should lave your eyes and hang them up in dreams.
Into the lowest sea swims the great sperm fish.
If I should rock you, the whole world would rock within my arms.

Your father is a greater architect than even you.
His structure falls between high Venus and far Mars.
He rubs the magic of the old and then peers through
The blueprint where lies the night, the plan the stars.

You will place mountains too, when you are grown.
The grass will not be so insignificant, the stone so dead.
You will spiral up the mansions we have sown.
Drop your lids, little architect. Admit the bats of wisdom into your
      head.

Here We Stand Before the Temporal World

Here we stand before the temporal world,
And whether we care to cast our minds
Or shiver from our words all that refutes
The clarity of thought . . .
Whether we wish to deflect the rudiments of source
. . . Bare bastard brats in summing up the whole . . .
These things I do not know.

Words have been to me like steps
Revolving and revolving in one cell.
Perhaps others have felt the limits of the pendulum,
Looking to the vast confines of night,
And conscious only of the narrow head,
The brief skull imminent of life,
Gray granules that, like Time, run through the hours.

Caesar walked quietly in his garden.
Two scribes walked gravely at his side.
The smooth pink marble of the fluted column passed
Reminded him of warm wine from the grapes,
The glitter of a spear dropped carelessly,
And caught by a hand quicker than he could see
Its slanting fall,
Reminded him of the shallow eyes that glinted
As he passed between two worlds, their own and his.
His thoughts tended toward irrelevance,
But his words cut out the veriest patterns
Of an eastern drive toward the steeples of far Babylon.

An Epithalamium

THE YOUNG WOMEN

We have loved the self, each other, and the rounded slope,
For being young abrupt shapes with abrupt words hurt.
Finding that we could not know ourselves, we turned to catch our
    reflection,
And meeting our difference, we felt less apart.
Where the shallow hills are curved, the grain may run iron ore,
And every heartless height holds some slight green.
Daughters of rock-climbers, fumbling in dark valleys,
Naturally drawing from our history the sure step, and the lean
Unpampered war cry, or instructor of immediate action,
Yet we choose an airy present of not giving, hugging the slope against
    the shale.
Now our virginity has gone, with the first step,
And our minds—allowing growth—have already dreamt the male and
    the female.
These are no longer boys that we see, but men. We are no longer girls
    but women.

THE YOUNG MEN

Now we shall listen to the tall grass and the trees.
More beautiful than our morning song that clapped back from
    the peak
Are the things that breathe about us on this day.
We put down our hands and kneel upon the ground to hear it speak,
Returning an unpremeditated dream in glad reply.
What is the time, the hour? On the hill we see a child plucking
    flowers:
The round face of the day is seeded with infinities.
In our minds the children stamp, the strict parent frowns, the infant
    cowers
Behind random clusters, the flower-symbol, to smother laughter.
Compact and kneeling, we smoothe the wet grass to one side,

Learning to touch the earth with consideration,
Knowing that we must be less militant and young to stroke the things
   that hide.
Even the bright dew weeps from the stem at our inept and
   thoughtless touch.

THE YOUNG WOMEN

Fear with us was care. Nature had commended us to life,
And flocking, smiling, nodding, we hid our exactions closed
   beneath lids.
Some of us paused, some gambled and unflowered at the brink;
Most of us knew cathedral choirs and envisioned noisy steeples in
   our heads;
But now all the images of earth have soared and bedded down
   in space.
Care is the mother of the moment whose arms we drop.
Thrusting aside blossoms from the face, we open our eyes and stare.
Released from our guard, we see the night birds swoop
Across unlidded pools down to the hollowed valleys
The day is here! Run, and lift the small child with its flower.
The little ones have been gathering since the first streak.
Old mouths, calling the new dawn with remembered clatter,
Have not left unblessed our history, the crevice or the crags.

THE YOUNG MEN

Let us speak long together of this wooing and our thought.
Beside the water, each of us must strip and take direction,
Knowing that we must move within a destined pattern.
Bending our steps alone from the bank to the liquid desolation,
We perceive that an act of life will fling us through the void,
The spirit of possession, whirling us, with insensate sound
That thins at last, and pointing out, ejects us into quiet.
Marvelous are those stars that hold, and those waters that wind,
The inert mountains, lashed down by the pines and streams.
No lover, considering the day of his marriage, should envy the hawk
   its height!
We anticipate many whispers

In which death extends to life some portion in the brood-world of
    the night.
It is not only the female fact that we meet here: it is the river into sea
    and the bared peninsula.

THE YOUNG WOMEN

Dance while we are young. (There is an old dance of the mind.)
Articulate all the movements that are mute in step.
The deep mouth of the wind sucks in its breath.
Our skirts are so high in blowing, a little wild are the notes that keep
The time, that sing out of the past the tune of the deleted swan.
Our betrothed come to us over the flower-rabble of the hill,
Glad that we learned to smile, for laughter would have tired us,
And tears appeared to be denial of the will.
We took all the variations of the self and pressed about the one
Until every particle of fact was faced and we were no longer
    wine-sick on love,
Nor laughter-ridden, nor tear-dazed, but strangely open,
As conscious innocents who understand and do not reprove.
O wind, put down our skirts! Let us fold our hands, be firm and neat.
The Puritan, poised in brief reminder, cracks the placid pond,
And we would not remind the correct back or the tight beak of our
    wedding night.
If some of us have stretched upon dark grass for other hearts to tend,
More have turned up pebbles or shouted down the channels of wells.

THE YOUNG MEN

We mount the irregular land and halt the advance,
As people expanding into dreamt-of but unmapped country.
Only by the celt and the sign, the earthwork and the roads,
Shall we be able to give form to the early inhabitants, the free
Intrepid man. You have said that yours was the heritage of
    rock-climbers.
Together we shall give the seed and the fruit that grows explicit in
    its step.
Rejecting no light or shade, leaping from crag to slope in the sun,

Drumming with the heels on the earth, the head on the rim of the
    day, till the inanimates weep,
And generations hold their pain with knowledge of impending
    laughter,
The wide becomes unfathomable, and the parent, stiff with history,
Exhorts the spirit of the future in the child.
Room for the irrelevant allows our act of love its mystery
In which the cult of nights abound and images of life take on the
    attitudes of sleep.

THE YOUNG WOMEN

Look into our eyes, for there is nothing there unknown.
At every turn we see some black direction that grows grave with light.
We pity those who lift back the morning and sink into barren dark,
Where there is no deviation from a lasting end in sight.
Here is the harvest, the hand extending, a floor to the sea and the
    air above.
We are not waters to be drowned in, nor have we submerged rocks
    for wrecking.
Where storms are, you have met our temper; the crackle of high
    leaves our talk.
Our love is a whip to the winter wind, and our sleep the corn clinging
Over the full round acres of inhabited land.
What wisdom can we bring you that we have not found together?
Each morning we wake up out of the same mother place,
With the same animal blinking as the lizard, paused and neuter,
Before discovering ourselves and then our shape.
Our life is a nakedness moving through tormented weather with
    a will.
Living with man, we cannot be apart from any fraction of the kind.
Come, O come to us, so that we shall know more of the pine against
    the hill.
Lovers may touch, but the marriage bond is a link without
    distraction.

There Has Been More Than
Beginning and End to Face

There has been more than beginning and end to face,
More than thirst and eventual storm and famine:
There is the strange disharmony of mind and spirit
(Gift of time, family and uncertain heritage)
Oh, and the unhealth of wrong thought and fear! —
The dullness, arch naïveté and infanthood!
For here lies sin against the simplest law,
Leisure, satanic slough, and rude despond
(The image-worship building in the so-called abstract mind,
Where channels made never may unscar themselves).
Death acts: freak masks the crimes against symmetrical law.

What I have not done, but seeded in my thought,
Felt quivering into half-life through my frame
(And so attempted to drown in shout and noise,
In loud primitive ejaculation, and brute moving
Against the logic and sweetness of my proper brain)
Are unforgivable, in the ways of balancing;
In the truth, that we surmise — unquestioning — to be human;
In the beauty, that is inherent in our meaning:
These are the deeds that have broken tablets and disinherited!

Come, let me grasp the power and the basic law!
Let me know the hand that is of a peculiar coolness!
I give the simple promise of self-will, of abstinence, all that
        is conquering:
That mind be grave and life be adequate.

Men and Women Have Meaning
Only as Man and Woman

Men and women have meaning only as man and woman.
The moon is itself and it is lost among stars.
The days are individual, and in the passage
The nights are each sleep, but the dreams vary.
A repeated action is upon its own feet.
We who have spoken there speak here.
A world turns and walks away.
The timing of independent objects
Permits them to live and move and admit their space
And entity and various attitudes of life.
All things are cool in themselves and complete.

And As I Came Out from the Temples

And as I came out from the temples and stared,
I saw to the left and to the right the fair-haired,
The sea-eyed, the rough-throated and the slender young.
Out of the temples I take breath, and count among
The hoard, all the resilient sheen of armor and of sword.

My people, O my people! Lift the sea of your eyes
So that I may remember life from the incensed halls.
Let me drown in the reflection of your corn-gold life;
Spare me and lift my soul with the shoot of many glances.

Behind the temple, the sun has set and risen to the gazing ones.
The smell of incense has given way to salt tang as the high seas run,
Boats drawn high to each strand and companion shore.
My sons are waving from four hills, like four
Sovereign eagles, with memories that the father has forgotten.

My children, O my children! How you do sway, my children!
For each newborn I feared and hated and wept against the wall;
I died, my face and tears within my hands; the palms wore thin
    and wet,
Wept until at last I learnt to feel one with old trees and new shoots.

My land! Land where my children and my people wait!

After man's passion for strange lands grew tired within me,
I went to the well that still holds fruit beside the desert sea.

Horan makes verse of considerable artifice using forms of his own device. He was a member of the Activists (a group of poets in the Berkeley area who collected around Lawrence Hart in the 1940s), and in line with that movement his poems work hard on their diction, using assonance, alliteration, and the curious placement of verbs. There is a good deal of religious reference in this book, though rather less religious argument, for with the exception of a few uneasy and unhappy love poems, most of Horan's verse is purely descriptive.

Robert Horan was born in Oakland, California, in 1922. He was still a teenager when he came in contact with Lawrence Hart at a night-school class. By 1947 he had moved to New York State, where he lived in Mount Kisco and was associated with Gian Carlo Menotti and Samuel Barber. Although his Yale book achieved a modest reputation, in his *A Beginning* was his end: it was the only volume of poetry he ever published. Eventually, he returned to the San Francisco Bay area, where he lived with his parents. He died in 1981.

Little City

Spider, from his flaming sleep,
staggers out into the window frame;
swings out from the red den where he slept
to nest in the gnarled glass.
Fat hero, burnished cannibal
lets down a frail ladder and ties a knot,
sways down to a landing with furry grace.

By noon this corner is a bullet-colored city
and the exhausted architect
sleeps in his pale wheel,
waits without pity for a gold visitor
or coppery captive, his aerial enemies
spinning headlong down the window to the trap.

The street of string shakes now and announces
a surprised angel in the tunnel of thread.
Spider dances down his wiry heaven to taste the moth.

A little battle begins and the prison trembles.
The round spider hunches like a judge.
The wheel glistens.
But this transparent town that caves in at a breath
is paved with perfect steel.
The victim hangs by his feet, and the spider
circles invisible avenues, weaving a grave.

By evening the web is heavy with monsters,
bright constellation of wasps and bees,
breathless, surrendered.
Bronze skeletons dangle on the wires
and a thin wing flutters.
The medieval city hangs in its stars.

Spider lumbers down the web
and the city stretches with the weight of his walking.
By night we cannot see the flies' faces
and the spider, rocking.

Prometheus

*"God help thee, old man, thy thoughts have created a creature in thee;
and he whose intense thinking thus makes him a Prometheus; a vulture
feeds upon that heart forever; that vulture the very creature he creates."*
— MELVILLE, *Moby Dick*

He pales at pleasure,
dives in his drenched rack
toward the dark;
lies in his ropes and weeps
but wrenched past care
for the hummingbird in passage
through blue air,
past joy in the sparrowed air.
Suns and the planet pearls

sit silent near him, poise
white in their vacant worlds
and strike his chains.
Weak on his rock he smiles
at their fresh fires, free lights
that flesh the morning miles;
feels his body sealed,
the coffin open and the rubbed bone
assailable. A tempest of blood
blinds the rash prisoner in stone,
wet in his midnight flood.

He prays some wilderness of water
to wash over these;
some sea and undulant savior
restore these agonies
out of the random flesh
into the spirit; make Spartan
this small splendor, and wash
clear the clotted curtain.

The church of chains has breath,
breathes with his breath,
moves at his neck and wrist
delaying death.
He feels for the key, wreathed
as he is in slow lead,
bruised by serpents, clothed
in a blaze, diseased.
His hands knock against final bone;
and the molten bird, bright on his billowing stone,
picks at the locks, now strikes
where the heart storms most,
drives with the dagger beak through the lost
islands of his face.

Prometheus, granted this grace,
mistakes devil for deliverer, who sings
brilliant in his embrace,
unknotting the metal strings.
He will not see, when once he is released,
the dark blood shine in the eye of the beast.

Soft Swimmer, Winter Swan

The sun shows thin through hail, wallpaper-pale, and falls
grey from its royal world toward colder poles.
Gone, like a grave swan gone blossoming in bone,
a white tree of feathers, blown singly down.

A last, a light, and caught in the air-ladder lark,
south-driven, climbing the indian, swift dark, and listen!
Sped by the building cold and rare in ether, birds hasten
the heart already taxed with cloud and cherubim—
fretted heaven, strained songless and flown dim.
Out from the house that held them in safe summer,
small ponds and blue counties, the chequered swimmers
in air, spring sudden through the closing vault of frost.
(The last, awakened by a late storm, are forever lost.)

But the calm swan, adamant in autumn, passes
through still willowed water, parting the yellow rushes.
His eye, like a lighted nail, sees the vast
distance of amethyst roll under him, the marble beast.

Seen from the shore, this bird but luminous boat,
so motionless in speed, quiet, will float
forward in cold time, disdaining harbor; marooned
in infinite roads of rivers, his wings wrought around
to muffle danger and battle with the wind;
safe, slow, calm, a ship with frail lights, a white swan.

But seen from beneath, the soft statue hardens; the wild feet
must wrest from this pure prison some retreat,
outdistance winter and oblivion; now, in feverish motion, foam
the careless waters, throat, wing, heart, all spotless in arched bone.

Pressed, must push farther on through lakes where winter lies
secret and dumb in shallows, building bright fields of ice
to trap the transparent fish, turn the wet world to stone,
surprise the soft swimmer and capture the winter swan.

We see, serene, this desperate passage through perfect seas;
taught to see ease in agony, see only ease.
In the battle of snow against snow and wind upon wind
the dead lie fooled in the ice, too far to find.

ROSALIE MOORE   *The Grasshopper's Man and Other Poems,* 1949

Rosalie Moore's book presents a puzzling dream world shot through with a compulsive awareness of mortality. Like Horan, Moore was an Activist, and in accordance with the group's tenets her verse strives for intensity through compression. (The Activists theoretically followed Hart Crane in this, though Moore appears more interested in Gerard Manley Hopkins.) A reader must enjoy winkling out meaning to take pleasure in Moore's particular combination of death and parataxis, but the pleasure and meaning are both there to be had. This book will repay persistence.

Moore was born in 1910 in Oakland, California, and received her M.A. in literature from the University of California, Berkeley. Both she and her husband, the science-fiction writer William Brown, were associated with Lawrence Hart. Moore is the author of three other books of poetry, including *Gutenberg in Strasbourg* (1995). She taught communications at the College of Marin and lives in Novato, California.

The Mind's Disguise

The mind's disguise is permanence.
Whether on rock, or on wrecked surfaces,
Wrests the uncluttered wind for the needed enemy,
Watches with many turns at once,
Confronts a century.

Learn early, unletter
Your alphabet decision,
Coming down to
Accident's corner of fence:
Enigma, protector of mighty.

And the winged, divisible sorrow,
Granted, almost—like love,
Is shunt from the high forbidder,
Forehead of No.

Still Without Life

The mind's circle increases death,
Not weakly, but with
A close and capital waiting.

Death is your ignorance of constants and horribles, and surely
Your knowledge of this, and walking behind a friend,
Are the same thing.

Never touch, never see, never counter in all your life
The solid that owns everything;
Only the objects, not us, have
The purpose to live like people,
The patience to love like boards.

Shipwreck

Watching, watching from shore.
Wind, and the shore lifting,
The hands raising on wind
And all the elements rising.

Calmly the wreck rides,
Turns like leviathan or log,
And the moon-revealing white turns upward
(Upward of palms, the dead);
And all of the sea's attack, small tangents and traps,
Is wasted on it, the wind wasted,
Helpless to wreck or raise.

Often in sleep turning or falling
A dream's long dimension
I rock to a random ship:
The one like a broken loon,

Clapping its light and calling;
The one bug-black, signing its sign in oil;
The telegraph-tall, invented—
Moved by a whine of wires;
The *Revenge* riding its crossbar,
Raising its sword hilt:

And I know their power is ended, and all of the dreams
Too vacant and inhabited:
The ships with lights on their brows, the mementos, the messages,
The cardinals, couriers to Garcias; and after it all, they say,
The ships make more noise than the sea.

And I look again
At the equal ocean
With its great dead ship.

Doors

Exists, like blinder or mistake:
Door without face.
You never outlive a door,
Pursues you in front,
Predicts absence.

Doors I fear. Hide
In the cattle of page writing,
In your Drydens of old leaves.

Dirge for the Living

I am the mover of other eyes,
Of other hands than these
That hang from my tree of bones—

   (The old knights, ringing their bones for battle)

I am the mover of other hands:
They came at the pitch of dawn,
Planting their spears;
The quick shrank from their crosses.

   (Winds paling the land, blow again
   The rafters of many men!)

And one came in his iron—in the low evening;
And looking above, he saw the birds at crossbow,
And a horn sounds in his throat,
And he knew he was dead amid valleys on valleys of horns.

They are dead, they are dead in their bones
And their hands are multiplied;
Their eyes have struck; their bodies
Reel in the faceless sky.

How often, mornings, hoping to hear rise horns,
Hear—(or the antler-crashing dawn!)—no sound
But the sound of my ear's bees.

With our levy of bones and nakedness of leaves
We wake in the cold plateaus,
And the stone in the chest is there—
The crows passing and passing
In blind men's eyes by daylight.
All of the streams are flattening the birds.

How last, how loom those we imaged—
As, turning on a sky, a mountain's horn.
They are a gallery of air away; they are
An iron of cold away.

They bury their dying in us,
Under some cross-sword stars.

Ripeness Is Rapid

Ripeness is rapid as plum-drop, as invader.
Plume-fall of evening captures the Turk's East, and I wonder—
The bright-ribbed Alexander . . .

Many in the berried light, riper,
The women.
But he came with a stiffness of swan,
With a tongue thick with galleys.

As one with toads or jewels at mouth speaking,
(And the waves pounding at Cypress)
He came, left hanging in air
The shaking cliffs and carrions.

Moonlight, wilderness cover:
The small wind dries on the bush,
The sail folds in Marmora.

Oh when will he return to this wooden moonlight, when uncover
All we were ever to see—that unfilled tomb
The women murmur for.

Personal Atlas

Moon: the lighted hall of a bell.

Down on the slopes, the cows brilliant as ants
Move in the floated grass.
Listen, their warm bells.

This, after the seas—
The racket of rocks on rocks,
Or vessels spilling anvils.
No longer the old ships,
Their whale hulls.

On imaginary voyages through races,
Through odysseys of ashes I have been
And calendars of stars:
Nations—their moss, their twigs,
Their men and histories,
Their tower-making of piled boughs.

By the low, waving sea they drove their axes;
In groves, with bees warming the air.
Then all the swarmed leaves came down about them,
And they stopped for the saws of wind;
And the morning came,
And it showed in the East like a shell,
And they knew they had thorns of eyes
And feet of trees.

Or raising buildings out of stone and eyes,
Wait in the narrow pass:
The night breaks walls,
Its granite crumbs leaking,
And the hero descends—
Hacking through space like a buzz saw.

Turn, turn to the night,
Though cities are shaking in water,
Though nations be knots of birds:

To the pound of light on these knolls,
The alternate stars,
And the cows—their island stopping,
Their backs like moon-maps.

ADRIENNE RICH   *A Change of World,* 1951

A*Change of World* was published when Rich was just twenty-one, and it is both a precocious and an uneven book. The best work in the volume, however, is notable for its nuance and control. In light of her subsequent career, one might remark that Rich's first book is on the whole unpolitical. In fact, Auden's distinctly condescending introduction commends her poetry as well mannered. In her 1971 essay, "When We Dead Awaken," the poet reflects on her early work: "In those years formalism was part of the strategy—like asbestos gloves, it allowed me to handle materials I couldn't pick up barehanded." With time, she would take off those gloves.

Born in Baltimore in 1929, Adrienne Cecile Rich was a senior at Radcliffe when her manuscript was selected for the Yale series. The author of eleven subsequent books of verse (*The Fact of the Doorframe, Poems Selected and New,* 1985), Rich has also written essays (*Blood, Bread, and Poetry,* 1986) and a sociological study of motherhood (*Of Woman Born,* 1976). Among the many awards she has received are the National Book Award, a Bollingen Foundation grant, and two Guggenheim fellowships. She lives in Santa Cruz, California.

Storm Warnings

The glass has been falling all the afternoon,
And knowing better than the instrument
What winds are walking overhead, what zone
Of gray unrest is moving across the land,
I leave the book upon a pillowed chair
And walk from window to closed window, watching
Boughs strain against the sky

And think again, as often when the air
Moves inward toward a silent core of waiting,
How with a single purpose time has traveled
By secret currents of the undiscerned
Into this polar realm. Weather abroad
And weather in the heart alike come on
Regardless of prediction.

Between foreseeing and averting change
Lies all the mastery of elements
Which clocks and weatherglasses cannot alter.
Time in the hand is not control of time,
Nor shattered fragments of an instrument
A proof against the wind; the wind will rise,
We can only close the shutters.

I draw the curtains as the sky goes black
And set a match to candles sheathed in glass
Against the keyhole draught, the insistent whine
Of weather through the unsealed aperture.
This is our sole defense against the season;
These are the things that we have learned to do
Who live in troubled regions.

Mathilde in Normandy

From the archaic ships the green and red
Invaders woven in their colored hosts
Descend to conquer. Here is the threaded headland,
The warp and woof of a tideless beach, the flight,
Recounted by slow shuttles, of swift arrows,
And the outlandish attitudes of death
In the stitched soldiery. That this should prove
More than the personal episode, more than all
The little lives sketched on the teeming loom
Was then withheld from you; self-conscious history
That writes deliberate footnotes to its action
Was not of your young epoch. For a pastime
The patient handiwork of long-sleeved ladies
Was esteemed proper when their lords abandoned
The fields and apple trees of Normandy
For harsher hunting on the opposite coast.
Yours was a time when women sat at home
To the pleasing minor airs of lute and hautbois,

While the bright sun on the expensive threads
Glowed in the long windless afternoons.
Say what you will, anxiety there too
Played havoc with the skein, and the knots came
When fingers' occupation and mind's attention
Grew too divergent, at the keen remembrance
Of wooden ships putting out from a long beach,
And the grey ocean dimming to a void,
And the sick strained farewells, too sharp for speech.

At a Bach Concert

Coming by evening through the wintry city
We said that art is out of love with life.
Here we approach a love that is not pity.

This antique discipline, tenderly severe,
Renews belief in love yet masters feeling,
Asking of us a grace in what we bear.

Form is the ultimate gift that love can offer—
The vital union of necessity
With all that we desire, all that we suffer.

A too-compassionate art is half an art.
Only such proud restraining purity
Restores the else-betrayed, too-human heart.

As he announced by his choice of nomenclature (recalling both Eliot and Auden), W. S. Merwin was determined from the first to take his place among the most eminent poets of his time. His Yale volume accordingly sets out to impress, beginning with two formidably dense poems and maintaining a highly rhetorical tone throughout. The spare style and vatic voice that came to be identified with this author are not yet present, but the neo-classicism and the wide range of learning that underpin Merwin's work make themselves felt immediately. There are opacities in this book that the poet later elected to avoid, but his gift is such that the reader is often delighted by leaps of language and the rightness of wording.

William Stanley Merwin was born in New York City in 1927. He was educated at Princeton and traveled to Europe, where he was tutor to the family of Robert Graves on Majorca. Merwin is the author of fifteen volumes of verse (*Selected Poems,* 1988) and four books of prose. He has also translated extensively from Latin and various Romance languages. The winner of the Pulitzer Prize (1970) and the Bollingen Prize, he has received a Guggenheim fellowship, a Rockefeller Foundation grant, and a grant from the Lila Wallace–Reader's Digest Fund. In 1994 he was the first recipient of the Dorothea Tanning Prize from the Academy of American Poets. Merwin lives in Haiku on the island of Maui in Hawaii. He is the current judge of the Yale Series of Younger Poets.

Ballad of John Cable and Three Gentlemen

He that had come that morning,
One after the other,
Over seven hills,
Each of a new color,

Came now by the last tree,
By the red-colored valley,
To a gray river
Wide as the sea.

There at the shingle
A listing wherry
Awash with dark water;
What should it carry?

There on the shelving,
Three dark gentlemen.
Might they direct him?
Three gentlemen.

"Cable, friend John, John Cable,"
When they saw him they said,
"Come and be company
As far as the far side."

"Come follow the feet," they said,
"Of your family,
Of your old father
That came already this way."

But Cable said, "First I must go
Once to my sister again;
What will she do come spring
And no man on her garden?

She will say 'Weeds are alive
From here to the Stream of Friday;
I grieve for my brother's plowing,'
Then break and cry."

"Lose no sleep," they said, "for that fallow:
She will say before summer,
'I can get me a daylong man,
Do better than a brother.'"

Cable said, "I think of my wife:
Dearly she needs consoling;
I must go back for a little
For fear she die of grieving."

"Cable," they said, "John Cable,
Ask no such wild favor;
Still, if you fear she die soon,
The boat might wait for her."

But Cable said, "I remember:
Out of charity let me
Go shore up my poorly mother,
Cries all afternoon."

They said, "She is old and far,
Far and rheumy with years,
And, if you like, we shall take
No note of her tears."

But Cable said, "I am neither
Your hired man nor maid,
Your dog nor shadow
Nor your ape to be led."

He said, "I must go back:
Once I heard someone say
That the hollow Stream of Friday
Is a rank place to lie;

And this word, now I remember,
Makes me sorry: have you
Thought of my own body
I was always good to?

The frame that was my devotion
And my blessing was,
The straight bole whose limbs
Were long as stories—

Now, poor thing, left in the dirt
By the Stream of Friday
Might not remember me
Half tenderly."

They let him nurse no worry;
They said, "We give you our word:
Poor thing is made of patience;
Will not say a word."

"Cable, friend John, John Cable,"
After this they said,
"Come with no company
To the far side.

To a populous place,
A dense city
That shall not be changed
Before much sorrow dry."

Over shaking water
Toward the feet of his father,
Leaving the hills' color
And his poorly mother

And his wife at grieving
And his sister's fallow
And his body lying
In the rank hollow,

Now Cable is carried
On the dark river;
Not even a shadow
Followed him over.

On the wide river
Gray as the sea
Flags of white water
Are his company.

Dictum: For a Masque of Deluge

for Dido

There will be the cough before the silence, then
Expectation; and the hush of portent
Must be welcomed by a diffident music
Lisping and dividing its renewals;
Shadows will lengthen and sway, and, casually
As in a latitude of diversion
Where growth is topiary, and the relaxed horizons
Are accustomed to the trespass of surprise,
One with a mask of Ignorance will appear
Musing on the wind's strange pregnancy.

And to him one must enter from the south
In a feigned haste, with disaster on his lips,
And tales of distended seas, continents
Submerged, worlds drowned, and of drownings
In mirrors; unto this foreboding
Let them add sidelong but increasing mention,
With darkening syllables, of shadows, as though
They stood and traded restlessness beneath
A gathering dark, until their figures seem
But a flutter of speech down an expense of wind.

So, with talk, like a blather of rain, begun,
Weather will break and the artful world will rush
Incontinent. There must be a vessel.
There must be rummage and shuffling for salvation
Till on that stage and violence, among
Curtains of tempest and shaking sea,
A covered basket, where a child might lie,
Timbered with osiers and floated on a shadow,
Glides adrift, as improbably sailing
As a lotus flower bearing a bull.

Hills are to be forgotten; the patter of speech
Must lilt upon flatness. The beasts will come;
And as they come, let one man, by the ark,
Drunken with desolation, his tongue
Rounding the full statement of the seasons,
Tremble and stare, his eyes seeming to chase
A final clatter of doomed crows, to seek
An affirmation, a mercy, an island,
Or hills crested with towns, and to find only
Cities of cloud already crumbling.

And these the beasts: the bull from the lotus flower
With wings at his shoulders; and a goat, winged;
A serpent undulating in the air;
A lion with wings like falling leaves;
These are to wheel on a winged wheel above
The sullen ark, while hare, swine, crocodile,
Camel and mouse come; and the sole man, always,
Lurches on childish limbs above the basket—
To his mere humanity seas shall not attain
With tempest, nor the obscure sky with torches.

(Why is it rumored that these beasts come in pairs
When the anatomies of their existence
Are wrought for singularity? They walk

Beside their shadows; their best motions are
Figments on the drapery of the air.
Their propagation is a redoubling
Merely of dark against the wall, a planetary
Leaning in the night unto their shadows
And stiffening to the moment of eclipse;
Shadows will be their lean progeny.)

At last the sigh of recession: the land
Wells from the water; the beasts depart; the man
Whose shocked speech must conjure a landscape
As of some country where the dead years keep
A circle of silence, a drying vista of ruin,
Musters himself, rises, and stumbling after
The dwindling beasts, under the all-colored
Paper rainbow, whose arc he sees as promise,
Moves in an amazement of resurrection,
Solitary, impoverished, renewed.

A falling frond may seem all trees. If so
We know the tone of falling. We shall find
Dictions for rising, words for departure;
And time will be sufficient before that revel
To teach an order and rehearse the days
Till the days are accomplished: so now the dove
Makes assignations with the olive tree,
Slurs with her voice the gestures of the time:
The day foundering, the dropping sun
Heavy, the wind a low portent of rain.

Carol

On vague hills the prophet bird
Chants now the night is drained;
What was the stem this night stirred
And root from the winter ground?

Lord, Lord, and no night remained,
But heaven only, whence comes
Light such as no sun contained,
And the earth shook, and our limbs.

By song we were brought to stand
By that flower where frail our eyes
Strayed among beasts and found
Dim kings dreaming on their knees.

Lord, Lord, and earth's hours were torn
To dreams and we beheld there
On that silence newly born
Heaven's light in the still flower.

From such a quiet wakened,
After the vision has burned
On such birth, to what end
Have dew and hours returned?

Lord, Lord, and what remember
We of dreams when the day comes,
And the loud bird laughs on wonder
And white sheep lying like tombs?

We who are flesh have no word
And distraction is our music,
Who on the anxious night heard
Peace over our voices break.

Bogardus writes highly formal, highly skeptical poems, most of them satires on the subjects of sex and fond attachment. Though this satire rarely rises above mere cynicism, the sentiment seems genuine, a matter of instinct rather than affectation. Auden singles out many lines from this book for praise, possibly because in their dry derision one hears echoes of the crisp authority found in his own work.

Edgar Bogardus was born in 1928 and received his B.A. and M.A. from Yale University. He taught at Carnegie Tech in Pittsburgh and the University of Connecticut before moving on to Kenyon College. There he was a member of the English department and managing editor of the *Kenyon Review.* Bogardus was a protégé of John Crowe Ransom, to whom his Yale volume is dedicated, and the recipient of a Guggenheim fellowship. He died in his home in Gambier, Ohio, of carbon monoxide poisoning in 1958. His *Last Poems* was brought out by the *Kenyon Review* in 1960.

Narcissus to Echo

What troubles you, wild sleepyhead?
Is it that I can make you sad
With all my puckered silences?
Ah sweet, to question quiet is
To question love, for I am mute
In keeping with this narrow cot,
The close hug, the constrained sob,
The pinching shadow we describe.
Love is a well in the world's backyard,
Fetid, outdated, black, unstirred,
Its still waters rank with romance—
Be reticent as it this once.
What stops your lips from wandering loose
Except the closet of my kiss?
And if our love is so divine,
Why talk in its soft church? So then
Beware of Psyche's bad mistake
Whose candle gave Love one good look,

And never try to know too well
The lineaments of my vague soul.
The rich in words have made poor lovers.
Quick meetings, corners, keys, hush, fevers,
The garbaged alleyways love prowls,
At these tight things your light soul fails,
And you would have me mix myself
In your full day of friends and golf
Until what energy we share
Is a pretty rug for your hard floor.
You smile at me and quote the wide
And courteous Christ, but what of God?
Eve learned how secrets have His grace,
And Heaven holds no open house.
You hate my girls and yet adore it
When your soft harlots milk my spirit.
Ah sweet, somewhere I too was taught
This slender thing of ours is but
A Romeo itself and woos
The fattest Juliet there is,
Who is all disparate acts, all breadth,
All leaps that burst the heart with width.
Yet Capulets and Montagues
Will never mix without the fuss
That leads to childish tragedy.
Cards, cookbooks, irons, gardening, play,
The household remedies love takes,
These things your bustling bosom likes,
And you would level us the space
To build for love a stalwart house,
But love wants balconies and paint
Before surveying and cement.
O I am sick of love that needs the excuse
Of names like husband, classmate, niece,
Neighbor, whore, or even friend,
Names to weld some homely bond.
I wish that love were a spring ignored

And not a well in the world's backyard,
A spring that leapt from mountains of mind
To travel the fields where buds are found.
No one has ever been in love,
But drink what water heaven will give.
Come stretch by me and my dark thrusts
And let my tight lips dart your breasts
Till countless kisses drive you numb
With tiny ecstasies of shame.
Silent as a secret, green,
Then lie and listen to the moon,
And we will try some nameless troth
To keep us from that homemade death.

This book contains verse that is both made with care and freighted with care, for it is much concerned with large metaphysical questions. Hoffman rhymes resourcefully, on one occasion casting couplets across stanza breaks, and his titles often form the first lines of his poems, à la Marianne Moore. Many of Hoffman's poems are set on the New England coast, and the book perhaps owes something to the littoral landscape of Elizabeth Bishop's *North & South*. In any case, this is a consciously literary volume, and the reader will hear echoes of Housman, Stevens, and Yeats. Auden, too: one finds a poem about Icarus that mentions Breughel.

Born in New York City in 1923, Daniel Hoffman was educated at Columbia University and served in the Army Air Corps during World War II. In addition to his Yale volume, he is the author of ten books of verse (*Hang-Gliding from Helicon: New and Selected Poems,* 1988), as well as criticism and translations (from Hungarian). He has been a Guggenheim fellow and Consultant in Poetry to the Library of Congress. Hoffman teaches at the University of Pennsylvania and lives in Swarthmore, Pennsylvania.

The Seals in Penobscot Bay

hadn't heard of the atom bomb,
so I shouted a warning to them.

Our destroyer (on trial run) slid by
the rocks where they gamboled and played;

they must have misunderstood,
or perhaps not one of them heard

me over the engines and tides.
As I watched them over our wake

I saw their sleek skins in the sun
ripple, light-flecked, on the rock,

plunge, bubbling, into the brine,
and couple & laugh in the troughs

between the waves' whitecaps and froth.
Then the males clambered clumsily up

and lustily crowed like seacocks,
sure that their prowess held thrall

all the sharks, other seals, and seagulls.
And daintily flipped the females,

seawenches with musical tails;
each looked at the Atlantic as

though it were her looking-glass.
If my warning had ever been heard

it was sound none would now ever heed.
And I, while I watched those far seals,

tasted honey that buzzed in my ears
and saw, out to windward, the sails

of an obsolete ship with banked oars
that swept like two combs through the spray

And I wished for a vacuum of wax
to ward away all those strange sounds,

yet I envied the sweet agony
of him who was tied to the mast,

when the boom, when the boom, when the boom
of guns punched dark holes in the sky.

An Armada of Thirty Whales

(Galleons in sea-pomp) sails
over the emerald ocean.

The ceremonial motion
of their ponderous race is

given dandiacal graces
in the ballet of their geysers.

Eyes deep-set in whalebone vizors
have found a Floridian beach;

they leave their green world to fish.
Like the Pliocene midge, they declare

their element henceforth air.
What land they walk upon

becomes their Holy Land;
when these pilgrims have all found tongue

how their canticles shall be sung!
They nudge the beach with their noses,

eager for hedgerows and roses;
they raise their great snouts from the sea

and exulting gigantically
each trumpets a sousaphone wheeze

and stretches his finfitted knees.
But they who won't swim and can't stand

lie mired in mud and in sand,
And the sea and the wind and the worms

will contest the last will of the Sperms.

At Provincetown

Over the wharves at Provincetown
we watched the hooded gulls manoeuvre.

As one last gull, in late arrival,
flung his wings before our face

crying *"Wait!,"* . . . *"Wait!,"* in a race
to ride their aerial carousel,

we saw his dark-dipt head, eye-bead,
each individual grace recede

as all swooped up, then spun, and fell
unmoving in motion. Here was pure flight,
free from all bird-appetite.

Then the highest soarer saw
the *Mary Magdalena* yaw
laden low with mackerel.

       ✿   ✿   ✿

Beauty is the moment moving
toward unpremeditate perfection.†

Over the wharves at Provincetown
the gulls within our arteries soaring

† The author notes that this couplet has since been deleted.

almost complete the great mobile
that all but froze gullsblood to steel.

Other wings across the harbour
flash like swords and dive for garbage.

Lobsterpot Labyrinths

Lobsterpot labyrinths wait. A porridge
of sand dries slowly. Sunlight in cages
and tides that seep below the cordage

have some connection with their waiting.
Ternmewed winds pour past their ribs
gathering old fishheads gaping

with the smell of death; there is a splendour
in their ramshackle spined ridgepoles
structural as architecture.

But drop one where the current yaws
unlit, its ramp wrought miniature
tensing to tread of knuckled claws

that probe the cordage aperture:
Primordial patterns close like doors
upon the crusted Minotaur.

That's what lobsterpots are for;
yet traps hold pleasure free, abstract.
Did Daedalus need a beast to spur

artist to art or artifact?

Ephemeridae

Dark specks whirr like lint alive in the sunlight.
The sky above the birches is disturbed.

Swarms swarm between pure heaven and treetops:
it's the mayflies' four-hour frenzy before their fall.

Waterward, they lay eggs in their dying
spasms, having then endured it all.

For five long shimmering afternoons that summer
we walked beneath the birchgroves on the shore

and watched the empty light on leaftips pour
and out of nowhere whirled the nebulae,

gadding gilded, all green energy, toward death.
After, the birches stirred, and we beneath

saw south-flying mallards bleak the air.
Green turns husk now. The world's shrunk to the bone.

Our thin flesh alone
through this long, cold, fruitless season

scampers frantic in wild whirligig motion
while larvae of the mayfly wait

and mallards migrate and the sap runs slow;
ours alone from time strains to purchase

pleasures mayflies find among the birches.

JOHN ASHBERY *Some Trees,* 1956

Constantly shifting in stance and tone, Ashbery's first book continues to puzzle readers today, forty years after its publication. In retrospect, *Some Trees* does seem an early effort—it contains many imitations of Stevens and a number of slight poems—yet the elements that would make up the poet's mature style are already in evidence: the lyric gift, the camp flippancy, the concomitant interest in the vernacular and the archaic, the high seriousness smuggled in under cover of irony, the outrageous obstacles placed in the way of a reader's attempt at synthesis.

John Ashbery was born in Sodus, New York, in 1927. He was educated at Harvard and Columbia and was a Fulbright scholar in France. Ashbery has been an art critic for the *International Herald-Tribune* in Paris and *Newsweek* magazine, and he was for a period executive editor of *Art News.* In addition to seventeen volumes of poetry (*Selected Poems,* 1985), Ashbery has published three plays, a novel (with James Schuyler), and a volume of art criticism. He has been a Guggenheim fellow (twice) and has won the Pulitzer Prize (1976), the Bollingen Prize, the National Book Award, and the National Book Critics Circle Award. He lives in New York City.

The Instruction Manual

As I sit looking out of a window of the building
I wish I did not have to write the instruction manual on the uses of a
    new metal.
I look down into the street and see people, each walking with an
    inner peace,
And envy them—they are so far away from me!
Not one of them has to worry about getting out this manual on
    schedule.
And, as my way is, I begin to dream, resting my elbows on the desk
    and leaning out of the window a little,
Of dim Guadalajara! City of rose-colored flowers!
City I wanted most to see, and most did not see, in Mexico!
But I fancy I see, under the press of having to write the instruction
    manual,
Your public square, city, with its elaborate little bandstand!
The band is playing *Scheherazade* by Rimsky-Korsakov.

Around stand the flower girls, handing out rose- and lemon-colored
   flowers,
Each attractive in her rose-and-blue striped dress (Oh! such shades of
   rose and blue),
And nearby is the little white booth where women in green serve you
   green and yellow fruit.
The couples are parading; everyone is in a holiday mood.
First, leading the parade, is a dapper fellow
Clothed in deep blue. On his head sits a white hat
And he wears a mustache, which has been trimmed for the occasion.
His dear one, his wife, is young and pretty; her shawl is rose, pink,
   and white.
Her slippers are patent leather, in the American fashion,
And she carries a fan, for she is modest, and does not want the crowd
   to see her face too often.
But everybody is so busy with his wife or loved one
I doubt they would notice the mustachioed man's wife.
Here come the boys! They are skipping and throwing little things on
   the sidewalk
Which is made of gray tile. One of them, a little older, has a toothpick
   in his teeth.
He is silenter than the rest, and affects not to notice the pretty young
   girls in white.
But his friends notice them, and shout their jeers at the laughing girls.
Yet soon all this will cease, with the deepening of their years,
And love bring each to the parade grounds for another reason.
But I have lost sight of the young fellow with the toothpick.
Wait—there he is—on the other side of the bandstand,
Secluded from his friends, in earnest talk with a young girl
Of fourteen or fifteen. I try to hear what they are saying
But it seems they are just mumbling something—shy words of love,
   probably.
She is slightly taller than he, and looks quietly down into his
   sincere eyes.
She is wearing white. The breeze ruffles her long fine black hair
   against her olive cheek.

Obviously she is in love. The boy, the young boy with the toothpick,
    he is in love too;
His eyes show it. Turning from this couple,
I see there is an intermission in the concert.
The paraders are resting and sipping drinks through straws
(The drinks are dispensed from a large glass crock by a lady in
    dark blue),
And the musicians mingle among them, in their creamy white
    uniforms, and talk
About the weather, perhaps, or how their kids are doing at school.

Let us take this opportunity to tiptoe into one of the side streets.
Here you may see one of those white houses with green trim
That are so popular here. Look—I told you!
It is cool and dim inside, but the patio is sunny.
An old woman in gray sits there, fanning herself with a palm leaf fan.
She welcomes us to her patio, and offers us a cooling drink.
"My son is in Mexico City," she says. "He would welcome you too
If he were here. But his job is with a bank there.
Look, here is a photograph of him,"
And a dark-skinned lad with pearly teeth grins out at us from the
    worn leather frame.
We thank her for her hospitality, for it is getting late
And we must catch a view of the city, before we leave, from a good
    high place.
That church tower will do—the faded pink one, there against the
    fierce blue of the sky. Slowly we enter.
The caretaker, an old man dressed in brown and gray, asks us how
    long we have been in the city, and how we like it here.
His daughter is scrubbing the steps—she nods to us as we pass into
    the tower.
Soon we have reached the top, and the whole network of the city
    extends before us.
There is the rich quarter, with its houses of pink and white, and its
    crumbling, leafy terraces.
There is the poorer quarter, its homes a deep blue.

There is the market, where men are selling hats and swatting flies
And there is the public library, painted several shades of pale green
     and beige.
Look! There is the square we just came from, with the promenaders.
There are fewer of them, now that the heat of the day has increased,
But the young boy and girl still lurk in the shadows of the bandstand.
And there is the home of the little old lady—
She is still sitting in the patio, fanning herself.
How limited, but how complete withal, has been our experience of
     Guadalajara!
We have seen young love, married love, and the love of an aged
     mother for her son.
We have heard the music, tasted the drinks, and looked at colored
     houses.
What more is there to do, except stay? And that we cannot do.
And as a last breeze freshens the top of the weathered old tower, I
     turn my gaze
Back to the instruction manual which has made me dream of
     Guadalajara.

The Young Son

   The screen of supreme good fortune curved his absolute smile into
a celestial scream. These things (the most arbitrary that could exist)
wakened denials, thoughts of putrid reversals as he traced the green
paths to and fro. Here and there a bird sang, a rose silenced her expres-
sion of him, and all the gaga flowers wondered. But they puzzled the
wanderer with their vague wearinesses. Is the conclusion, he asked,
the road forced by concubines from exact meters of strategy? Surely
the trees are hinged to no definite purpose or surface. Yet now a won-
der would shoot up, all one color, and virtues would jostle each other to
get a view of nothing—the crowded house, two faces glued fast to the
mirror, corners and the bustling forest ever preparing, ever menacing
its own shape with a shadow of the evil defenses gotten up and in fact
already exhausted in some void of darkness, some kingdom he knew
the earth could not even bother to avoid if the minutes arranged and

126

divine lettermen with smiling cries were to come in the evening of administration and night which no cure, no bird ever more compulsory, no subject apparently intent on its heart's own demon would forestall even if the truths she told of were now being seriously lit, one by one, in the hushed and fast darkening room.

Some Trees

These are amazing: each
Joining a neighbor, as though speech
Were a still performance.
Arranging by chance

To meet as far this morning
From the world as agreeing
With it, you and I
Are suddenly what the trees try

To tell us we are:
That their merely being there
Means something; that soon
We may touch, love, explain.

And glad not to have invented
Such comeliness, we are surrounded:
A silence already filled with noises,
A canvas on which emerges

A chorus of smiles, a winter morning.
Placed in a puzzling light, and moving,
Our days put on such reticence
These accents seem their own defense.

The Painter

Sitting between the sea and the buildings
He enjoyed painting the sea's portrait.
But just as children imagine a prayer
Is merely silence, he expected his subject
To rush up the sand, and, seizing a brush,
Plaster its own portrait on the canvas.

So there was never any paint on his canvas
Until the people who lived in the buildings
Put him to work: "Try using the brush
As a means to an end. Select, for a portrait,
Something less angry and large, and more subject
To a painter's moods, or, perhaps, to a prayer."

How could he explain to them his prayer
That nature, not art, might usurp the canvas?
He chose his wife for a new subject,
Making her vast, like ruined buildings,
As if, forgetting itself, the portrait
Had expressed itself without a brush.

Slightly encouraged, he dipped his brush
In the sea, murmuring a heartfelt prayer:
"My soul, when I paint this next portrait
Let it be you who wrecks the canvas."
The news spread like wildfire through the buildings:
He had gone back to the sea for his subject.

Imagine a painter crucified by his subject!
Too exhausted even to lift his brush,
He provoked some artists leaning from the buildings
To malicious mirth: "We haven't a prayer
Now, of putting ourselves on canvas,
Or getting the sea to sit for a portrait!"

Others declared it a self-portrait.
Finally all indications of a subject
Began to fade, leaving the canvas
Perfectly white. He put down the brush.
At once a howl, that was also a prayer,
Arose from the overcrowded buildings.

They tossed him, the portrait, from the tallest of the buildings;
And the sea devoured the canvas and the brush
As if his subject had decided to remain a prayer.

The Pied Piper

Under the day's crust a half-eaten child
And further sores which eyesight shall reveal
And they live. But what of dark elders
Whose touch at nightfall must now be
To keep their promise? Misery
Starches the host's one bed, his hand
Falls like an axe on her curls:
"Come in, come in! Better that the winter
Blaze unseen, than we two sleep apart!"

Who in old age will often part
From single sleep at the murmur
Of acerb revels under the hill;
Whose children couple as the earth crumbles
In vanity forever going down
A sunlit road, for his love was strongest
Who never loved them at all, and his notes
Most civil, laughing not to return.

This volume is conservative in style, even as it seeks to be daring in its mores. Like Whitman and Williams before him, Wright felt that no subject was inherently unpoetic, and his poems wish to be untrameled by respectability and unprejudiced with respect to culture or class. This poet later became a leading practitioner of a species of symbolism known as the "deep image." His early work is more formal and less mystical than his mature verse, but it is already symbolist in method, repeating key words (*apple, stone, flute*) from poem to poem until they acquire totemic weight.

Born in Martins Ferry, Ohio, in 1927, James Wright was educated at Kenyon College and the University of Washington. The author of ten volumes of verse, Wright was a Fulbright fellow, a Guggenheim fellow (twice), and received the Pulitzer Prize for his *Collected Poems* (1971). He died in 1980.

The Horse

. . . the glory of his nostrils is terrible.

—JOB 39:20

He kicked the world, and lunging long ago
Rose dripping with the dew of lawns,
Where new wind tapped him to a frieze
Against a wall of rising autumn leaves.
Some young foolhardy dweller of the barrows,
To grip his knees around the flanks,
Leaped from a tree and shivered in the air.
Joy clawed inside the bones
And flesh of the rider at the reins
Flopping and bounding over the dark banks.

Joy and terror floated on either side
Of the rider rearing. The supreme speed
Jerked to a height so spaced and wide
He seemed among the areas of the dead.
The flesh was free, the sky was rockless, clear,
The road beneath the feet was pure, the soul
Spun naked to the air

And lanced against a solitary pole
Of cumulus, to curve and roll
With the heave that disdains
Death in the body, stupor in the brains.

Now we have coddled the gods away.
The cool earth, the soft earth, we say:
Cover our eyes with petals, let the sky
Drift on while we are watching water pass
Among the drowsing mass
Of red and yellow algae in green lanes.
Yet earth contains
The horse as a remembrancer of wild
Arenas we avoid.

One day a stallion whirled my riding wife,
Whose saddle rocked her as a cradled child,
Gentle to the swell of water: yet her life
Poised perilously as on a shattered skiff.
The fear she rode, reminded of the void
That flung the ancient rider to the cold,
Dropped her down. I tossed my reins,

I ran to her with breath to make her rise,
And brought her back. Across my arms
She fumbled for the sunlight with her eyes.
I knew that she would never rest again,
For the colts of the dusk rear back their hooves
And paw us down, the mares of the dawn stampede
Across the cobbled hills till the lights are dead.
Here it is not enough to pray that loves
Draw grass over our childhood's lake of slime.
Run to the rocks where horses cannot climb,
Stable the daemon back to the shaken earth,
Warm your hands at the comfortable fire,
Cough in a dish beside a wrinkled bed.

A Presentation of Two Birds to My Son

Chicken. How shall I tell you what it is,
And why it does not float with tanagers?
Its ecstasy is dead, it does not care.
Its children huddle underneath its wings,
And altogether lounge against the shack,
Warm in the slick tarpaulin, smug and soft.

You must not fumble in your mind
The genuine ecstasy of climbing birds
With that dull fowl.
When your grandfather held it by the feet
And laid the skinny neck across
The ragged chopping block,
The flop of wings, the jerk of the red comb
Were a dumb agony,
Stupid and meaningless. It was no joy
To leave the body beaten underfoot;
Life was a flick of corn, a steady roost.
Chicken. The sound is plain.

Look up and see the swift above the trees.
How shall I tell you why he always veers
And banks around the shaken sleeve of air,
Away from ground? He hardly flies on brains;
Pockets of air impale his hollow bones.
He leans against the rainfall or the sun.

You must not mix this pair of birds
Together in your mind before you know
That both are clods.
What makes the chimney swift approach the sky
Is ecstasy, a kind of fire
That beats the bones apart
And lets the fragile feathers close with air.
Flight too is agony,

132

Stupid and meaningless. Why should it be joy
To leave the body beaten underfoot,
To mold the limbs against the wind, and join
Those clean dark glides of Dionysian birds?
The flight is deeper than your father, boy.

The Angel

Last night, before I came to bear
The clean edge of my wing upon the boulder,
I walked about the town.
The people seemed at peace that he was dead:
A beggar carried water out of a door,
And young men gathered round the corner
To spell the night.

I walked, like a folded bird, about the towers
And sang softly to the blue levels of evening,
I slid down treeless, featherless, bemused:
At curious faces whispering round a fire
And sniffing chestnuts sugared by a woman;
At a vague child heaving a beetle over
In dust, to see it swimming on its back.

Under an arch I found a woman lean
Weeping for loneliness: away from her
A young man whistle toward the crowds;
Out of an open window pigeons flew
And a slow dove fluted for nothing—the girl
Blew to the air a melody lost on me.

Laid in a pile of stone, how could he weep
For that calm town?
Looped in a yoke of darkened garden,
He murmured blood out of his heart for love,

Hallowed a soldier, took the savage kiss
And gave it back a warm caress;

Yet no one changed.

Tossing aside the worry of the place,
As someone threw an apple core across
A wall I walked beside, I sought delight
Pebble by pebble, song by song, and light
By light, singly, among the river boats.
Down to the river at the end I came.

But then a girl appeared, to wash her hair.
Struck stupid by her face,
I stood there, sick to love her, sick of sky.
The child, the beetle, chestnut fires, the song
Of girl and dove
Shuddered along my wings and arms.
She slipped her bodice off, and a last wave
Of shadow oiled her shoulder till it shone;
Lifting her arms to loosen the soft braids
She looked across the water. I looked down
And felt my wings waving aside the air,
Furious to fly. For I could never bear
Belly and breast and thigh against the ground.

Now, having heaved the hidden hollow open
As I was sent to do, seen Jesus waken
And guided the women there, I wait to rise.
To feel a weapon gouge between the ribs,
He hung with a shut mouth:
For curious faces round a chestnut fire,
For the slow fluting doves
Lost on a trellis, for the laughing girl
Who frightened me away.

But now I fumble at the single joy
Of dawn. On the pale ruffle of the lake
The ripples weave a color I can bear.
Under a hill I see the city sleep
And fade. The perfect pleasure of the eyes:
A tiny bird bathed in a bowl of air,
Carving a yellow ripple down the bines,
Posing no storm to blow my wings aside
As I drift upward dropping a white feather.

Hollander's distinctive combination of the learned with the earthy may already be seen in his early work, which offers both formal proficiency and intellectual challenge. Much of this volume is seventeenth century in tone, as the author frequently resorts to Jacobean and Elizabethan verse forms. Auden selected several poets whose first books demonstrated great technical ability, but Hollander's debut as a formalist was perhaps most impressive of all.

John Hollander was born in New York City in 1929 and was educated at Columbia University and Indiana University. He has written sixteen volumes of poetry (*Selected Poems,* 1993), as well as books of criticism and a manual of prosody (*Rhyme's Reason,* 1981). The recipient of a MacArthur fellowship, a Guggenheim fellowship, and the Bollingen Prize, Hollander has taught for most of his career at Yale University. He lives in Woodbridge, Connecticut.

Carmen Ancillae

Burgundy c. 1430

Wider than winter
Lying over the river
Or the frosty sky through the window
That stretches forever
Around the white pennants
Above the battlements;
Wider than all I remember
Is the bed in my Lady's chamber.

Whiter than my Lady
Gazing along the river
At the sunny grass where lately
Her liking had led her
Away from the remnants
Of frost on the battlements;
Whiter than was December
Was the bed in my Lady's chamber.

Cold is the basin
I dip into the river
When the morning sun is blazing
Beyond the crisp weather.
  With its cold contents
  I cross the battlements.

  My Lady's bed is colder,
  Almost, than the river.
  When we were younger
  We warmed it together,
  Warmer than the anger
  She showed as she grew older.

Gold shines in the water
I carry from the river.
Gold given a king's daughter
Can only enrich the giver.
  And what of my penance
  Along the battlements?

  What I bring her looks golden:
  Will it avail me ever?
  Today she will be married,
  Clothed in gold like the river.
  I have fetched and carried:
  She will think of it seldom.

Black as the pearl she gave me
To tie among my tresses
Was her face as she bade them save me
Old robes and dresses
As parting presents.
I can see from the battlements
How she stands in a temper
Of tears and rage in her chamber.

For Both of You, the Divorce Being Final

We cannot celebrate with doleful Music
The old, gold panoplies that are so great
To sit and watch; but on the other hand,
To command the nasal krummhorns to be silent,
The *tromba marina* to wail; to have the man
Unlatch the tail gate on his cart, permitting
The sackbut player to extend his crook
And go to work on whimpering divisions;
For us to help prepare the masque itself,
Rigging machinery to collapse the household
Just at the end, rehearsing urchins who
Will trip, all gilded, into the master bedroom
And strip the sheets, is, finally, to confess
That what we lack are rituals adequate
To things like this.
                    We tell some anxious friends
"*Basta!* They know what they are doing"; others
Whom we dislike and who, like queens, betray
Never a trace of uneasiness, we play with:
"No, it could never work, my dears, from the start.
We all knew that. Yes, there's the boy to think of,"
And so on. Everyone makes us nervous. Then,
For a dark instant, as in your unlit foyer
At sundown, bringing a parcel, we see you both
And stifle the awkward question: "What, are *you* here?"
Not because it has been asked before
By Others meeting Underground, but simply
Because we cannot now know which of you
Should answer, or even which of you we asked.
We wait for something to happen in the brown
Shadows around us. Surely there is missing
A tinkle of cymbals to strike up the dirge
And some kind of sounding brass to follow it,
Some hideous and embarrassing gimmick which
Would help us all behave less civilly and

More gently, who mistook civility
So long for lack of gentleness.
                              And since
Weeping's a thing we can no longer manage,
We must needs leave you to the Law's directive:
"You have unmade your bed, now lie about it."
Quickly now: which of you will keep the *Lares*,
Which the *Penates?* And opening the door
We turn like guilty children, mutter something,
And hide in the twilit street.
                              Along the river
The sky is purpling and signs flash out
And on, to beckon the darkness: THE TIME IS NOW . . .
(What time, what time?) Who stops to look in time
Ever, ever? We can do nothing again
For both of you together. And if I burn
An epithalamium six years old to prove
That what we learn is in some way a function
Of what we forget, I know that I should never
Mention it to anyone. When men
Do in the sunny Plaza what they did
Only in dusky corners before, the sunset
Comes as no benison, the assuring license
Of the June night goes unobserved. The lights
Across the river are brighter than the stars;
The water is black and motionless; whatever
Has happened to all of us, it is too late
For something else ever to happen now.

Late August on the Lido

To lie on these beaches for another summer
Would not become them at all,
And yet the water and her sands will suffer
When, in the fall,
These golden children will be taken from her.

139

It is not the gold they bring: enough of that
Has shone in the water for ages
And in the bright theater of Venice at their backs;
But the final stages
Of all those afternoons when they played and sat

And waited for a beckoning wind to blow them
Back over the water again
Are scenes most necessary to this ocean.
What actors then
Will play when these disperse from the sand below them?

All this is over until, perhaps, next spring;
This last afternoon must be pleasing.
Europe, Europe is over, but they lie here still,
While the wind, increasing,
Sands teeth, sands eyes, sands taste, sands everything.

Science and Human Behavior

for B. F. Skinner

Feeling that it is vaguely undignified
To win someone else's bet for him by choosing
The quiet girl in the corner, not refusing
But simply not preferring the other one;
Abashed by having it known that we decide
To save the icing on the chocolate bun
Until the last, that we prefer to ride
Next to the window always; more than afraid
Of knowing that They know what sends us screaming
Out of the movie; even shocked by the dreaming
Our friends do about us, we vainly hope
That certain predictions never can be made,
That the mind can never spin the Golden Rope
By which we feel bound, determined, and betrayed;

But rather, if such a thing exists at all,
Three nasty Thingummies should hold it, twisting
Strand onto endless strand, always resisting
Our own old impulse to pull the string and see
Just what would happen, or to feel the small
But tingling tug upon the line, to free
The captives so that we might watch them crawl
Back into deeper water again. It is well
To leave such matters in their power, trusting
To the blasé discretion of disgusting
Things like the Two who spin and measure, and
The Third and surely The Most Horrible,
Whom we'd best forget, within whose bony hand
Lies crumpled the Secret she will never tell.

Which Secret concerns the nature of the string
That all Three tend, and whether it be the wire
Designed to receive the message or to fire
The tiny initial relay. In the end,
The question is whether merely Determining
Or really Knowing is what we most pretend
To honor because it seems most frightening
Or worship because we hold it most to blame.
I once saw Dr. Johnson in a vision;
His hat was in his hand, and a decision
Of import on his lips. "Our will," he said,
"Is free, and there's an end on't." All the same,
Atropos and her sisters, overhead,
Grinned at this invocation of their name.

William Dickey's is a short book containing short poems. He writes formal and fastidious verse obsessed with the way of all flesh. The poems show a marked repugnance for bodily function, and for sex in particular. Although the poet's diction presents no barrier, his word choice is consistently interesting and his rhymes are sometimes of unusual sophistication. This is another poet whose later work, which often celebrates homosexuality, differs markedly from his first efforts.

Born in Bellingham, Washington, in 1928, William Hobart Dickey was educated at Reed College, Harvard, the University of Iowa, and Oxford University, where he was a Fulbright fellow. He wrote fifteen books of poetry (*In Dreaming: Selected Poems,* 1994) before his death in 1994. Dickey taught for many years at San Francisco State University.

For Easter Island or Another Island

We are the last that there are anywhere.
The changeless figures, the great heads sitting on stones,
Look out of place. We, too, who put them there
Look out of place, ribbed in these cages of bones
Where the heart hangs and hangs like a yellow gourd,
And the eyes, divest of covering, lean and sway;
Throat's edge shines out bright as the edge of a sword.
We are the last. Everyone goes away.

They fall like leaves, the cities of the past,
Endlessly into rock and the endless streams.
Our minds fall shut on each, fall at the last
With the great-lipped faces of our merciless dreams
In the red-colored dust. It with its various reds
Like the first leap of anger fills our heads.

The Plot

Beatrice lay naked on the narrow bed;
"I'm half in love with easeful death," she said.
"And so am I," I said without delay,
"But once you've got him, how will you make him stay?"
"By woman's wiles, and by ambitious kisses;
He can't be satisfied with those skeleton blisses,
Those beds on which an atomy reposes—
I'll give him flesh like concentrate of roses.
The change will make a man of him again."
"I grant you that," I said. "What happens then?"
"Then I deceive him carefully," she said;
"I leave him soundly sleeping, and I tread
On airy foot in search of certain potions,
Somniferous drugs and faint Lethean lotions.
I scatter poppy near him as he slumbers,
I tell off charms and cabalistic numbers—"
"He sleeps?" "He sleeps forever and a day,
He sleeps the ages of the world away."
"He leaves us free for our desired pursuing?"
"He leaves us free for doing and undoing;
And safe from traveling through that ominous portal,
We'll have our pleasure, mortal and immortal."

Memoranda

The scars take us back to places we have been,
Cities named Masochism or Inaccuracy.
This little one between the finger and the thumb
Is something that my brother did to me
On a hot Washington's Birthday in the past,
When we were young and cruelly competent;
In a miniature world like a glass fishing float
He was the total image of intent.

143

Who stuck the pencil point into my palm?
It is so long ago that I cannot say,
But the black stick of graphite under the skin—
Some friend, some enemy put it there that way
To succeed in calling himself always to mind.
Action has consequence, and though his face
Has faded into the city of the lost,
I look at my hand and see the injured place.

Like hasty marks on an explorer's chart:
This white stream bed, this blue lake on my knee
Are an angry doctor at midnight, or a girl
Looking at the blood and trying not to see
What we both have seen. Most of my body lives,
But the scars are dead like the grooving of a frown,
Cannot be changed, and ceaselessly record
How much of me is already written down.

Cassandra

This is because I am spiteful. You see, I hate
What hates me: houses, women with children, serpents, stones
Ringed viciously round with their blemishes looking me over:
What they do is too late now, nothing atones,
Nothing helps when the high god hate hits out at the sides of my head
And in moans with my tongue like a tripped snare dangling before
I sum them chapter and verse of their intricate ends.

But nothing ends. All of their war-splintered bones
I cry like candies or kisses the length of their towns,
All of the blood on the street spilt still will not let itself fall
Where I see it will be: it is all
Ahead, hard, terrible, simple to see but to tell?

Yet I will tell what I see:
Craft coiling like night in a pit, like a murderous bird's skull's

Word for their ear: will they hear? will the sweet smile
Stop on their lips where their grave-teeth now are beginning to grow?
Once they are dead I am free. I shall know

What I know now in a harmless historian's mouth,
Saying walls of a long-dead king's son fell
Time out of mind in the north, in the night,
And a ship stood wait for me under the isle and I came
With that treasure of word sometime spent
For my stay in this south.

This book is a harbinger of things to come, being as much a product of its anxious times as any of the Yale volumes published in the 1960s. Starbuck is preoccupied with the threat of nuclear war, and one poem in the book is inspired by the hearings of the House Un-American Activities Committee. A good deal of this poet's verse is formalist, though of an unusual sort, written in startling stanzas eager for the opportunity to rhyme. Starbuck's home-made formalism is shaped in part by his quirky sense of humor, an aspect of his work that later became a signature trait.

George Edwin Starbuck was born in Columbus, Ohio, in 1931. He attended many schools—the University of California at Berkeley, the California Institute of Technology, the University of Chicago, and Harvard University—but did not obtain a degree. The author of eight books of verse (*The Argot Merchant Disaster,* 1982), Starbuck was an editor at Houghton Mifflin for several years, thereafter teaching at the University of Iowa and Boston University. The recipient of the Prix de Rome and a Guggenheim fellowship, he died in Tuscaloosa, Alabama, in 1996.

Technologies

On Commonwealth, on Marlborough,
the gull beaks of magnolia
were straining upward like the flocks
harnessed by kings in storybooks
who lusted for the moon. Six days
we mooned into each other's eyes
mythologies of dune and dawn—
naked to the Atlantic sun,
loving and loving, to and fro
on Commonwealth, on Marlborough,
our whole half-hours. And where our bloods
crested, we saw the bruise-red buds
tear loose the white, impeded shapes
of cries. And when our whitest hopes
tore at the wind with wings, it seemed
only a loony dream we dreamed,
such heavy machination of

cars and motels confronted love
on Commonwealth, on Marlborough.
They do the trick with rockets now—
with methodologies of steel—
with industry or not at all.
But so, sweet love, do these white trees
that dare play out their lunacies
for all they are, for all they know
on Commonwealth, on Marlborough.

Communication to the City Fathers of Boston

Dear Sirs: Is it not time we formed a Boston
Committee to Enact a Dirge for Boston?

When New York mushrooms into view, when Boston's
townspeople, gathered solemnly in basements,
feel on their necks the spiderwebs of bombsights,
when subway stations clot and fill like beesnests
making a honey-heavy moan, whose business
will it be then to mourn, to take a busman's
holiday from his death, to weep for Boston's?

Though dust is scattered to her bones, though grieving
thunderheads add hot tears, though copper grapevines
clickety-clack their telegraphic ragtime
tongues at the pity of it, how in God's name
will Boston in the thick of Armageddon
summon composure to compose a grave-song
grave and austere enough for such a grieving?

Move we commit some song, now, to the HOLD files
of papers in exotic places. Helpful
of course to cram our scholars with hogs' headfuls
of Lowells, khaki-cap them, ship them wholesale
to Wake or Thule—some safe base, where heartfelt

terror may milk them of a tear; but Hell's fire,
what'll they have on us in all those HOLD files?

You want some rewrite man to wrap up Boston
like garbage in old newsprint for the dustbin?
The Statehouse men convivial at Blinstrub's,
the textile men, the men of subtler substance
squiring Ledaean daughters to the swan-boats,
the dockers, truckers, teen-age hotrod-bandits—
what could he make of them, to make them Boston?

Or even make of me, perched in these Park Street
offices playing Jonah like an upstart
pipsqueak in raven's clothing—First Mate Starbuck
who thinks too much? Thinking of kids in bookstores
digging for dirty footnotes to their Shakespeares,
while by my window the Archbishop's upstairs
loudspeaker booms redemption over Park Street.

Thinking of up the hill the gilded Statehouse
where just last night the plaster-of-paris faces
of Sacco and Vanzetti craned on flannel
arms at the conscientiously empaneled
pain of a state's relentlessly belated
questioning of itself. (Last year the Salem
Witches; next year, if next year finds a Statehouse . . . ?)

Thinking of Thor, Zeus, Atlas. Thinking Boston.
Thinking there must be words her weathered brownstone
could still re-whisper—words to blast the brassbound
brandishers on their pads—words John Jay Chapman
scored on her singlehanded—words Sam Adams,
Garrison, Mott, Thoreau blazed in this has-been
Braintree-Jamaica-Concord-Cambridge-Boston.

There were such men. Or why remember Boston?
Strange how not one prepared a dirge for Boston.

April, 1959

Prognosis

Petrarch watched a plague: it took
half of Europe, says my book.
Now of course we've found the rat.
Anyway, half lived. And yet

something very like a plague
propagates, and while our vague
fears breed fear, the insecure
vaccinate themselves — with fear.

Flesh, that to uranium
seems a power vacuum,
cannot linger uncommitted:
sooner, later, all are pitted.

Saved from Mao and Molotov,
millions leave the clinic of
Doctor Dulles, Doctor Nixon,
rabid with their antitoxin.

Millions more, on Khrushchev's serum,
rage with fear of those that fear them.
Shadows prowl at every back.
All precaution is attack.

Still, the books will skimp it, if
here and there a spasm of life
raises on the ruins one
knowing cross of bone on bone.

Schoolboy Chaucer feared the bog,
fled from shapes of mist and fog.
We can grin, and blame the flea:
air, we know, kills boundlessly.

Dugan writes fiercely intelligent and bitterly dyspeptic poems. The language of his first book does not yield easily, and the reader must work to register the full measure of the poet's disaffection. For all its contemporary idiom and imaginative obscenity, this is a neoclassical book, and its harsh ironies at the expense of human pretension allude directly to the literature of ancient Greece. Dugan's anger and disgust sometimes run the risk of self-pity, but he works to avoid such failing by being hard-bitten.

Alan Dugan was born in 1923 in Brooklyn, New York. He attended Queens College, served in World War II, and graduated from Mexico City College in 1951. Dugan's Yale volume won both the Pulitzer Prize and the National Book Award. The poet has also received a Guggenheim fellowship, a Rockefeller fellowship, and the Prix de Rome. His numerically titled books have by now arrived at *Poems 6* (1989). He lives in Truro, Massachusetts.

Prison Song

The skin ripples over my body like moon-wooed water,
rearing to escape me. Where would it find another
animal as naked as this one it hates to cover?
Once it told me what was happening outside,
who was attacking, who caressing, and what the air
was doing to feed or freeze me. Now I wake up
dark at night, in a textureless ocean of ignorance,
or fruit bites back and water bruises like a stone:
a jealousy, because I look for other tools to know
with, and another armor, better fitted to my flesh.
So, let it lie, turn off its clues, or try to leave:
sewn on me seamless like those painful shirts
the body-hating saints wore, this sheath of hell
is pierced to my darkness nonetheless: what traitors
labor in my face, what hints they smuggle through
its itching guard! But even in the night it jails,
with nothing but its lies and silences to feed upon,
the jail itself can make a scenery, sing prison songs
and set off fireworks to praise a homemade day.

Weeds as Partial Survivors

The chorus of the weeds, unnameably
profuse, sings Courage, Courage, like
an India of unemployables who have
no other word to say and say it.
Too bendable to break, bowing away
together from the wind although
the hail or hurricane can knock them flat,
they rise up wet by morning. This
morning erection of the weeds
is not so funny: It
is perseverance dancing: some of them,
the worst, are barely rooted and
a lady gardener can pull them out
ungloved. Nevertheless, they do do
what they do or die, surviving all
catastrophes except the human: they
extend their glosses, like the words I said,
on sun-cracked margins of the sown
lines of our harrowed grains.

Letter to Eve

The lion and lioness are intractable,
the leaves are covered with dust,
and even the peacocks will not
preen. You should come back,
burnish us with your former look,
and let the search for truth
go. After a loud sleep last night
I got up late and saw a new
expression on the faces of the deer;
the shrews and wolves are gaunt
and out of sorts: they nosed
their usual fruits and do not know

what they intend to do. The dogs
got tangled up in an unusual way:
one put its urinary tube
into the other's urinary tract
and could not get it out.
Standing tail to tail for hours,
they looked at me with wise,
supplicatory eyes. I named
two new sounds: snarl and shriek,
and hitherto unnoticed bells,
which used to perform the air,
exploded!, making a difference.
Come back before the garden does
what I'll call "die," not that it
matters. Rib, Rib, I have a new
opinion of your Eve, called "lust"
or Love, I don't know which,
and want to know how I will choose.

How We Heard the Name

The river brought down
dead horses, dead men
and military debris,
indicative of war
or official acts upstream,
but it went by, it all
goes by, that is the thing
about the river. Then
a soldier on a log
went by. He seemed drunk
and we asked him Why
had he and this junk
come down to us so
from the past upstream.

"Friends," he said, "the great
Battle of Granicus
has just been won
by all of the Greeks except
the Lacedaemonians and
myself: this is a joke
between me and a man
named Alexander, whom
all of you ba-bas
will hear of as a god."

Actual Vision of Morning's Extrusion

Grey smoke rose from the morning ground
and separated into spheres. The smoke
or fog of each sphere coiled upon itself
like snakes at love, and hardened into brains:
the corals in the ocean of first light.
Those brains grow shells. Mother of pearl, out
clattered the bones! Two ivies intertwined
ran down them searchingly, the red and white
of arteries and nerves, and found their ends.
Nerves hummed in the wind: the running blood,
in pulsing out a heart, induced a warm,
red haze of flesh around a hollow tube,
writhing with appetite, ejection, love,
and hardened in the temperature of dawn.
"Done!" said the clocks, and gave alarm.
Eyes popped into heads as tears amazed.
All hair stood out. All moved and rose
and took a breath: two gasping voids
turned blue with it around the heart.
Shocked into teeth and nails and wrapped
in winding sheets of skin, all souls walked
to test their creatures in their joints,

chinks, and armors as the walking dead,
curious as to what the water, partial sun-
light, ground and mobile air, combined
reactively, could have in mind.

On the Elk, Unwitnessed

The frantic elk climb from the valleys to escape the flies.
Then, on the heights, they leap, run, and play in snow
as Alces, Alces, glad to be relieved of goads
and ready to get married, due to the wholesome airs.
Those gads downhill, buzzing in armor causative,
must have their joys in cycles too, if the escape
from them in dancing Io!, Io!, on the heights is how,
oh Alces!, Alces!, Hymen triumphs and the roaring stags
fight to assemble harems in the trampled snow
while gad-eggs cradle in their hides and nostrils.

They set out every year diagonally to make
the grand tour of their corner of the world in Oregon,
spurred by a bug at base and climbing up to love
on the apex, and without that lightning touch of Zeus
to slap them, Ha!, Epaphus!, out of the cycling dark
and innocent present of the locally driven beasts,
and toward the widening drive all over Asia and up
into the sky, too, that is the cycle of the really stung.

Europe on the cheap and Greenwich Village cool enter the Yale series with Jack Gilbert, who is poised somewhere between beatnik and hippie and is both captivated and amused by the scene he surveys. His most successful poems are telegraphic in style, but no one style predominates. Instead, the poet tries on various stances and sorts through disparate elements of high and popular culture. In the midst of confusion, Gilbert does achieve some perspective, not least upon himself. His claim to have made his art out of a "concern for whales and love, / For elephants and Alcibiades" captures the distinct flavor of his verse.

Born in Pittsburgh in 1925, Jack Gilbert was educated at the University of Pittsburgh and San Francisco State College. An interval of twenty years separated Gilbert's Yale volume and the appearance of his second book (*Monolithos: Poems, 1962–1982* (1982), and a further twelve years passed before his third publication, *The Great Fires: Poems 1982–92* (1994). Gilbert has been a peregrine poet, living in Italy, Japan, and Greece. He lives now in San Francisco.

Perspective He Would Mutter Going to Bed

for Robert Duncan

"Perspective," he would mutter, going to bed.
"Oh che dolce cosa è questa
Prospettiva." Uccello. Bird.

And I am as greedy of her, that the black
Horse of the literal world might come
Directly on me. Perspective. A place

To stand. To receive. A place to go
Into from. The earth by language.

Who can imagine antelope silent
Under the night rain, the Gulf
At Biloxi at night else? I remember

In Mexico a man and a boy painting
An adobe house magenta and crimson
Who thought they were painting it red. Or pretty.

So neither saw the brown mountains
Move to manage that great house.

The horse wades in the city of grammar.

Malvolio in San Francisco

Two days ago they were playing the piano
With a hammer and blowtorch.
Next week they will read poetry
To saxophones.
And always they are building the Chinese Wall
Of laughter.
They laugh so much.
So much more than I do.
And it doesn't wear them out
As it wears me out.
That's why your poetry's no good,
They say.
You should turn yourself upside down
So your ass would stick out,
They say.
And they seem to know.

They are right, of course.
I do feel awkward playing the game.
I do play the clown badly.
I cannot touch easily.
But I mistrust the ways of this city
With its white skies and weak trees.
One finds no impali here.
x
And the birds are pigeons.

The first rate seems unknown
In this city of easy fame.
The hand's skill is always
From deliberate labor.

They put Phidias in prison
About his work on the Parthenon,
Saying he had stolen gold.
And he probably had.
Those who didn't try to body Athena
They stayed free.

And Orpheus probably invited the rending
By his stubborn alien smell.
Poor Orpheus
Who lost so much by making the difficult journey
When he might have grieved
Easily.
Who tried to go back among the living
With the smell of journey on him.
Poor Orpheus
His stubborn tongue
Blindly singing all the way to Lesbos.

What if I should go yellow-stockinged
And cross-gartered?
Suppose I did smile
Fantastically,
Kissed my hand to novelty,
What then?
Still would they imprison me in their dark house.
They would taunt me as doctors
Concerned for my health
And laugh.
Always that consuming,
Unrelenting laughter.

The musk deer is beguiled down from the great mountain
By flutes
To be fastened in a box
And tortured for the smell of his pain.

Yet somehow
There is somehow

I long for my old bigotry.

The Abnormal Is Not Courage

The Poles rode out from Warsaw against the German
Tanks on horses. Rode knowing, in sunlight, with sabers.
A magnitude of beauty that allows me no peace.
And yet this poem would lessen that day. Question
The bravery. Say it's not courage. Call it a passion.
Would say courage isn't that. Not at its best.
It was impossible, and with form. They rode in sunlight.
Were mangled. But I say courage is not the abnormal.
Not the marvelous act. Not Macbeth with fine speeches.
The worthless can manage in public, or for the moment.
It is too near the whore's heart: the bounty of impulse,
And the failure to sustain even small kindness.
Not the marvelous act, but the evident conclusion of being.
Not strangeness, but a leap forward of the same quality.
Accomplishment. The even loyalty. But fresh.
Not the Prodigal Son, nor Faustus. But Penelope.
The thing steady and clear. Then the crescendo.
The real form. The culmination. And the exceeding.
Not the surprise. The amazed understanding. The marriage,
Not the month's rapture. Not the exception. The beauty
That is of many days. Steady and clear.
It is the normal excellence, of long accomplishment.

It Is Clear Why the Angels Come No More

It is clear why the angels come no more.
Standing so large in their beautiful Latin,
How could they accept being refracted
So small in another grammar, or leave
Their perfect singing for this broken speech?
Why should they stumble this alien world?

Always I have envied the angels their grace.
But I left my hope of Byzantine size
And came to this awkwardness, this stupidity.
Came finally to you washing my face
As everyone laughed, and found a forest
Opening as marriage ran in me. All

The leaves in the world turned a little
Singing: The angels are wrong.

Sandra Hochman writes a poetry of reaction and rejection. Her verse arises in response to unhappy love affairs, as well as to what the poet feels to be the bourgeois values and stifling atmosphere of her native New York City. As Dudley Fitts notes in his foreword, this book remains steadfastly unexperimental. Unlike many of her contemporaries, Hochman is more interested in creating emotional space for herself than in creating a new art.

Born in New York in 1936, Hochman was educated at Bennington College and Columbia University. She has lived in Hong Kong and Boston and has published six books of verse (*Earthworks: Poems 1960–1970,* 1970), as well as four novels (*Playing Tahoe,* 1981) and two volumes of essays. She has now returned to New York, where she writes plays.

Manhattan Pastures

On our wedding day we climbed the top
Of Mount Carmel. To keep our promises
We lay down in maize.
Who can tell us how to lead our lives?
Now in Manhattan's pastures I hear
Long processions of the compact cars
Nuzzling their gasoline.
The day is springtime. Have I come too late
To hear the Zen Professor speak of peace?—
One thing is as good as another, he says, and eats
Salad, wheat germ, and all natural foods.

Voices out of records: terrible sounds.
Wagner's music is a tongue.
My radio announces man in space. This
Was once my city. Who will tell us
How to lead our lives?

Eichmann stalls in the judicial stables.
His children saddle him to a black horse
Motoring through six million beds of grass.

He wears a light-wool suit tailored for summer.
The doctors say that we are doing well. We shall
Be cured of childhood if we keep
Counting our nightmares in the fields of sleep.
I shear black cars and records in my sleep.

Eichmann drops as man is shot in space
Out of a pop-gun. In our universe
A lonely husband needs a hundred wives. Who

Can tell us how to lead our lives?

Cannon Hill

A farm. A cannon on a hill.
Long ago I sat beneath that cannon
And picked clover. Often, at sunset,
I walked down to the barn, and held my arm
Around a calf, or took the one-eyed pony for a ride.
Later, I walked in the forests of corn.
The stalks were palm-boughs, strands of yellow sun.
Evenings, I picked tomato vines.
Earth clung to them, they prickled in my hand.
And our house was always lit. My grandfather
Furnished it from his *Broadway Theatrical Warehouse*.
Everything only seemed to be what it was: cupboards
Didn't open, prop tables had three sides,
Books were cardboard thick, lamps dimmed on,
Statuettes were paper silhouettes—
Papier-maché, they seemed to have no weight upon the farm.
Even the cannon had come home
From a play about war. It had been in
A smash hit in which Nazis, like
Chippewas, lost. There it stood,
Up on our hill, made out of wood,

Soggy and warping from the summer rain.
Cannon Hill Farm was sold. Black
Out. Nothing works but a kitchen knife.

Sphinxes

We clawed through Paris
And said, "Let's be alone
And talk to the dead." We spoke to Baudelaire.
Good morning,
Hookers are gone,
Artists are all over Montparnasse
Tinkering with fenders and ice-boxes,
Creating statues
That destroy themselves.
Good morning, grunted Baudelaire,
How are the ragpickers? The lesbians? The vampires?
Only art is left, we said.
And the poets?
Dead.
And the hellcats? The dangerous girls? The children
Tearing maps? The hangmen? The carrion boys
Swinging in the belfry of their bones?
All gone.
And what about the tears of snow? The
Scratching virgins? The libertines?
They pose for PARIS MATCH, we said.
Paris is dead.

The Hairbrush

In the end
There will be nothing but a hairbrush.
I shall find the bristles to be soft. Brush
My hair, and with my hair my mind
And unknown cavities of water.
I shall brush and tease. Until pools of memory
Are like all strands of hair: soft,
So clean, or singed.

As first books go, this volume is exceptional for its sustained tone and consistent style, and the result is a self-assured beginning. Davison has a welcome appetite for ambiguity, a quality much in evidence in the title sequence exploring the author's mixed religious heritage. The book is dedicated in part to the memory of "R.F.," but although Davison was a student of Frost's and went on to reflect his influence, these early poems more often show the impact of T. S. Eliot.

Born in New York City in 1928 and raised in Colorado, Peter Davison was educated at Harvard University and Cambridge University. He is the author of ten books of poetry (*The Poems of Peter Davison, 1957–1995,* 1995), two books of criticism, and a memoir. Beginning as an editor at Harcourt, Brace in 1950, Davison has had a distinguished career in publishing. He is currently an editor at Houghton Mifflin, where he has his own imprint, and poetry editor of the *Atlantic Monthly.* He lives in Boston.

The Star Watcher

(for R. F.)

Stars had the look of dogs to him sometimes,
Sometimes of bears and more than once of flowers,
But stars were never strange to him because
Of where they stood. We knew him jealous
And in his younger days a little sly
About his place among the poesies;
Yet when his eyes showed envy or delight
They rested upon knowledge, not on distance.
All that he saw, up close or farther off,
Was capable of being understood,
Though not by him perhaps. He had enough
Of science in him to be optimistic,
Enough of tragedy to know the worst,
Enough of wit to keep on listening,
Or watching, when it came to stars. He knew,
Across the distance that their light might travel,
That nothing matters to the stars but matter,

Yet that their watchers have to learn the difference
Between the facts of knowledge and of love,
Or of love's opposite, which might be hate.
Therefore he taught, and, like the best of teachers,
Often annoyed the students at his feet,
Whether they learned too much or not enough,
Whether or not they understood him wrong.
Two was his pleasure, and the balance held
In love, in conversation, or in verse.
With knuckles like burled hemlock roots, his hands
Had, in his age, smooth palms as white as milk;
And, through the massy cloudbanks of his brows,
His eyes burned shrewdly as emerging stars.

from The Breaking of the Day

2. *The Birthright*

A half-and-half affair, I grew from the union
Of a buxom, vital, Titian-haired New Yorker
And the cockerel moodiness of a Tyneside orphan.
She in the gabble of Upper-West-Side tea dances,
Looked feverish when her father, the cotton merchant,
Stumped off to synagogue to pray for his brothers' funerals.
Later, she chose not to explain to me the difference
Between the Talmud and the Pentateuch,
And I, unlearned in the ways of Shabbas and Seder,
Had to read them up later in the works of Wouk.
Not until I got to be thirteen
Did it cross my mind I might be half a Jew,
And not until a malicious schoolmate told me:
I heard the malice rising in his voice.

To take a step backward, look once more at my father,
Who never saw a Jew till he was twenty.
Sweet-voiced, he was made much of by the Rector
As he raised his boy soprano at St. Simon's

And learned his Apostles' Creed and Catechism.
For him a Jewess was rich with secret knowledge
And raven-haired—he'd read Scott and Disraeli.
Jews, on the other hand, were money-lenders.

When the schoolboy told me of my being Jewish
I asked my parents: was he telling truth?
My mother said that they had *meant* to tell me.
My father said that it didn't really matter
Because I was Anglican by half.
The question I had asked was left unanswered
And all the knowledge that I got for asking
Was learning that they had no wish to answer
And that my questions led to other questions.

4. *The Gift of Tongues*

God my father spoke in the calm of evening.
He spoke in iambs beating in the darkness.
His pipe glowed and its vapor blossomed upward.
The child at his feet drank in the heady honey
Of his voice, his presence, his attention
While the elm-leaves rustled their assent.
The words he spoke—from Oreb or from Sinai—
Were, had I known it, many times outworn
Except for those that burned as his alone:

> *I shall come back to die*
> *From a far place at last,*
> *After my life's carouse*
> *In the old bed to lie*
> *Remembering the past*
> *In this dark house.*

His voice wore all the costumes of our tongue,
And in the dark I trembled at the golden
Din of the past resounding in my ears.
These were the words that God had always spoken,

As, "This is my beloved Son, in whom
I am well pleased." The words belonged to him,
And now, as their custodian, he gave
His hoard to me at night beneath the trees.
I counted them for years before I learned
The spending of them: yet I did not know
That he had given them away for good
And that from that night forward he would walk
The earth like any natural man,
His powers incomplete, his magic gone.

6. The Dead Sea

Shore people worshipped, we are told, the Mother
In preference to the Horseman, Father Poseidon.
My gods were naked. He was wrinkled, massive,
Bearded, with eyes that gleamed in wrath or kindness;
She, mother-sister, of an unloosing softness,
Had breasts that flowed with all I knew of bounty.

The womb that held me in its lake is dry,
The bounty parched and powdered. He that held
A weapon or a sceptre or a cross
Has lost the good of his grasp and sits in silence,
Who took it on himself to shake the earth.

Mother Jew, you gave me an endearment
For my inheritance, but hid your race away,
Withholding what I had to learn to want.
You, mother, rocked me bloodless in my cradle
And yearned to free me from my ancestors:
The womb of the Goddess denied she had been born.

My Father Christian never knew his father
And had to fashion sceptres for himself.

So both were outcasts from their ancestry.
No offerings for them, no worshippers —

Except for me, who worshipped in myself
Crude copies of their skilled originals,
To find at last, on the baked earth of this shrine,
That I am no more Christian, no more Jew.

The afternoon is dark and not with rain.

7. Delphi

The crackle of parched grass bent by wind
Is the only music in the grove
Except the gush of the Pierian Spring.
Eagles are often seen, but through a glass
Their naked necks declare them to be vultures.
The place is sacred with a sanctity
Now faded, like a kerchief washed too often.
There lies the crevice where the priestesses
Hid in the crypt and drugged themselves and spoke
Until in later years the ruling powers
Bribed them to prophesy what was desired.
Till then the Greeks took pride in hopelessness
And, though they sometimes wrestled with their gods,
They never won a blessing or a name
But only knowledge.

                   I shall never know myself
Enough to know what things I half believe
And, half believing, only half deny.

Sober and well made, Valentine's Yale volume is compounded of family memories and pervaded by a sense of depression. In this, as well as in style and setting, her early work appears much influenced by that of Robert Lowell, the Lowell of *Life Studies* and *For the Union Dead.* Fitts makes it clear in his foreword that he was taken with this book, praising in particular its complex eroticism and classical allusion.

Born in Chicago in 1934, Jean Valentine was educated at Radcliffe College. She has written seven volumes of verse, including *Home Deep Blue: New and Selected Poems* (1988). The recipient of a Guggenheim fellowship and a Rockefeller fellowship, Valentine teaches at Sarah Lawrence College and lives in New York City.

Lines in Dejection

for my sister

Remember how we spread our hair on the sea,
Phosphorous fans, the moon's edge crumbling under
Moving pieces of sky? Ghostly weeds loitered
Like misty Thetis's hair, or some sea-monster's
Ancient whiskers, floating around our knees;
Moony children, we drifted, and no god or monster
Could have seemed foreign then to our globe of water.
Remember
Lying like still shells on the glass water?
The paper moon opened, a Japanese water flower
Drifting free of its shell in the bowl of the sky.

Who poured it out? In twenty years
The bay is still in its place, they are still there,
Walking slowly by the water.
Have they been here, all along? Have we?
Back, back, I strike out from the ancestral stare
And now the bowl's shadow composes what I see:
The weeds cradle me and draw me under, under.

But there they are, on the pitch-black ocean floor,
Hands out, hair floating: everywhere!
Holding us in their charred arms like water.

Sleep Drops Its Nets

Sleep drops its nets for monsters old as the Flood;
You are not you, no more than I am I;
If our dead fathers walk the wall at night
Our hands when we wake up are white on white
Betraying neither wounds nor blood;
The voice is mist that made us cry.

And then day sweeps the castle dry.

Sunset at Wellfleet

A spit of sky, awash with Venetian gold
Hangs over the Congregational bell-tower, where
Last night the Northern Lights sifted their fire,
Shot through with the airless dark, romantic and cold.
The sun doesn't move, but suddenly is gone,
The cloudy tide goes out, and leaves a ring.
Easy to die: we knew it all along:
Knee-high to the dark as of old:
These words I tell you smoking in my eye:
The tree-frog is the tree-frog. The sky is the sky,
The rattling bay runs night and day *I, I, I,*
Over and over, turning on itself: there,
Where it curls on emptiness: there I sing.

Waiting

Ask, and let your words diminish your asking,
As your journal has diminished your days,
With the next day's vanity drying your blood,
The words you have lost in your notebooks.
Ask—do not be afraid. Praise Him for His silence.

What I love to ask is what I know,
Old thoughts that fit like a boot.
What I would hazard clings in my skull:
Pride intervenes, like an eyelid.

All sound slows down to a monstrous slow repetition,
Your times of reflection become a dark shop-window,
Your face up against your face.
You kneel, you see yourself see yourself kneel,
Revile your own looking down at your looking up;
Before the words form in the back of your head
You have said them over and answered, lives before.
O saints, more rollicking sunbeams, more birds about your heads!
Catherine, more Catherine-wheels!

Sic transit gloria mundi,
The quick flax, the swollen globe of water.
Sic transit John's coronation, mortal in celluloid.
Underground roots and wires burn under us.
John outlives the Journal's 4-color outsize portrait
Suitable for Framing, flapping, no color,
No love, in the rain on the side of the paper-shed.

Into Thy hands, O Lord, I commit my soul.
All Venice is sinking.

Let us dance on the head of a pin
And praise principalities!

Life is a joke and all things show it!
Let us praise the night sounds in Connecticut,
The Czechoslovak's parakeet,
Whistling *Idiot, Idiot!*

The moon's disk singes a bucketing cloud
Lit by the sun lit by a burning sword
Pointing us out of the Garden.

Turn your back on the dark reflecting glass
Fogged up with the breath of old words:

You will not be forgiven if you ignore
The pillar of slow insistent snow
Framing the angel at the door,
Who will not speak and will not go,

Numbering our hairs, our bright blue feathers.

To My Soul

AFTER HADRIAN AND RONSARD

for Michael

Scattered milkweed, valentine,
Moonlighting darling, leonine
Host and guest of my château,

Tender, yawning concubine,
Vine of my summer in decline,
Uncut, unribboned mistletoe,

Monstrous footprint in the snow,
Hypnotizing, gemmy toad,
My generations' cameo,

Symplegadês of every road,
Closet bones, unflowered sod,
Laugh, my little nuncio!

JAMES TATE *The Lost Pilot,* 1967

J ames Tate's book consists of short, thin poems that are open to slang and
  popular culture. They reflect the social ferment of the era at a certain re-
  move, however, remaining mild and unfrenzied. This poet often chooses
to end his poems with sudden and humorous revisions in perspective, a tac-
tic later adopted by Charles Simic, among others. Though the pilot referred
to (the poet's father) was lost during World War II, this volume's title was of
immediate relevance in 1967, the height of the Vietnam conflict.

Born in Kansas City, Missouri, in 1943, James Vincent Tate was educated
at the University of Missouri, Kansas State College, and the University of Iowa.
The author of more than twenty volumes of poetry, his *Selected Poems* (1991)
won the Pulitzer Prize. In 1995 he was given the Dorothea Tanning Award by
the Academy of American Poets. Tate lives in Amherst, where he teaches at
the University of Massachusetts.

Coming Down Cleveland Avenue

The fumes from all kinds
of machines have dirtied
the snow. You propose
to polish it, the miles
between home and wherever
you and your lily
of a woman might go. You
go, pail, brush, and
suds, scrubbing down
Cleveland Avenue
toward the Hartford Life
Insurance Company. No
one appreciates your
effort and one important
character calls you
a baboon. But pretty
soon your darling jumps
out of an elevator
and kisses you and you

sing and tell her to
walk the white plains
proudly. At one point
you even lay down
your coat, and she, in
turn, puts hers down for
you. And you put your
shirt down, and she, her
blouse, and your pants,
and her skirt, shoes—
removes her lavender
underwear and you slip
into her proud, white skin.

The Descent

I imagine that these thousand
sleek, invisible zebras are
leading me somewhere;

it is the moment before
birth, I expect, and follow.
The air that pursues us

is as warm and moist
as the breath of a young
rhinoceros. The sky rumbles

with televisions. Harry
Langdon in *The Life
of Abu Bakr.* None of the little

anthracite rabbits with carrot
pink eyes are real.
I know that now and feel

burdened with all the eternal
verities. The ground beneath me
is as soft as the tongue

of an old giraffe. Where
are we now, darlings? This
suitcase has lost its charm.

The Cages

The insular firebird
(meaning the sun) gives up
the day, and is tucked into

a corner. Order, like
a giant janitor, shuttles
about naming and replacing

the various humanities.
I look at you, you look
at me—we wave again

(the same), our hands like
swollen flags falling, words
marooned in the brain.

Rescue

For the first time the only
thing you are likely to break

is everything because
it is a dangerous

venture. Danger invites
rescue—I call it loving.

We've got a good thing
going—I call it rescue.

Nicest thing ever to come
between steel cobwebs, we hope

so. A few others should get
around to it, I can't understand

it. There is plenty of room,
clean windows, we start our best

engines, a-rumm . . . everything is
relevant. I call it loving.

Death on Columbus Day

Sometimes you can hear the naked will
working, like the ocean becoming a shore
yesterday, and the day before,
the trees shrinking away,
even the mere transitional phase of seasons,
the tenacious skidding of a gone summer,
the cleaving to lusciousness,
and (you can see all this
from your window if you wash it
regularly, if you are afraid to go out)
even whole environments,
giants of varying kindness,
dissolve, and you, your pupils,
yes, blue as they may appear,
are, when you think about it,
acolytes to all destruction.

The Book of Lies

I'd like to have a word
with you. Could we be alone
for a minute? I have been lying
until now. Do you believe

I believe myself? Do you believe
yourself when you believe me? Lying
is natural. Forgive me. Could we be alone
forever? Forgive us all. The word

is my enemy. I have never been alone;
bribes, betrayals. I am lying
even now. Can you believe
that? I give you my word.

Coming Close is one of several volumes in the Yale series that are informed by the chaotic energies of American society in the sixties. A virtual compendium of cultural totems, this book treats of sex and supermarkets, addiction and orbit, civil rights and uncivil language, UFOs, napalm, hippies, shrinks, immolated monks, acid trips, you name it. The popular crazes are juxtaposed with personal disorders, however, and in that correspondence lies Chasin's particular art: the most resonant of these poems concern the intersection of public and private madness.

Helen Chasin was born in 1938 and grew up in Brooklyn. After graduating from Radcliffe College, she studied verse writing with Robert Fitzgerald, Robert Lowell, and John F. Nims. She was a Bread Loaf Scholar in Poetry in 1965 and a fellow at the Bunting Institute from 1968 to 1970. A second volume of Chasin's poetry, *Casting Stones,* appeared in 1975. She lives in New York City and Rockport, Massachusetts.

In Communication with a UFO

Objects clutter the shiny air and flash
through the night sky, parsing its darkness
into the telegraphic grammar of space:

Here! We are here! Believe!
We hover but will not fix, we wheel
in the skeptical atmosphere. Beyond the reach
of your vision we skim curves of the universe
and splash like otters in its large drafts,
uttering shrieks of light, bellywhopping
to where you hang. Each sighting irks you
into a flurry of hope. Blind
with anticipation, earthlings, you want us
to be serious, bring the good news, disclose
that we are what you want us to be.

Strength

Lord, surely you took the position designed to infuriate
and held it until the end
when you spread your arms in a blessing
and gesture of union with the assemblage of comrades, catching
and hauling them like fish in the enraging net
of your unconditional love.
From the beginning, above all suffering all,
unweaponed, you opened and shrugged
into your inhuman posture

which was unlikeable:
a cellular message, the adrenalin clue
for animals met on disputed ground,
the stance that triggers attack. Words
are too recent a skill to do good—we decode
bodies.

      A Buddhist monk on the cover of *Life* droops
on his shadow like a man on a cross;
quiet men walk into flak. In a primitive language
they ask for it. The undefended stand
like victims. Signalling *unfit!* mistaken
for fair game, the loving unfold.
Christ I could have told you how few
would be pacified.

Getting the News

There's no sense in listening to it, except
that it's really happening.

In the crazy house it's easy
to trust the bulletins: everyone's doing well, considering
what everyone's doing here.

Dear Mom, a lady asked me how I was.
When I (after I flicked the bugs
off my arm) told her she said I shouldn't think
in terms of that word, dear,
it wasn't useful. But. Who's
taking care of whom? Please send
something.

Places are situations.
Everyone turns in his own bed, out
of sight, out of mind. Some acts
are more insane than others.
Where are the soldiers, and those gone mad
from giving the facts?

Man, what goes on here is where it's at.
Like when this cat jammed the broadcast
from the lightbulbs and tried to shove something
up my veins, the whole time
pushing love like it was H — crazy!

In the asylum they put easy questions
(the year, the President), but no one says
Fit them together, Make them mean,
Move the scalded babies to where you live.

The poetry in this volume is exuberantly vernacular and aggressively experimental, disconcerting in its appearance and resolute in its avoidance of any punctuation beyond a slash. This feels at first like beat poetry, but it is rather more literary than that, as the author is much given to puns and poetic allusions. The book is organized around metaphors drawn from uranium mining, and readers will be reminded once again of the profound moral and psychological crisis occasioned by the atomic age.

Judith Johnson was born in 1936. She attended Radcliffe College and the Juilliard School, as well as Barnard, from which she graduated in 1958. The author of five books of verse (*How the Dead Count,* 1978) and one volume of short stories, Johnson (she now goes by that name) is a past president of the Poetry Society of America and currently teaches at the State University of New York, Albany.

to Whom it may concern

Lord in the matter of your ninety-second element
(rare, heavy, greyish, found especially in pitchblende and uranite
eager for evil, made for misrule)
let me most earnestly advise you:

       alter the weight, let the nucleus be
       lighter or heavier, as you please to imagine,
       but cohesive, resistant to bombardment
       and the shocks metal inherits;

       let the substance be black or blue
       or scarlet as sin, that we may know what we do;

       let it be common as dirt, that all may use
       it as they choose,
       the head of state
       and the atomized states of individual hunger
       who are his body politic;

or let it be found filigreed, entwined in veins
of marble in art's most valued monuments,
that we may fear to scratch it out
lest we crack the image of civilization;

this element, if it be apt to evil, educate
it to elude us, not cooperate
when we break it to our desire.
redeem it, stand in fire
at Hiroshima or blister under the skin
with your fishermen in the pacific sea
when the element is tried and found wanting
or not wanting
as waywardly it may seem to be:
wanting: in its very breaking to be
your death, mine, transubstantiate you or me;
not wanting: that what was should be
your universe unchanged, the element
fixed in its rank, obedient
as a star to do your will.

if it is still
incorrigible
after your sacrifice by blister
your radiation of passion,
after the very seed and day
in you of all our years turn mutant,
cast it into the fires of greatest heat
that it may meet
the hurt it brings you and your fishermen
this dawnless day
enduring still Hiroshima, here.
let it be broken in hell, let the fires there
burn out each other, let that heat fuse to silence
in the ice-clear sight of unchanged charity.
now, while you may,

let this element die
in us; mine
it from our minds,
delve
it out of ourselves
where it lies rare, heavy, greyish, in pitchblende
of our desires.
let man your self-reflecting universe
be made without uranium.

Lord, while you may, i earnestly advise
you, lift this destructive element from your mind, excise
it, let it be
in the void, unmade, unnamed, unthought, let this be
our dream of salvation.

Nightpiece

not to touch, she said to me, anything sticky
oil hairgoo pitgooch rancid facecream spoilt
vegetables, overripe and stepped down around
the dried crud at the curb, shaking flaked soot from her hair
any kind of filth that could rub off on me, not
to feel, she begged me, wash swallow and swirl of just any
old slime sloshing, and the little white scaly seeds
scattered the riding winds of a city's dandruff
not to break down inside me, she promised, the barrier
that keeps what i use from touching what i am, and took
one giant step over the rainbow rings on the black
skin of an oil pool, not not not to absorb
in my veins the jackhammer jolt
of what i despise, and tripped delicately past
the red splat of pizza, waded the tiny pink
bobbing faces trapped in the vomit marsh
on the IND stairs, raking

her dress from her thighs with the fingers of their smell,

walked through the glass showcase
stares of queers in the mirror doors *sweetheart when you sat*
at the mirror i saw that longhair greaseball Death
with hands toothed as plows, harrow
right through the ticketed marked-down sale
merchandise that would have raped her if she had looked
one come-on *and jerking his head, with an ingratiating smile comb*
the meat from your bones in strings and right on through
all the people that might rub off, the blood lymph mucous that
    bubbles
over the line between it and you inside you, doesn't know when
to stop *pretty*
you up for the night, carding
your wool with his knotted fingers

C*ollecting Evidence* is very much a product of the sixties, with its student protests, ghetto riots, and sexual revolution. The public upheaval forms a background to the private agonies of the poet, for this volume is almost entirely devoted to the self-absorbed psychology of young love rejected. The two poems given here, which open and close the book, are exceptions.

Hugh Seidman was born in Brooklyn in 1940 and was educated at Columbia University. He is the author of four books of poetry (*Selected Poems, 1965–1995,* 1995) and has taught at the University of Wisconsin, Yale, Columbia, Wilkes College, and the New School for Social Research. He lives in New York City.

Tale of Genji

In Murasaki's time
they wept at the sunsets

It was easy

      If you were the Prince
      & in love

Calligraphy could do it

      The total life
      in the nuance of a line

& later

      The sun that had changed

The cold light defining shadow
Poetry leading nowhere

Occurrence made meaningless
The injustice of history

Not that it mattered

Or the light
they wept at

The Making of Color

WHITE

Parchment and paper left clean
or the lead, called white, or ceruse

The stack of vinegar and lead
embedded in tanbark or dung;
the temperature of fermentation,
moisture, carbon dioxide,
and the acid vapor of vinegar—
until a crust is formed on the coils of metal:
the white carbonate and hydroxide of lead

The metal may be wrapped in marc,
the refuse of grapes from the wine press,
or else in the waste from beer

The fundamental character is density,
opacity, and brilliant whiteness

Those who work this are warned of
the poisonous dust of this residue—
retained in the human system as
the body's tolerance incurably declines

There is the white of bone,
or of egg shell, or of oyster,
calcined and powdered,
or a pigment of chalk
to be mixed with orpiment

BLACK

Certain insects sting in oak
nodules called galls from which
tannic and gallic acids are soaked

Mixed with a salt of iron
to form a purple-black liquid
that blackens with age

The color of iron-inks
oxidized in the fibers
of parchment and paper

incaustum — burnt in

or less frequently
suspensions of graphite
or of lampblack

RED

Minium in the sense of cinnabar
the native red sulphide of mercury

Pliny reports
the excellent mines are in Spain
the property of the State

Forbidden to break up or refine
but sent under seal to Rome

Ten thousand pounds per year
the price sustained by law
seventy sesterces a pound

Liver-colored or occasionally scarlet
but a bright red when ground

BLUE

Cloth dyed blue
licensed by the Crown

Ultramarine—lapis lazuli
pounded in a bronze mortar
Cennino relates

Eight ducats an ounce
for the patrons to purchase

PURPLE

The color of cheeks and the sea
Purpureus—the porphyry
The shellfish or the whelk
The murex—the purples of antiquity
Porphyrygenetos—born to the purple
A single drop from a skeleton

The stripes of the Roman togas
The purple of the ancient courts
The purple of Byzantium   The purple
of the great codices written in gold
The purple ink of the Patriarch
in the letters to the Pope of Rome

Parchment dyed shellfish-purple
crimson, plum-color, black
and the true purple—rivaling gold

GOLD

Sheet metal, foil the thickness of paper,
leaf that is thinner than tissue

Malleable but difficult to powder

Sawed or filed into coarse particles
ground with honey or salt and washed

Hardened with a base metal
filed and crushed and retrieved in acid

Brittle amalgams which are ground
mercury driven off by heat

The goldbeaters place a thin square
at the center of parchment and over this
more parchment and metal—hammered
until the gold spreads to the edges—
cut and the process repeated—
for the finest leaf, a sheet
of ox intestines—goldbeater's skin

One hundred and forty-five leaves
beaten from a ducat
Venetian—fifty-four troy grains

Powdered gold in suspension
chrysography
                    letters
on the reds and purples and blacks
of purple-dyed parchment
polished with a smooth hard stone
or with a tooth
                         the appearance
of filings of metallic gold

FIRE

The pages are stained with purple
The letters are written in gold
The covers are encrusted with gems
St. Jerome remonstrates

The curling writhes
Molten gold on carbon
Ink burnt ash grey
Emerald into vapor
The book, the codex, the manuscript
The canvas, the panel, the wall
Conflagrant world against world

K lappert's agile and unpredictable book is sometimes wildly funny. He writes complex poems built out of competing ironic voices, and his tone veers from silly to sober to scabrous. In all of this, as well as in his fondness for throw-away lines, goofy rhymes, orotund expressions, and literary allusions, his poetry has some of the quicksilver motion (though none of the lyric plangency) of John Ashbery's. Presumably it is a case of parallel evolution, as Ashbery was living abroad for much of the sixties and had barely begun to make an impact at home.

Born in 1942 in Rockville Centre, New York, Peter Klappert was educated at Cornell University and the University of Iowa. The author of four books of verse (*The Idiot Princess of the Last Dynasty,* 1984), Klappert currently teaches at George Mason University. He lives in Washington, D.C.

from Pieces of the One and a Half Legged Man

THE COURT OF DIVINE JUSTICE

He has a ticking in his soul, and prays;
his heart is infected with doubt, forgive him,
he has a ticking in his soul.

Will the remnant please
be carried forward:
Name? (look when you answer)
Objection, we are not interested
in the remnant's name
                 Oc-cupation?
Objection we are not and so forth but
Now Mr. Remnant, is it or is it not true/
you came here intending to sue/
Miss Thanwich Nograter who/
denied you the Power of Screw/ yes or no
what were you doing when the leg
came off? how do you *objection we are not* plead
filthy or not filthy? up on your stumps

yes or filthy the remnant must answer for himself
(speak up please)
        ORDER IN THE COURT
        REMNANT WANTS TO
anyone who speaks is a remnant for life
speak up on your stumps: what were you up to
when your tongue fell out *ShutUp!*

(. . . I created, or someone has told me)

                it says here
ears remnant, pink pulpy *ears,* pendulant
succulent *ears,* ponderous preposterous *ears,*
swimming in ears, diving in ears, dreaming
of gallons of ears
        EARS?
           Jesus Christ Remnant
what were you *doing?* (speak up please)
what was his job? triangle-sitter yes yes
but what does that mean? look remnant: what the hell
were you doing with all those ears? (face the jury)
(there is no jury) what kind of fantasy
life is that remnant? *trinity divinity unity infinity yes*
yes, but cut 'em into bacon strips I'd say. Catechism
remnant repeat after me: this man is a state of mind
this man is a state of mind (repeat after me after me)
Ears! Catechism remnant repeat after me: trinity is a delta
in the stream of traffic, trinity is a playground for scholars,
trinity is a pretty ring in the orchestrated chaos, trinity

                "erase me"

Who mangled the monument remnant?

              "erase me,
                 backward in time
                Love   "   193

Stand up in your head remnant, I can't erase you.
You have swallowed the point-handed clock remnant,
feel it there ticking like a heart ticking
in your belly? tick-ing. Eat of the point-handed
ticking remnant, *I can't erase you.*
Good luck to those who can.

To Whom

Enter mine host
With a sheaf of foundation grants
And a neatly pressed pants.
He is the social Eumenide,
Provider of these amenities.
We sit in his vacuous affair
His palace in the very air
We breathe
And we conceive
From his suggestions. Oh, *he was no forpynëd goost*
But the monk who keeps learning alive.
A fat goose lovëd he best
Or else a breast.

Our wives start stalking each other
They bristle and ripple their gristle.
Suddenly there's a crowd and sulky Yvette
Steals out of her Mexican shroud. She laughs
Out loud. And our condescending confucian
Focuses into a yawn: rebirth is reborn.

    (who had his ears in the clouds and failed to sleep
    who was a walking catatonic
    who carefully had not neglected to breathe
    who made up schedules of himself, who made up timetables,
        who stood in the rain and missed every bus

who touched on the subject touching the subject
who defined himself by the lighting around him
who sat Monday morning in the bar without his glasses and
     memorized in the mirror the blurred face of the clock
who started nothing —
who ate cashews who ate butternuts who ate peanuts who ate
     sunflower seeds
who suffered a partial eclipse
who was there, who saw what was coming (probably) and stayed
     where he was
who did what had to be done as if he hadn't heard the news
who woke up dying, who died
waking up. Who ran away with himself who ran . . .

Mine host does his introductions:
He conjures names with one hand, with the other
He opens a can of applause
                 —Outbursts of
Orchids emblossom and cascade
From the neck of America's finest champagne,
We are all caught up in a masquerade,
It's in moments like these that poets get made.

In Memory of H. F.

d. Man of War Key, March 1, 1965

I found the land above the river, where
the river meets the sea, fallen off
into the Sound
            Ann writes to me, Hobey,
that you have drowned in your own years.

There was no fault in the massed earth,
nor was there in the sea. The fault

fell at birth, and whatever rooted
in the broken land—cedars, rockwart,
or the great and other sea birds:
dependent creatures, nested in the bluff—
knew it was there, and loved
the hollow where the sea resounded.

Summer upon summer the Sound
fell upon the mouthing river,
striped bass and bluefish wandered
among the rocks, weed creatures scavenged
in the breakwater wash. Broad summers
we have known the land would shift;
we could not catch the momentary trembles
but saw, on morning walks, sand fill
our footprints, and found new boulders
in the sea below the bluff. We know
of sea, that it breaks the whole world down,
or builds it, in some other sea.

Friday . . . cedars, terns, crustaceans.
But as if a part of the land mass had fallen,
it is quiet as the sun rises above the Sound.

O*bscenities* is a Vietnam War diary made up of brief, cheerfully grim poems couched in the jocular vernacular common to soldiers. The book aims at journalism and does a good job of reporting, for the author rarely editorializes and never sermonizes.

Born in Lowell, Massachusetts, in 1947, Michael Casey was drafted upon graduation from the Lowell Institute of Technology in 1968 and served as a military policeman in Vietnam. He returned to study at the State University of New York, Buffalo. Casey is the author of a second book of poems, *Millrat* (1997). He lives in Andover, Massachusetts.

On What the Army Does with Heads

Most Americans like kids
GI's is no exception
They likes to play with kids
Walking up to them
Pattin them on the head
Hey   ya cute lil fucker
Now
If you see a little bald-headed kid
Don't do that
Don't go pattin him on the head
This kid's Buddhist
An it's against his religion
You do that
An to them
To these people here
You've fucked with the kid's head
An no one can
Convince that kid's mama
You didn do it on purpose

The LZ Gator Body Collector

See
Her back is arched
Like something's under it
That's why I thought
It was booby trapped
But it's not
It just must have been
Over this rock here
And somebody moved it
After corpus morta stiffened it
I didn't know it was
A woman at first
I couldn't tell
But then I grabbed
Down there
It's a woman or was
It's all right
I didn't mind
I had gloves on then

Learning

I like learning useless things
Like Latin
I really enjoyed Latin
Caesar and the Gallic Wars
Enjoyed his fighting
The Helvetians and Germans
And Gauls
I enjoyed Vietnamese too
The language
Its five intonations
Its no conjugations
A good language to learn
Vietnam is divided in
Three parts too
It makes me wonder
Who will write their book

This is a watershed volume in the Yale series, the first of many books that pursue their sustenance in simplicity and view the full appreciation of the passing moment as a moral obligation. Hass might be called a nature poet—he writes lovingly plain descriptions of landscape, mostly Californian—but he is a politicized one, unsurprisingly so given his time and place. The conscientious regard for nature in Hass's work may be traced back to certain aspects of Romantic poetry, and to think of the Romantic project come to San Francisco and galvanized by antiwar protests and a deteriorating ecology might provide one entrance into this book.

Robert Hass was born in San Francisco in 1941 and was educated at St. Mary's College and Stanford University. The author of four books of poetry (*Sun under Wood,* 1996), Hass has also published two books of criticism and translated the poetry of Czeslaw Milosz. Poet Laureate of the United States from 1995 to 1997, Hass has received a MacArthur fellowship, a Guggenheim fellowship, and the National Book Critics Circle Award. He lives in Inverness, California, and teaches at the University of California, Berkeley.

Bookbuying in the Tenderloin

A statuary Christ bleeds sweating grief
in the Gethsemane garden of St. Boniface Church
where empurpled Irish winos lurch
to their salvation. When incense and belief
will not suffice: ruby port in the storm
of muscatel-made images of hell
the city spews at their shuffling feet.
In the Longshoremen's Hall across the street,
three decades have unloaded since the fight
to oust the manic Trotskyite
screwballs from the brotherhood. All goes well
since the unions closed their ranks,
boosted their pensions, and hired the banks
to manage funds for the workingman's cartel.
Christ in plaster, the unions minting coin,
old hopes converge upon the Tenderloin

where Comte, Considerant, Fourier
are thick with dust in the two-bit tray
of cavernous secondhand bookstores
and the streets suffuse the ten-cent howl
of jukebox violence, just this side of blues.
Negro boy-whores in black tennis shoes
prowl in front of noisy hustler bars.
Like Samuel Gompers, they want more
on this street where every other whore
is painfully skinny, wears a bouffant,
and looks like a brown slow-blooming annual flower.
In the places that I haunt, no power
to transform the universal squalor
nor wisdom to withstand the thin wrists
of the girls who sell their bodies for a dollar
or two, the price of a Collected Maeterlinck.
The sky glowers. My God, it is a test,
this riding out the dying of the West.

After I Seized the Pentagon

Washington was calm, murderous, neo-classical.
More lies than cherry trees and nothing changed.
And drowsing home through northern Pennsylvania
the dawn light fooled me. Dreams. We talked
and, half-asleep, my body hummed. We were too excited.
After dark searchlights had cast troopers
in huge shadow on penitential stone. I saw
two shadows raising clubs to beat a girl,
a sickness in my stomach and a worse one in my head,
a pleased sense of historical drama, of the aesthetics
of evil. We were too excited. Eyes open, eyes closed,
I saw frost bleach the hills to western grass
and dreamed of small-breasted girls,
jack cheese, the smell of sweat, the acrid

smell of sage. Hiking, and morning woke me
to a maple blaze.
            I thought of pepper trees,
survivors, modest local gods, tough-barked,
of an easy grace and bitter fruit
which grow in riven country near the sea
where spring is clement and the land an aftermath.

The Pornographer

He has finished a day's work.
Placing his pencil in a marmalade jar
which is colored the soft grey
of a crumbling Chinese wall
in a Sierra meadow, he walks
from his shed into the afternoon
where orioles rise aflame from the orchard.
He likes the sun and he is tired
of the art he has spent on the brown starfish
anus of his heroine, the wet duck's-feather tufts
of armpit and thigh, tender and roseate enfoldings
of labia within labia, the pressure and darkness
and long sudden falls from slippery stone
in the minds of the men with anonymous tongues
in his book. When he relaxes, old images
return. He is probably in Central Asia.
Once again he is marched to the wall.
All the faces are impassive. Now
he is blinded. There is a long silence
in which he images clearly the endless sky
and the horizon, swift with cloud scuds.
Each time, in imagination, he attempts
to stand as calmly as possible
in what is sometimes morning warmth,
sometimes evening chill.

Measure

Recurrences.
Coppery light hesitates
again in the small-leaved

Japanese plum. Summer
and sunset, the peace
of the writing desk

and the habitual peace
of writing, these things
form an order I only

belong to in the idleness
of attention. Last light
rims the blue mountain

and I almost glimpse
what I was born to,
not so much in the sunlight

or the plum tree
as in the pulse
that forms these lines.

Letter to a Poet

A mockingbird leans
from the walnut, bellies,
riffling white, accomplishes

his perch upon the eaves.
I witnessed this act of grace
in blind California

in the January sun
where families bicycle on Saturday
and the mother with high cheekbones

and coffee-colored iridescent
hair curses her child
in the language of Pushkin—

John, I am dull from
thinking of your pain,
this mimic world

which makes us stupid
with the totem griefs
we hope will give us

power to look at trees,
at stones, one brute to another
like poems on a page.

What can I say, my friend?
There are tricks of animal grace,
poems in the mind

we survive on. It isn't much.
You are 4,000 miles away &
this world did not invite us.

Ryan writes abstract, existentialist poetry about the finality of human isolation, the dread of death, and the complications of sex. His book is dedicated to his father, who we are told "drank himself to death," and Ryan's memories of growing up the child of an alcoholic seem to lie at the heart of his work. This is conceptual verse, which resorts to the concrete only to evoke the faint surrealism lurking in everyday situations.

Michael Ryan was born in Saint Louis, Missouri, in 1945 and educated at Notre Dame, Claremont College, and the University of Iowa. He has published three books of verse, as well as a memoir, *Secret Life* (1995). A Guggenheim fellow, Ryan has taught at the University of Iowa and Warren Wilson College and was an editor of the *Iowa Review.* He lives in Irvine, California.

Talking About Things

for Jon Anderson

For a moment, the idiot inside me who shouts *death* constantly blacks out & here I am, hobnobbing with objects: I ask myself, have you thanked the pillow for muffling that bickering? And what would I do without this fork to my hot pot pies? Good light bulbs, I appreciate not descending stairs in the dark . . .

Surely we all are included by objects, even if my shirt could care more about which body slides around inside it. From now on, let's only use nouns: knife, widow, fume, penis, idiot. Of course the little fellow's still unconscious. Yes I'll still call him *Man with a past which is not his* . . .

Your Own Image

When by mistake you miss
the urinal in a public place,
there's no bending down, cleaning
up, or betting others won't
step in it. So you zip

205

your zipper with a flourish,
hoping the guy in the nearest
stall is admiring your follow
through & not the spreading puddle
which at least is your very own.
You stroll casually to the wash-
stand, avoiding thoughts
of barefoot little kids & cripples
whose leather laces brush
the floor and the curious eyes
that compare you to Pontius Pilate
as you wash your hands,
but you can't help meeting
your own image as you finish
the ablutions. It says,
You are dark and handsome.

This Is a Poem for the Dead

fathers: naked, you stand for their big faces,
mouths stuffed flat, eyes weighted, your miserable dick
sticking out like a nose. Dressed, you're more
of a mother making dinner: those old dirt bags,
the lungs, sway inside your chest like tits
in a housedress. Perhaps you're frying liver
which shrinks like your father getting older.
You still smell him breathing all over
your skin. He drank himself to death.

Now each woman you meet is a giant.
You'd crawl up their legs & never come down.
Even when you think you're big enough
to touch them, his voice flies from under
your throat & "I love you" comes out
a drunk whimper. All you can do

is breathe louder. You're speaking
to the back of your mouth. Finally,
you admit you know nothing
about sex & drown the urge slowly
like a fat bird in oil.

Still, those wings inside you.
At the hot stove all day you feel yourself
rising, the kids wrapping themselves
around your legs oh it's sexual
this nourishing food for the family
your father stumbling through the door
calling to you Honey I'm home.

Stanton is a visionary, and her poems are obsessive in their fascination with the imagining mind. They are obsessed by the body, too, but that fascination is more problematic for the poet. The book's frigidly pleonastic title is apt. Snow turns up everywhere in this intelligent, accomplished, and uncomfortable volume (there is even an "Elegy for Snow"), often in psychic response to sex. The author is aware of the psychomachy that underlies her art, however, and she uses her compulsions as much as they use her.

Born in 1946 in Evanston, Illinois, Maura Stanton received her B.A. from the University of Minnesota and her M.F.A. from the University of Iowa. The author of four books of poetry (*Life Among the Trolls,* 1994), she has also published a novel and a collection of short stories. She lives in Bloomington, Indiana, where she teaches at Indiana University.

A Voice for the Sirens

Oh they came, their eyes blank.
I pinned their souls under rocks
wanting only their shocked flesh
as the ships broke up, again, again . . .
Years now. Unlike the others I remember
a hand, some coarse hair against my cheek.
Now I stare at the sea all day
singing about strange events
for I've passed through their souls
inadvertently, thinking them shadows—
their souls were particles of odd happenings
or geography or touch,
tainting my immortality with memory.

As the sea roiled around him, one sailor
dreamed of his wife's tomb,
the steep, sweating walls & dead pigs
killed to entice away worms.
Another rubbed sea salt into his eyes
as if it were home, the desert;

while the one I murmured over, sweetly
dead in my young, implacable arms
saw his father turn in another sea.
In this fairyland, their strenuous lips
only blub loosely like the octopus
crossing my feet with lank, amorous
tentacles; their fingers dissolve
into the sharp, familiar bone.

Sometimes I hear mariner's wives chanting
over the water, like us, forlorn;
I remember the charmed wedding nights,
& each man's last embrace snow-
flake patterned into his soul, now mine.
Yet I keep singing, my dangerous voice
joined in sad irresponsibility with those
on this rock who forget why
each time until the next ship crashes.
Into the haunted music I weave my warning
carefully, as if my language were decipherable.

In Ignorant Cadence

The chemical tapestry of your brain
amazes the heart of you,
all those ions & neural protons

clicking into scenes or wishes.
Your tongue is alive
in your mouth like a slippery fish

so why can't you say anything?
Even Philomela, throat stanched with rags,
managed to shred her weaving fingers

until the thread equaled
recklessness from once upon a time.
The tongue of a bird is a delicacy—

yours, a distraction you never understood,
a hopeless slab of muscle
forever wobbling on the edge of song.

Judith Recalls Holofernes

While he slept, I poured salt in his ears.
Yes, it was easy
until the wasps escaped from the first hole in his neck
to blind me with wings
settling iridescent on my arms while I hacked
fiercely into the spine.
When it was over, I kissed his lips
then thumbed the eyes open
looking for my reflection in the dark pupil.
Actually, it was my maid
wielding the sword with strong, anonymous fingers.
I hid in the sheets, imagining
how many soldiers in the mountains
north of Bethulia dreamed of me each night.
Excuse me, it's hard to remember:
the blue tent, the olives,
Holofernes leaning into my breasts
describing something called "snow."
Did he have a beard or was that Anchior?
Perhaps I poisoned him first, yes, of course.
He drank greedily, his muscles
rippling silver in the light while he pulled
my left earlobe in fun.
Let me try out your sword, I said.

His wife writes me sad letters, asking for detail.
Did he eat well? Or catch cold?
Judith, you're the heroine, she says, I can't complain
about history, but didn't he call
my name in his sleep?
I write back: I'm not sure, I think the sword
flew by itself, a miracle, into his throat.
I'm not responsible for God.

This is our shipwrecked anniversary
which I celebrate by lighting a candle
inside his skull above the town gate
except, this year, they've torn it down.
Listen, his heart simply burst—
he was singing, he was so lonely
he stuffed flowers in his mouth
just to entertain me a moment longer.
Why did he hang his sword on the bedpost?
No, I don't remember.
Something is buzzing in my head,
something that sounds like a thousand
transparent wings rising behind my eyes.

The Conjurer

In a mayonnaise jar I keep the tiny
people I shrank with my magic; I didn't
know they'd hold each other's hands & cry
so sharply when I said, no, the spell's
irreversible, do you eat grass or breadcrumbs?
Two are lovers who claim the air's bad
down there, & bite my fingers when I offer
a ride. They don't understand me.
I keep the jar by a window, washing
soot off the glass walls periodically . . .
When I gave them a flower, some ants

in the stamen attacked viciously,
gnawing the man-in-the-fur-cap's leg
completely off, while the others squealed
at the punched lid for his rescue:
I thumbed the ant dead, but were they grateful?
Lately they've begun to irritate me,
refusing raw meat, demanding more privacy
as if they were parrots who need cage covers
for daytime sleep. The awkward lovers
break apart at my shadow, nonchalant . . .
They're weaving something out of grass,
a blanket maybe, growing thin to save
their stalks, eating only breadcrumbs.
Don't they see? I could dump them
out into a real garden, let them tunnel
through the weeds to an anthill.
One night I dreamed those lovers crawled
inside my left ear with candles,
trying to find my brain in a fog.
They moved deep among the stalactites
searching for the magic spell they thought
I'd lost in sleep. I knew better.
Still, I woke with something resurrected
in my memory, maybe only a trick,
yes, a trick, I'll tell them to close
their eyes I've something for them.

CAROLYN FORCHÉ   *Gathering the Tribes,* 1976

As the title of her book implies, Forché is interested in any person, place, or thing that appears tribal: primitive, ritualistic, tied to the earth. She believes that the instinctive wisdom that can accompany a simple existence offers a higher understanding than whatever Western culture, scholarship, and poetry in particular have left to offer. Forché's style is unusual. Though each line is spare, her poems move rapidly in many directions, swept on by casual bursts of descriptive clause.

Forché was born Carolyn Sidlosky in Detroit in 1950. The eldest of seven children (the tribes gathered in this volume thus include her immediate family, as well as the American Indians among whom she has lived), she was educated at Michigan State University and Bowling Green University. Forché, who has worked as a correspondent in El Salvador and Beirut, is the editor of an anthology, *Against Forgetting: Twentieth-Century Poetry of Witness* (1992). The recipient of the Lamont Prize, a Guggenheim fellowship, and a Lannan Foundation fellowship, she has published three books of verse and has translated from both Spanish and French (*Selected Poems of Robert Desnos,* 1991). She teaches at George Mason University in Fairfax, Virginia.

Skin Canoe

Swallows carve lake wind,
trailers lined up, fish tins.
The fires of a thousand small camps
spilled on a hillside.

I pull leeks, morels from the soil,
fry chubs from the lake in moonlight.
I hear someone, hear the splash, groan
of a waterpump, wipe my mouth.
Fish grease spits at darkness.

Once I nudged a canoe through that water,
letting its paddle lift, drip.
I was sucked down smaller than the sound
of the dropping, looked out
from where I had vanished.

Ancapagari

In the morning of the tribe this name Ancapagari was given to these mountains. The name, then alive, spread into the world and never returned. Ancapagari: no footstep ever spoken, no mule deer killed from its foothold, left for dead. Ancapagari opened the stones. Pine roots gripped peak rock with their claws. Water dug into the earth and vanished, boiling up again in another place. The water was bitten by aspen, generations of aspen shot their light colored trunks into space. Ancapagari. At that time, if the whisper was in your mouth, you were lighted.

Now these people are buried. The root-taking, finished. Buried in everything, thousands taken root. The roots swell, nesting. Openings widen for the roots to surface.

They sway within you in steady wind of your breath. You are forever swinging between this being and another, one being and another. There is a word for it crawling in your mouth each night. Speak it.

Ancapagari has circled, returned to these highlands. The yellow pines deathless, the sparrow hawks scull, the waters are going numb. Ancapagari longs to be spoken in each tongue. It is the name of the god who has come from among us.

Kalaloch

The bleached wood massed in bone piles,
we pulled it from dark beach and built
fire in a fenced clearing.
The posts' blunt stubs sank down,
they circled and were roofed by milled
lumber dragged at one time to the coast.
We slept there.

Each morning the minus tide—
weeds flowed it like hair swimming.
The starfish gripped rock, pastel,
rough. Fish bones lay in sun.

Each noon the milk fog sank
from cloud cover, came in
our clothes and held them
tighter on us. Sea stacks
stood and disappeared.
They came back when the sun
scrubbed out the inlet.

We went down to piles to get
mussels, I made my shirt
a bowl of mussel stones, carted
them to our grate where they smoked apart.
I pulled the mussel lip bodies out,
chewed their squeak.
We went up the path for fresh water, berries,
Hardly speaking, thinking.

During low tide we crossed
to the island, climbed
its wet summit. The redfoots
and pelicans dropped for fish.
Oclets so silent fell
toward water with linked feet.

Jacynthe said little.
Long since we had spoken *Nova Scotia,*
Michigan, and knew beauty in saying nothing.
She told me about her mother
who would come at them with bread knives then
stop herself, her face emptied.

I told her about me,
never lied. At night
at times the moon floated.
We sat with arms tight
watching flames spit, snap.
On stone and sand picking up
wood shaped like a body, like a gull.

I ran barefoot not only
on beach but harsh gravels
up through the woods.
I shit easy, covered my dropping.
Some nights, no fires, we watched
sea pucker and get stabbed
by the beacon
circling on Tatoosh.

2

I stripped and spread
on the sea lip, stretched
to the slap of the foam
and the vast red dulce.
Jacynthe gripped the earth
in her fists, opened—
the boil of the tide
shuffled into her.

The beach revolved
headlands behind us
put their pines in the sun.
Gulls turned a strong sky.
Their pained wings held,
they bit water quick, lifted.
Their looping eyes continually
measure the distance from us,
bare women who do not touch.

Rocks drowsed, holes
filled with suds from a distance.
A deep laugh bounced in my flesh
and sprayed her.

3

Flies crawled us,
Jacynthe crawled.
With her palms she
spread my calves, she
moved my heels from each other.
A woman's mouth is
not different, sand moved
wild beneath me, her long
hair wiped my legs, with women
there is sucking, the water
slops our bodies. We come
clean, our clits beat like
twins to the loons rising up

We are awake.
Snails sprinkle our gulps.
Fish die in our grips, there is
sand in the anus of dancing.
Tatoosh Island
hardens in the distance.
We see its empty stones
sticking out of the sea again.
Jacynthe holds tinder
under fire to cook the night's wood.

If we had men I would make
milk in me simply. She is
quiet. *I like that you*
cover your teeth.

Broumas devotes her energetic poems to anger and to love, celebrating sisterhood and castigating the patriarchy. Female figures drawn from Greek myth and European fairy tales are the starting points for much of her verse, but the poet reimagines this material in order to illustrate the plight and encourage the independence of women everywhere. This volume is notable for its enthusiastic and metaphorically resourceful treatment of lesbian sex, a frankness that seems unsurprising now but verged on taboo a mere twenty years ago.

Born in Syros, Greece, in 1949, Olga Broumas spent two years in the United States as a child but did not move there permanently until 1967. She was educated at the University of Pennsylvania and the University of Oregon. The author of six books of verse (*Black Holes, Black Stockings,* 1985, written with Jane Miller), Broumas has translated Odysseus Elytis and has been the recipient of a Guggenheim fellowship. She lives in Provincetown, Massachusetts.

Sometimes, as a Child

when the Greek sea
was exceptionally calm
the sun not so much a pinnacle
as a perspiration of light, your brow and the sky
meeting on the horizon, sometimes

you'd dive
from the float, the pier, the stone
promontory, through water so startled
it held the shape of your plunge, and there

in the arrested heat of the afternoon
without thought, effortless
as a mantra turning
you'd turn
in the paused wake of your dive, enter
the suck of the parted waters, you'd emerge

clean caesarean, flinging
live rivulets from your hair, your own
breath arrested. Something immaculate, a chance

crucial junction: time, light, water
had occurred, you could feel your bones
glisten
translucent as spinal fins.
                                        In rain-
green Oregon now, approaching thirty, sometimes

the same
rare concert of light and spine
resonates in my bones, as glistening
starfish, lover, your fingers
beach up.

Artemis

Let's not have tea. White wine
eases the mind along
the slopes
of the faithful body, helps

any memory once engraved
on the twin
chromosome ribbons, emerge, tentative
from the archaeology of an excised past.

I am a woman
who understands
the necessity of an impulse whose goal or origin
still lie beyond me. I keep the goat

for more
than the pastoral reasons. I work
in silver the tongue-like forms
that curve round a throat

an arm-pit, the upper
thigh, whose significance stirs in me
like a curviform alphabet
that defies

decoding, appears
to consist of vowels, beginning with O, the O-
mega, horseshoe, the cave of sound.
What tiny fragments

survive, mangled into our language.
I am a woman committed to
a politics
of transliteration, the methodology

of a mind
stunned at the suddenly
possible shifts of meaning—for which
like amnesiacs

in a ward on fire, we must
find words
or burn.

Beauty and the Beast

For years I fantasized pain
driving, driving
me over each threshold
I thought I had, till finally
the joy in my flesh would break

loose with the terrible
strain, and undulate
in great spasmic circles, centered
in cunt and heart. I clung to pain

because, as a drunk
and desperate boy once said, stumbling from the party
into the kitchen and the two
women there, "Pain
is the only reality." I rolled
on the linoleum with mirth. too close
to his desperation to understand. much less
to help. Years

of that reality. Pain the link
to existence: pinch your own tissue, howl
yourself from sleep. But that night was too soon

after passion
had shocked the marrow alive in my hungry bones. The boy
fled from my laughter
painfully, and I
leaned and touched, leaned
and touched you, mesmerized, woman, stunned

by the tangible
pleasure that gripped my ribs, every time
like a caged beast, bewildered
by this late, this essential heat.

Bin Ramke's poetry, which is vividly metaphorical and sometimes surreal, explores the lingering guilt and bodily unease that were evidently the residue of a Roman Catholic upbringing in east Texas. In both style and content, his verse calls to mind the work of Galway Kinnell. The inherently compelling subject matter of sex and shame is treated with detachment, giving this book an aloofness of tone which Richard Hugo notes in his foreword.

Bin Ramke was born in Port Neches, Texas, in 1947 and was educated at Ohio University. The author of five books of verse (*Massacre of the Innocents,* 1995), Ramke is editor of the Contemporary Poetry Series of the University of Georgia Press. He lives in Denver, where he teaches at the University of Denver and edits the *Denver Quarterly.*

The Difference Between Night and Day

The geography of dream is complex
so I look to the stars, I live
within a copper dome taking snapshots
of God. He is ugly, he burns
red and orange. He has names like Aldebaran
and Alpha Centauri, ugly as he.
But he is clean.
Astronomers know the texture of fish,
and how it shines in the moonlight,
and how fish move like stars in the dark
ocean, that they are clean.
Nothing like them under the sun.

I pick up a fish dead in the road
at three in the morning in the desert.
I put it in my pocket
and continue to look for love in the night.

If you watch the tracks of the stars
you will see how useless I am.
I have charts but cannot read them.

I tell you a star is green
but you cannot see it.
I predict the end of your sun
in twelve million years.

There is murder in the sky
like tossed bones
and counted teeth;
like water in which we breathe
the air shines planes and cones
that pop and glisten.
The fish grow ugly in heat,
mouths puff open, eyes
will not close properly.
The stars in the desert are a dream of fish.

Revealing Oneself to a Woman

The creaking of the universe must be, for those
large enough, slow enough to vibrate to its tune,
must be like what I heard on the river
when I lay waiting for sleep and the barge
we lived on listed and each separate plank
spoke and the lashings and moorings pulled
from the touch of slow water,
burned a wide sound to the bone.

Sometimes in the night I see
the flesh as flame circling the bone. Slow.
Surely it is to light my way into Orion to live
for the next one thousand years.

The birds, too, are blaze of flesh flying:
I hear them at night. Voices
dark and shrill as air, blue,
shine and cast bright shadows on the wall;

                              the dry house
catches and goes like the rug before the fire
from the spark of their song.

There is no defense in the night
but to catch flame and go
large-wheeling at the dance.
We shall die in the light of our making.

The Astronomer Works Nights: A Parable of Science

Lobachevsky . . . and Bolyai . . . first asserted and proved
that the axiom of parallels is not necessarily true.
— H. P. MANNING

Opusculum paedagogum. / The pears are not viols
— WALLACE STEVENS

What else in this dark world turns true?
Three pears and an apple in the bowl
on my table near the charts, dust,
the memory of silver stars, and breakfast.
Stars pop

like corn on a griddle if you watch them
as I do. The greatest calamities
the universe has known make no sound
like the deadliest trees in the forest.
Stars leave eggs under the fingernails
while you sleep.

I look at points and I make lines
to link stars in sleep which comes
with the sun. I have never touched
what alone I love, which is the light
which is clean and cold
as I am.

My wife and daughter loved me before
my skin grew translucent as a lampshade;
I can see stars through it when I hold
my hand against the night.

What I *do* is photograph
a section of the sky
smaller than the last
segment of the orange
after you took a bite.
Then I measure
the negatives.

While a student twenty
years ago I walked
the wet brick paths
on cooling afternoons;
I listened to the sky
crack as heat escaped;
I would not eat for days
because I liked
the strange dark feeling
(or sometimes half
an orange, closely peeled).

The bones glow white as stars
hidden in the map of flesh
and the universe laughs quietly
just over some dark ridge.

Perhaps I *can* hear it
ticking like an engine block
cooling on the side of the road
while adulterers walk
arm in arm in the woods.

Slow Hercules stalks Cygnus
and the Dragon insinuates between:
some nights I see it all come true;
I am the cosmic peeping Tom,
and what intimacies I spy on
through stars like wistful windows
while beauty lies sadly
with the world.

But when I wander home and hear
a wife and lover laughing in the shadows
I wonder whether some night I might watch
a dance much closer if not more slow;

our final hope is that we will not know.

Ullman's is the poetry of longing, sexual longing above all. Her languorous verse is ready to engage the world yet finds itself baffled at many turns. Low-key if not casual, this author is unlike many poets of the seventies in that she eschews angst for its own sake. Hugo appreciated the unanguished quality of Ullman's poems, characterizing them in his foreword as patient, quiet, matter-of-fact, and honest.

Born in 1947 in Chicago, Leslie Ullman was educated at Skidmore College and the University of Iowa. The author of a second book of verse (*Dreams by No One's Daughter,* 1987), she teaches at the University of Texas, El Paso.

Why There Are Children

The woman inside every woman
lights the candles.
This is the woman sons look for

when they leave their wives.
Daughters become wives
thinking they travel backward

to the dresser covered with lace,
the hairpins still scattered there
and the cameo earrings.

The same gnarled tree
darkens the bedroom window.
The hair coiled in a locket

conceals the hands of men and children.
When a woman shivers on the porch,
perhaps at dusk, it is the other

wanting a shawl. When a woman
in her middle years rises
and dresses for work, the other

reaches for the cameos
remembering a great love
and herself on the brink of it.

Rain

The slaves are dragging the last
bundles of figs
to higher ground. These figs
were to sweeten

and be passed among dignitaries.
The king's children
splash at the edge of the new ocean.
A man will walk here again

carrying a map.
He will let out his breath
suddenly. He will wrap
in a piece of soft cloth

a wedge of clay
from which all hair was pressed,
whose figs were eaten and eaten

and whose last
children, standing
on its last visible rise
sat down, tucking their

long shirts beneath them.
Their tutors must already know the story:
why else do they

rush from room to room
in the darkened
palace, not wondering,
talking of lamps, oil, and salt?

Memo

Touch was all.
Many nights of touch
and only yourself to trust.
Your hands led you
through the caverns of other hands.
You brought nothing from the journeys,
lost nothing each time the mind
took back its roots,
learned nothing
when people withdrew with pieces
of what you thought was heart.
The hands set out plates, opened cans.
Your age arrived, one corner
at a time. The familiar hungers turned
their backs. Only the hands
kept up with you,
folding the loose garments,
fingering the sheets
on the thin bed, showing more and more
of their frame, their muscle.

One Way to Reconstruct the Scene, 1980

Davis is possessed of an outlook at once homespun and grim. He writes spare poems in response to the pressure of memory, some of them appropriately cast in Stevensian tercets. The circumstances of these poems tend to be domestic and familial, but overall this is a chilly book in which the poet's favorite metaphors are bones and snow.

William Virgil Davis was born in 1940 in Canton, Ohio. He was educated at the Pittsburgh Theological Seminary (he is an ordained Presbyterian minister) and Ohio University. The author of three books of poetry (*Winter Light,* 1990) and several critical studies (on Robert Bly, among others), he has been a Fulbright fellow in Denmark and Austria. Davis teaches at Baylor University and lives in Waco, Texas.

The Sleep of the Insomniac

The body beside your body sleeps like death.

There is nothing to hear from your heart,
ghostly clock, full of collapse. Even your
breath, wind from the world's wind, breaks

unevenly, losing itself in itself. Suddenly,

the stars fall to fill your room. Time is
the thin spider you found along the fence
when you were five and kept to yourself

the way, for years, you kept your body

inviolate until you learned there was nothing
to be done for the flesh which would keep it
incorruptible. Death is as close as the wife

you sleep beside. Stars fasten to your forehead.

Spider

The web outside the window filled
with first light, the dew like small rain
stopped to seize the morning. We lie awake
without speaking or smoking. We have been together
this whole night, and never another.
That we both know.
Soon, the spider crouches, still, waiting,
off center but central in the web.
All the lines around him run through
his own wet eyes
and he waits for what the wind will deliver.

In a Room

It is like smoke escaping through a screened
window. When you enter an empty room,
with a chair in the center, when you
sit on the chair, waiting, and nothing happens,
and no one comes, you begin to notice
the size and shape of the room, the color,
or lack of color, of the walls, the cracks
in the floor beneath your feet, the ceiling
above you. After a time, when nothing
has happened and you have run out of ideas,
you look for the door. When you discover
that it has disappeared you begin to search
for it. You are certain there was a door,
reasonably certain you entered the room
through a door. When you cannot find it,
you sit down on the chair in the center
of the room. You wait for someone to come,
or to call. You notice, now, how the room
has begun to grow smaller, darker.

Snow

We are left, finally, to decide why
the world goes, and we with it,
toward some strange kind of return.

This morning, before morning, I dreamed
of snow falling thickly through trees.
When I awakened, snow was falling.

I put on the shoes of separation,
took the road of wandering, and walked out
to find a red heifer unblemished.

I spoke my name to the mountain
and waited to hear a word returned.
Nothing but the wind moved.

In less than an hour my tracks
were covered over, and still the snow
fell thick through the cedars

like dust, dust that at last would rise.

B ensko's poetry deals with psychological pressure come home to roost. The speaker in this book is both the veteran of a Southern upbringing, in which ancestral history is all important, and the veteran of many wars at once, particularly the two world wars and the Spanish civil war. Bensko alternates family narrative with wartime memory, and the disturbances caused by these recollections lend a shimmer to his undemonstrative verse.

Born in Birmingham, Alabama, in 1949, John Bensko was educated at Saint Louis University, Auburn University, the University of Alabama, and Florida State University. He has published a second book of poetry, *The Waterman's Children* (1994). Bensko, who has been a Fulbright professor in Spain, now lives in Tennessee and teaches at the University of Memphis.

A Last Look in the Sambre Canal

for Wilfred Owen

The bells of the Armistice wake his family.
The girls put on their best ribbons and sing
while they shake his clothes in the window.
When his mother comes back from the post and drops
the letter in the ditch, she understands

the sound of guns, the duckboards wet
and covered with mud, and the difficulty
of carrying anything, a letter, a poem, across
the canal and into the house. The letter fades
the way his body drifts,

plum and green and luxuriant in the water
with a charm that stops the guns. Like their farm
in Kent he'll sprout violets and moss. His face
rises in the water with a smile accustomed
to a world turning itself green.

The news of his death arrived in England
days after the war ended and the Sambre peasants

picked him clean of souvenirs. On the dresser
in his mother's house his last photo,
a notebook, and a drawing come to light.

In the shade of the few trees left, his body
stalls, poems float from his pockets
and his eyes follow them. What do the words
reflect? A letter, his mother, the girls singing?
The water, more than a mirror, dissolves them.

The Bones of Lazarus

"All the time we knew his corpse was rotting,
unseen as those things should be, wrapped in sheets."

But we let the old man go on
and walk among our children,
talking to the birds and animals.

We loved him and we decided he was harmless.
A penny here, a penny there.
So he went on for years.

His hands shook a little, and he was sometimes
forgetful, stumbling into the room
when he wasn't wanted. We ignored his failures.

Because we knew by then
age had taken its course. Only bones
were left. It was then he died.

That night we washed him. The bones
rode easily under the dried, yellow skin.
We thought of the old temptation
to believe in his second chance.

The Butterfly Net

One grandchild runs with a net
like an awkward wing. Another asks:

What in their wings gives them color?
A powder no one understands.

Why do some fly south?
They gather by the thousands and die.

He remembers his teacher bringing
her collection of delicate, rare butterflies,

shattering just as the glass shattered
when he dropped them. He remembers trying

to pick them up, and how useless it was.
Holding her best catch, one grandchild rubs

the large blue wings with eyes.
What's that in your hands? his mother

had asked. She couldn't believe
the colors of his powdery fingers.

DAVID WOJAHN   *Icehouse Lights,* 1982

Setting his lucid yet passionate poems in the desert border towns of the American Southwest and in the Minnesota of his childhood, Wojahn seeks to capture some of the average man's quiet desperation. This is deliberately down-to-earth verse that finds some relief in the examination of everyday objects from the bleakness of a whiskey-soaked, blue-collar existence. Wojahn is careful to avoid romanticizing the beautiful, preferring to aestheticize the unbeautiful instead.

David Wojahn was born in Saint Paul, Minnesota, in 1953, and educated at the University of Minnesota and the University of Arizona. The author of six books of poetry (*The Falling Hour,* 1997), Wojahn was co-editor of the Pushcart Prize anthology in 1986. An Amy Lowell Traveling Scholar in 1987–88 and a winner of the William Carlos Williams Book Award, Wojahn lives in Chicago and teaches at Indiana University, Bloomington.

Distance

Tonight the workmen
with red bandanas are building
a house across the street.
Light spills from the holes
they've left for windows.
They've inched across the roofbeams,
buckets of shingles in their arms.
This last man leans after
everyone's gone, his head
on a door that's propped on a tree.
I hear him singing to himself.

We both can't sleep—
his singing, and his hand
that drums a hammer again
and again into the ground.
The cats on the roof disturb him;
he stares and hammers,
hears me typing, or finds me

through the window, bent
to my lamp. I've come to admire

the distance between us,
the noises we make to ourselves
in the night, tired
as the lovers in a Japanese print
who've turned and wiped their genitals
with the blue silk scarves
they had stuffed in their mouths
while coupling.

Allegory: Attic and Fever

All day the fever tells lies.
The armchair vibrates with the train
from the yards below the window. The new snow
falls like moths on a soldier's collar,
like the long white dreams of those condemned.
They've moved great slabs of marble from the country
for building a new station in spring.
But now it's a huge icehouse from the window,
children climbing abandoned cranes and pulleys.

Fever is an allegory, like the tale I wrote
of the fire in the bookstore. No one wanted it,
as I don't want coal or bread. This morning,
bending down to look through the crack in the floorboards,
I watched Katya the whore undress her client—
a bald man in suspenders, stains on his shirtfront.
Her fraying garters, and his buttocks between them,
grunting forward. Finished, he took her towel
and wiped himself. Like me. Like me

erasing a page. It's not allegorical:
I begin again. This time, not a fire in a bookstore,

but the station house below me, burning.
And the train on fire pulling forward
across the trestle, lighting all Oslo
at midnight. The cries in the train are the beauty
of no escape, like a fever refusing to break.
I've a coal in my mouth, singing.
Hear it steaming in my mouth.

Let me tell you how the first snow comes
in the country of my dream. The lake's not frozen,
for the fever's in the water.
I'm in a glass bottomed rowboat, watching
the other world, the one below.
I'm King of Perch, Archduke of Cod.
But the fever's in the water and they die:
my hair falls out, all goes milky in snow.
But Katya's here, undressing me, telling me

how weary I am. No one would call her beautiful
or able to control her fate. I tell her this is not a dream,
but the fever and the vision we must live.

The Inside

Because this is the moment
when stars grow ominously small,
there's room again for passivity.
There's no pale green flooding the bed—
the corner bar has shut off its sign,
and love isn't even disease anymore,
not even a secret we're
forever disclosing. As a child

I feared bridges and nuns.
They kept me awake, staring at Christ,
his arms pinned into the wall.

Worry is better now.
You sleep beside me until morning,
a habit we'll repeat
until we've had enough. The stars

must collapse within themselves to rest.
In the mirror I know age
is the face imploding.
I hate the inner life—you snore
with your back against me.
The artistry of sleeplessness
is a mind as heavy as a landscape of trains,
coils of a mountain road.
I'm tired of the thoughts I steer by.
This is the inside, where stars
keep revolving, revolving.

CATHY SONG *Picture Bride,* 1983

This book is made up of reticent, calm, suggestive poems exploring family dynamics and the poet's subdued struggle with ancestral tradition. As this struggle is pursued, the constraints placed upon an oriental daughter are tacitly compared to the predicament of artists everywhere. Hugo seemed to feel that there might be an Eastern aesthetic at work in Song's preference for description and implication over imagination and analysis.

Cathy Song was born in Honolulu, Hawaii, in 1955 and was educated at Wellesley College and Boston University. She has published three books of poetry (*School Figures,* 1994) and has received the Shelley Memorial Award from the Poetry Society of America as well as the Hawaii Award for Literature. She lives in Honolulu.

Ikebana

To prepare the body,
aim for the translucent perfection
you find in the sliced shavings
of a pickled turnip.
In order for this to happen,
you must avoid the sun,
protect the face
under a paper parasol
until it is bruised white
like the skin of lilies.
Use white soap
from a blue porcelain
dish for this.

Restrict yourself.
Eat the whites of things:
tender bamboo shoots,
the veins of the young iris,
the clouded eye of a fish.

Then wrap the body,
as if it were a perfumed gift,
in pieces of silk
held together with invisible threads
like a kite, weighing no more
than a handful of crushed chrysanthemums.
Light enough to float in the wind.
You want the effect
of koi moving through water.

When the light leaves
the room, twist lilacs
into the lacquered hair
piled high like a complicated shrine.
There should be tiny bells
inserted somewhere
in the web of hair
to imitate crickets
singing in a hidden grove.

Reveal the nape of the neck,
your beauty spot.
Hold the arrangement.
If your spine slacks
and you feel faint,
remember the hand-picked flower
set in the front alcove,
which, just this morning,
you so skillfully wired into place.
How poised it is!
Petal and leaf
curving like a fan,
the stem snipped and wedged
into the metal base —
to appear like a spontaneous accident.

The White Porch

I wrap the blue towel
after washing,
around the damp
weight of hair, bulky
as a sleeping cat,
and sit out on the porch.
Still dripping water,
it'll be dry by supper,
by the time the dust
settles off your shoes,
though it's only five
past noon. Think
of the luxury: how to use
the afternoon like the stretch
of lawn spread before me.
There's the laundry,
sun-warm clothes at twilight,
and the mountain of beans
in my lap. Each one,
I'll break and snap
thoughtfully in half.

But there is this slow arousal.
The small buttons
of my cotton blouse
are pulling away from my body.
I feel the strain of threads,
the swollen magnolias
heavy as a flock of birds
in the tree. Already,
the orange sponge cake
is rising in the oven.
I know you'll say it makes
your mouth dry

and I'll watch you
drench your slice of it
in canned peaches
and lick the plate clean.

So much hair, my mother
used to say, grabbing
the thick braided rope
in her hands while we washed
the breakfast dishes, discussing
dresses and pastries.
My mind often elsewhere
as we did the morning chores together.
Sometimes, a few strands
would catch in her gold ring.
I worked hard then,
anticipating the hour
when I would let the rope down
at night, strips of sheets,
knotted and tied,
while she slept in tight blankets.
My hair, freshly washed
like a measure of wealth,
like a bridal veil.
Crouching in the grass,
you would wait for the signal,
for the movement of curtains
before releasing yourself
from the shadow of moths.
Cloth, hair and hands,
smuggling you in.

Spaces We Leave Empty

The jade slipped from my wrist
with the smoothness of water
leaving the mountains,

silk falling from a shoulder,
melon slices sliding across the tongue,
the fish returning.

The bracelet worn since my first birthday
cracked into thousand-year-old eggshells.
The sound could be heard
ringing across the water

where my mother woke in her sleep crying thief.
Her nightgown slapped in the wind
as he howled clutching his hoard.

The cultured pearls.
The bone flutes.
The peppermint disks of jade.

The clean hole
in the center, Heaven:
the spaces we left empty.

RICHARD KENNEY *The Evolution of the Flightless Bird,* 1984

Intricately constructed and intellectually restless, Richard Kenney's poems constitute both essays and excursions. The poet is acutely aware of humanity's insignificance in the face of overwhelming natural forces, and he posits love and human interaction as our only line of defense. Much that is mundane has been elided from Kenney's verse, but unexpected information is adduced from many fields, and the reader may be called upon to grasp astronomy, geography, nautics, paleontology, and more in the space of a few stanzas. This is a demanding book, and one that insists upon being reread.

Born in Glen Falls, New York, in 1948, Richard Kenney graduated from Dartmouth College and then studied in Scotland and Ireland on Dartmouth's Reynolds Fellowship. The author of three books of verse (*The Invention of the Zero,* 1993), he has received fellowships from the Guggenheim Foundation, the MacArthur Foundation, the Lannan Foundation, and the American Academy in Rome. He lives in Port Townsend, Washington, and teaches at the University of Washington.

In April

In April, in New England, the earth ball yields
under its own mass, gives in to dead
gravity, loses tone, relinquishing
the rigor of the last freeze like slack skin
fallen from the cheekbones of the Canadian Shield.
Even Yankees start to soften, thumb the dread
almanacs, shed mackinaws, maxims
sour in the mouth, and offer up halting, truculent
hearts like flushed chameleons—in that radical
instant god-struck as Ikhnaton or cold Incan
warlocks in their own mountains were, when power
flowed out of the sky again. It makes me think
of the reindeer men winding down from the shielings,
the high slopes of summer, following spoor

down forty thousand years, the sun cupped
in their frightened minds like a cinder—

smell them, seared fat, still. Von Humboldt, Lewis,
Clark, Amundsen—we shared ancient values
then as I stood, in my twelfth year, ankle
deep in the drowning sluiceway of our gravel
road. I watched the winter off in rivulets.
Those waters might have been birth-waters, torn loose
all at once as the snowveils bled back to wrinkled
tatters in the shade of the forest; like great unraveling
nets, they dropped their catch. I imagined distinct,
torn wings, the earth littered with wings of cicadas,
all the thousands of hours held perfect, incorruptible,
since the first heavy snows of mid-December.

In April, between the Champlain Valley and the Connecticut
River, a single mountain roadside remains
arrested forever: in indistinct, random patterns
of matted foliage and straw, I saw a delicate
arrangement of brown hair, exposed bone—a single
instant, discrete as a snowflake on a neuron
imperishable among millions in the gray moraine
of long accumulation (I can still feel that new
sun on my damp back like a mild alkaline
burn, intense and shallow—I saw the pick-up-sticks
complexity the earth assumed, and thought *Isn't
the sun the same as life?* and, grown fearful, yearned
for the first time for the brittle light, the fixed,
stupefying conservation of form that had been winter.

I fell back in that starving light of past time
when a white-tailed deer fell over on its ribs
and froze; here was the first dead juvenescence
of spring, stillbirth, when winterkill drops
across the season like stone. How plausible,
the ancient stone planet reborn each year a stone,
a watch-fob charm spun down some lazy, oval
fall through time, until a soft Pleistocene

wind drifted the mind of the first man whose lime-
dusted doppelgänger's form faced him like this: eyes full
to their pink rims with snow, the dead thought
and fish-stare still—behind the retinas, like loam,
the flat brain keeps the antique taproot of the
fear that spring is nothing more than a thaw.

We stand, imagining the strobe of afternoons
since earth began, the unregenerate gray
ground slacking weight all around us, once
more unfreezing, to be frozen again and thrown
back again in twigs and slag snow, and nowhere grace
or quick or leaf, the least flush or fragrance—
Then in some cold bedroom—as finely dreamt
as riffling cotton sleeves, and all the plant stems
like new copper by the road—a seine, a spill
of hair will fall and touch the face to simple
recognition, then: that blind instant caught,
in the absence of desire, out of the confusing sun,
when two of our species reach thoughtlessly
to groom one another, to smooth the other's skin.

Sailing

Flailing like a foal giraffe to keep his balance
on the flying skates, fast as tin pans
tied to a car he drags behind a tarpaulin
parachuting from red mittens, runs the narrows
of Lake George, aching to hold on, to sail Champlain,
the Chambly Rapids, beyond the great St. Lawrence
itself. I see him trudging home, half-frozen,
surprised by the distance, for once feeling his age,
feeling the wind's edge. High Adirondacks ringed
that gleaming plate, the lake, still as *Epidauros'*
empty amphitheater in stark arranged

elements of simple memory and stage-light—
Sometimes my memories of you are so, *ex machina,*
contrived, quiet as an actor's painted mask.

When I was twenty I went to Greece—that long-dreamt
crossing—and how reluctantly! I've jewelled
old memories in mind with such care: eventually
the shore-ice weakened, the lake changed, its drumhead
having rotted unnoticed in the March winds,
the red-sailed iceboats having disappeared all at once,
like birds. Then the lake split open, *doomed*
and *snapped,* hollow, implausible, awful as stage-thunder.
Once greenish metallic ice plates sheared on a thin
craze line in front of me, bleeding sudden gouts
of slush and water quick as mercury— I recognized
those sounds today, the unmistakable wrack
and cough in the Winooski River. The ice will go out
of the lake soon. I think of wind, and walking back—

And I see you, like my own hieratic figure
waving out of childhood, a scrap of scarlet
flannel in the distance, receding— I think
how we are swept, and changed. Bright runners score
the surface of a lake like fresh-sawn marble, unforgiving
and hard-edged in a shell-like, gleaming, Aeschylean
order; and for awhile the patterns seem secure,
and hold us. But even a child hears blood in the conch,
and feels the breaking away, bits of shell-coral
and life's lining carried away with the shattering
rush, rivers, and the sea, and across—the streaked gongbronze
corrodes, and cracks, and the child diminishes—a skirl
of snow blousing in the cold wind, small *choregos*
lost against a painted sky, and gone.

The Battle of Valcour Island

Although hindsight accords a degree of humored
panache to our performance that year, my heart
I own still lurches like a stallion fording
a rapid to remember my first battle, when Edward
shinned out to the tip of the bowsprit to free a fouled
jib, alone, and drew the fire that followed
from every more or less awestruck gunner aboard
the galley *Congress*. Balls and shells and shards
of every sort soughing around his deaf gallant
ears, and he chopping lines as nonchalant
as paring vegetables for his mother in a cooling rain
in England. His next birthday we drank *restraint
in action*, lest the natural span of adult
years lapse before one's ascent to the Admiralty —

It happened this way. We were on the lake at five
of the false dawn on 11 October, Sir Guy
Carleton aboard flotilla Captain Pringle's
ship the *Lady Maria*. Then the *Inflexible*,
the *Carleton*, the radeau *Thunderer* (the sow),
twenty gunboats, longboats, canoes, and bateaux,
following like farrow on a fresh north breeze,
and all for seven nutshells full of Yankees.
I sailed the *Carleton's* cutter, feeling like an ass.
The boat still bore the stencil *HMS
Blonde*, my ship and Edward's ship, anchored
in the St. Lawrence, while we scurried
down this freshwater wilderness farther and farther
from a decent sea. I felt — lost there.

At four bells we blew by them like grape.
Tucked in the channel behind Valcour Island, sheep
in a pen, Pringle said (though led by a brilliant
goat, as he later learned): and the north wind sent
us gaily past like clowns. It took the *Inflexible*

two miles to come about. On a tactical pretext
several of Arnold's vessels feinted from Valcour
Sound, into the lake, and Lieutenant Dacres
instantly committed the *Carleton* to pursuit.
She sheered off like a razor, bow guns shooting
wide, and the rebels turned. Dacres dogged
them straight up the channel. Gunboats followed with lug-
sails and oars, but of five British ships, the *Carleton*
engaged the rebel battle line alone.

It went very badly. With the first exchange, Lieutenant
Dacres fell wounded, and Edward assumed command
of the ship. Not twenty years old, then, already twice
the man that Captain Pringle was, or was
capable of being (we've since toasted his vulgarity,
all birthdays, George, old age and flag
rank for every Jack-tar, *skoal*)— In ragged
fall crosswinds sneezing off those miserable Valcour
bluffs, the *Carleton* lost control, her slack
sails flapping like shot gulls. Slowly the black
schooner swung round, until she lay still before
the crescent enemy line: like a focused mirror
throwing gunlight on a single point, the surface
of the water buzzing like bees, and fire from the *Congress.*

The naval history will read *The* Carleton *fought
like a British ship,* or some such phlegmy
platitude to explain her vicious mauling, needless
to say; though long before the *Maria's* recall
flag ran up it ceased to be a contest. The *Carleton*
was totally unresponsive by then, caught
bows into the breeze like a shivering compass needle,
helpless to come about, hulled, her flame-
lit decking raked by every shot from the galley
Congress, and at the same time powerless to lay
her own traversing guns. The command was saved by
one man, by the single most extraordinary

act of courage I had ever seen, high
on the bowsprit, the ship in his hands like a sword—

We rowed to him in longboats from the *Isis*
and the *Blonde;* Edward hurled a hawser,
and we towed the *Carleton* to safety. Soon it was night.
(Time for Pringle, the ninny, to dine—no doubt
he was helped to more than a gill of fine Madeira
to irrigate his spent, weary, dead
intelligence. Or as some later said, *courage.*
The British naval code is simple: *Engage
the enemy.* Engage: In 1766
a fleet admiral was shot for having neglected
to engage. The *Lady Maria* had hardly fired
a round— But the navy has had its inquiry;
that's done.) That night the plan was to blockade
the Americans in the sound, and sink them the next day.

We used only four ships! At night, half awake,
I still search my drowned memory for the clicks
of rowlocks, the breath of Benedict Arnold. . . . Lake
Champlain deep in fog that night; we'd
heard nothing. They went by like teal through marsh-reeds
and gently rocking masts, like thoughts
through a dreaming dog, whose feet paddle and eyelids
only quiver. What fools. The captain licked
his lips when he saw the sheepfold empty as the lake
below, and knew we all knew he was a horse's
ass beside his rebel adversary.
What came of that was Edward Pellew, Lieutenant
Dacres and I smelled no salt water all winter,
and kissed a number of ladies in Montreal.

Alexander is a relaxed poet, and her work is in no hurry to get to an end or jump to conclusions. She writes whimsical and engaging verse that is glad to make room for the curious and the old-fashioned. Though rarely formal, these poems do show an interest in language for its own sake. Offering oddments of information and the pleasure of puns, *Navigable Waterways* is one of those rare books of poetry that are simply fun to read.

Educated at Bates College and the University of Iowa, Pamela Alexander was born in 1948 in Natick, Massachusetts, where she still lives. The author of two subsequent books of verse (*Inland,* 1997), she has taught at the University of Iowa and is a writer-in-residence at the Massachusetts Institute of Technology.

A Marriage of Sorts

The maze is round and blue and green.
Clouds float over it,
and feathered ounces fly—
ouzels, loons; their cries sound
like miniature wine-glasses breaking
against the crusty earth.
The birds are white flares starting
from dark trees and viny swamps
as if in celebration. But what
festival is here? Are the droplets flung
from the hands of drowning men
tossed in joy like rice at weddings—
the worthless coins with which
they try to buy their breath back from the sea;
are their last cries
choked with gladness?
                          The globe is lovely. Colors
fit together in intricate designs
that wash away, and form again;
the planet in its veil of weather
wobbles, bright and dark. Clouds
and birds and cries

rise and turn together, fall.
Dissolving, they make circles
within the circles of the seas.
And land circles sea in
an ancient sort of dance.

A Well-Known Elizabethan
Double Entendre

If we are dying, let's do it slowly, together.
Are dolphins ever tired?
The way we have been leaping
about the steamship *Intercourse* and heaving
as if it ran on our hot breaths;
the way we have been yelling
as if our lungs were bellows for the furnace
of that gentle, violent vessel;
the way we gasp and clutch each other
like drowning sailors, then die to find
another life, ourselves transformed
and kissing easily as fish or playing
like dolphins over waves,
or tossing like the waves themselves
above the sea-bed, after
having beaten around our respective and
respectable bushes
on dry land for so long —
I am turned around, not sure
if we are found or foundering.
There is a storm above the waves
and one below, but for all our
sweet struggle, the churning all around,
our sporting in the wake,
the ship appears to be more or less
on course. We sight a new world daily.

Scherzo

She is a mermaid caught in a net,
feet merged into a tail-fin
in one webbed end of the hammock, or
she is a planet hung like a lantern in space.
The cords diverge
and line her back with longitude
and latitude, tropical waist
to temperate brain.
She is an angel lounging
on a stringy cloud, unleavened
cirrus.

Trees hang above her, their globy tops
bushy stars on stalks.
The leaves are busy with
all kinds of commerce and curious
emergencies—green flares go off,
and smallish gongs; there are raucous
goings-on in the palisade layers
where pairs of cells dance between the columns
and odd ones idling along the fibrous walls
look out through leaf-pores
at constellations of leaves,
galaxies of trees. Waiters circulate
with drinks, and wiry insects perform
skating tricks and acrobatics on the waxy decks.
A party! The leaf manufactures
streamers and lights and sweet liqueurs
from the cranky air.

Though she lies lazy as a land mass
between the hammock's polar regions,
nothing within her precincts
is still: while some cells, of quiet
disposition, tend the elevators

of respiration, others drive sports cars wildly
through the tumbling blue traffic
of the blood, or jockey trucks of produce
about the stomach rumblingly; some dash
along nerve paths with telegrams
and holler out *Halloo — halloo —*

                      She is

a red leaf! suspended between
the stout stems of trees and linked
to the living commotion
by the subtle twig of breath, that
ether
her mind has ridden on for years
like a flock of grey birds circling,
a school of planets swimming.

Poems concerning art, science, and travel make up this volume, which James Merrill selected not without reservation.

George Bradley was born in 1953 in Roslyn, New York, and was educated at Yale University and the University of Virginia. The author of two subsequent books of verse (*The Fire Fetched Down,* 1996), he lives in Chester, Connecticut.

E Pur Si Muove

Of course it had been madness even to bring it up,
Sheer madness, like the sighting of sea serpents
Or the discovery of strange lights in the sky;
And plainly it had been worse than madness to insist,
To devote entire treatises and a lifetime to the subject,
To a thing of great implication but no immediate use,
A thing that could not be conceived without study,
Without years of training and the aid of instruments,
And especially the delicate instrument of an open mind;
It had been stubbornness, foolishness, you see that now,
And so when the time comes you are ready to acquiesce,
When you have had your say, told the truth one last time,
You are ready to give the matter over and say no more.
When the time comes, you will take back your words,
But not because you fear the consequences of refusal
(Who looks into the night sky and imagines a new order
Has already seen the instruments of torture many times),
Though this is the conclusion your inquisitors will draw
And it is true you are not what is called a brave man;
And not because you are made indifferent in your contempt
(You take their point, agree with it even, that there is
Nothing so dangerous as a new way of seeing the world);
Rather, you accept the conditions lightly, the recantation,
Lightly you accept their offer of a villa with a view,
Because you have grown old and contention makes you weary,

Because you like the idea of raising vines and tomatoes,
And because, whatever you might have said or suffered,
It is in motion still, cutting a great arc through nothingness,
Sweeping through space according to a design so grand
It remains, just as they would have it, a matter of faith,
Because, whether you say yea, whether you say nay,
Nevertheless it moves.

Agoos is a poet of sensibility, and her suggestive poems present a calm surface glossing hidden emotion. This book centers around a sojourn in Florence, and it registers the impact on the mind of things foreign yet formative, offering evidence of whatever remains in our day of the refining effects of travel. Both graceful and cryptic, Agoos's poetry runs deep and refuses to be read quickly.

Born in Boston in 1956, Julie Agoos was educated at Harvard University and Johns Hopkins University. She has been a Robert Frost Residency Fellow, and her second book of verse, *Calendar Year,* appeared in 1996. Agoos is a professor of English at Brooklyn College and lives in Skillman, New Jersey.

Portinaio

Here is a room to come to,
one with chairs enough;
here are books to choose from
just as the stingy light does,
leaving its impress on each wall,
while the stone brute lies guarding us,
and this old portinaio
(far more capable
of movement than we are)
comes setting the floor astir

with something closer to grandeur
than impatience: pulling the broom,
a square bit of tapestry
drags into the room beneath it,
just like a hooked fish
half rising out of flystruck
water: how at home he is,
bending backward like an angler,
moving through the room
back first, his flexed thighs

and puffed-out ribs, blue-covered,
mirroring the sky—a perfect
Eastern reverence
now carrying him all around
the twelve chairs we're sitting in,
that girdle the lustrous table,
making the scene more metaphorical
to us; to him, more blessed—
for when I say *buon giorno,*
he does not turn—

his voice trembles—then he bows
as if the river shielded him. Ah,
for a man like that, who assumes
some majesty within me
without demanding it!
And I call to him again
and see the hot blush
start beneath his collar,
too late how his body, spine-arced,
his vision now altered, had been

preparing him to turn
from the western window, where
he stands straight at last,
gazing out—having left
a wide circumference,
a dull planet circled
on the wood stretching between us,
as if the sun had been
where he has been, not
yet heating the place I come from.

High on the mantel, a crowned
Madonna is as faithless
to the forms the world
holds out to us, and reaches

her hand around her child
into handpainted
scenes of Eden troubling
that high south wall. What wouldn't
she exchange, gladly,
for a single taste

of that cadmium yellow apple?
And Maddalena, what
type is she, beside
that other Mary covered
in dust he cannot reach?
Or, bearing her own child,
can she have quelled that rumor,
this repeated history?
Che bella giornata comes
to me on a rare lightwave,

and I am at home now.
But where is the third mother,
is that what his soft broom is asking?

To Atlas in the Attic

Stored in the attic, even in sleep
—dust-covered, greening, a careless package
underneath the eaves—the world
still clings to you, your thoughtless body.
Statue, what tale will you teach my children
at night as they climb to the attic to hide,
and hold you for the first time seeking history?

How long have you lain on your side, and is it
more peaceful there? You, who had glory
and speech: Aratus, Theocritus, all
Alexandria mourned you, though you are merely
a myth to me, once displayed

in sunlight. I read then on your burning back
the shape of things: continents, seas,
tracing and turning the map. Bronze man,
you would have cast the world aside
if you could, had you dared. But oh, from May
to November, given the world to endure,
only your size was certain; and patience
was given a meaning: the lasting shrug
of your shoulder blazed beneath the sky,
the bronze beads like tears rising.

The day you fell headlong from
your pedestal, had you decided
to split the pain, like open pages;
see the soldered globe returned
like melon at your feet? You toppled almost
innocently. Now only
a bronze head remains, your image
lonely, gracing the living room.

"Quite good," some say, but in passing. You
were the world. World-wide you were
renamed, remade. Once you became
a mountain. But whether of stone or plaster
always upholding the greater creation.

To a child the earth is a mystery,
like you a statue, or a round story:
his favorite fruit with neither bruise
nor fragrance like the orchard fruit
you carried home to Heracles
from the far Hesperides. And though sorrow
is everlasting, and heaven recedes,
your strong palms turned upwards still
move me to childish belief,
bearing the gift of the night sky
where every star is named by you.

BRIGIT PEGEEN KELLY   *To the Place of Trumpets,* 1988

Clever and various, the poems in this volume grapple with Roman Catholicism and record a departure from that faith. The atmosphere of Kelly's poetry is small town, and the voice she uses is at once poised and companionable. Her work feels homey, but it holds many surprises, moving in unpredictable directions and ending in odd places. Familial and familiar though it is, this book retains its secrets, being full of private references that are rarely made plain.

Born in 1951 in Palo Alto, California, Brigit Pegeen Kelly studied nursing at Ivy Tech State College and writing at the University of Oregon. The winner of the Lamont Poetry Prize from the Academy of American Poets, Kelly's second collection of verse, *Song,* was published in 1995. She is a professor of English at the University of Illinois, Urbana-Champaign.

The Leaving

My father said I could not do it,
but all night I picked the peaches.
The orchard was still, the canals ran steadily.
I was a girl then, my chest its own walled garden.
How many ladders to gather an orchard?
I had only one and a long patience with lit hands
and the looking of the stars which moved right through me
the way the water moved through the canals with a voice
that seemed to speak of this moonless gathering
and those who had gathered before me.
I put the peaches in the pond's cold water,
all night up the ladder and down, all night my hands
twisting fruit as if I were entering a thousand doors,
all night my back a straight road to the sky.
And then out of its own goodness, out
of the far fields of the stars, the morning came,
and inside me was the stillness a bell possesses
just after it has been rung, before the metal
begins to long again for the clapper's stroke.
The light came over the orchard.

The canals were silver and then were not,
and the pond was—I could see as I laid
the last peach in the water—full of fish and eyes.

The Visitation

God sends his tasks
and one does
them or not, but the sky
delivers its gifts
at the appointed
times: With spit and sigh,
with that improbable
burst of flame, the balloon
comes over
the cornfield, bringing
another country
with it, bringing
from a long way off
those colors that are at first
the low sound
of a horn, but soon
are many horns, and clocks,
and bells, and clappers
and your heart
rising to the silence
in all of them, a silence
so complete that
the heads of the corn
bow back before it
and the dog flees in terror
down the road
and you alone are left
gazing up
at three solemn visitors

swinging
in a golden cage
beneath that unbelievable chorus of red
and white, swinging
so close you cannot move
or speak, so close
the road grows wet with light,
as when the sun flares
after an evening storm
and you become weightless, falling
back in the air
before the giant oak
that with a fiery burst
the balloon
just clears.

To the Lost Child

(for Anna)

This is the field you did not come to, this
the damp November day confederate
clouds trail defeat across. The far hills
are purple as the ashes of old fires,
and black as guns or crutches the trees. But the fields
are oddly green, still, in this winter thaw.
Or perhaps it is late fall—the small
measures we find ourselves with
don't change the movement of things. We, like this crow,
passing over the cedars in lazy,
widening circles, wobbling and sliding
as it rights itself by some internal decree,
can only ride the currents that *are*,
and are not held, up and down.
                              I am glad

of the crows, they are like my own hands,

always here, always remembering the day
to itself, glad of the trees, of the startling
red weeds and blue pools of shale
in this field where one tulip poplar stands
brisk and tall as a good child, a bee box
at her feet, a bee box full of humming.
And this humming is the maker, the body
of the gold it broods over. This must be so.
Pollen would have no savor if it came
from colorless flowers, and silent bees,
for all their flying, would make no honey
but some watery substance, or nothing
at all. For sound does make things happen.
The cows wander and when they cry
I heave hay, rank with mold and the months
of dust that fly up in blue clouds, over
the fence; the red-hatted hunter shouts
and the deer careers into or away from
the arrow's whistling arc; planes moan,
the head rises to heaven. And, Anna,
had you called as our bull calf Moses did,
all night when he was first new, tied to a pine
under the window, bullying the thin air
he found himself in, wailing at the cows
on the other side of the fence
who would not see him for what he was
until he forgot what he was and thought
we were one of him and he a fine man
in his uniform—had you called you would
have brought the sweet milk trickling between
your lips to form its lovely, cloudy pool.
I will not be sad. I count the things
I put in a box for us, all I thought
you would see, the scrawny forsythia starters—
pulled from the mother plant that smothers
the gate and each year must be thinned—tottering
along the drive, the deer trail lined

with the yellow roses that are still foolishly
blooming, the pines that cut the gray sky,
and the brilliant burning bush that, all improbably,
Moses, then grown, ate most of
before he barrelled away through the woods
to the farmer's far barley field, where, proud and stupid,
he ate his fill until we took
him away to one whose sturdy fences
would keep him home.

                I can sit for a long
time now. Some war is over. Below me
the bog in the woods is black
and pungent with decay and the oil from
the red cans the old tenant left, and below that,
at the base of the hill, the rushing stream
is a gathering of voices. Many voices.
Yours. Mine. It moves, we move, and hands,
these things that find and belong
to each other, also move and carry like water
more than themselves, as they fly in their bird-
like ways toward whatever small purposes
they have been given.

THOMAS BOLT *Out of the Woods,* 1989

The excursion many younger poets make into foreign culture and distant locale, Thomas Bolt makes into the landscape of decay. His poems amiably explore a highly lapsarian world of waste and refuse, of household garbage, discarded appliances, rusted automobiles. The last section of this book consists of an impressive sequence of Dantesque cantos constructed entirely of woods, walking, and wreckage.

Born in Washington, D.C., in 1959, Thomas Bolt received his B.A. from the University of Virginia in 1982. The winner of the Peter I. B. Lavan Award from the Academy of American Poets as well as of the Prix de Rome, Bolt now lives in New York City.

Meditation in Loudoun County

The Pontiac
Is a natural object. Ice melting on its hood
Trickles along a warp to the front end,
Drips from chromed fenders to the gravel
Making ticking sounds. Expanding metal,

Late spring.
Bloomed honeysuckle wavers in the chainlink,
Wilting. Still the car sits still: its metal,
Bled up through dulled enamel, rusts
In the hot sun of the front yard,

Throttled
By dried weeds. Punctures open into crusts.
Dead, flat enamels pucker into blisters.
Chromes flake and sprinkle gravel. A pale dust
Coats the hubcaps.

If truth
Is up on cinderblocks in the noon sun,
The color leaches from its dented door.
All day sun burns into the battered hood.
The earth is conservative. The car sits still.

Glimpse of Terrain

One kind of logic is a road cut into the side of a steep, wooded hill.
Its engineering makes travel of several kinds possible.
The road describes itself
(From a train I saw the profile
Of road and hill, the hill without the road
Covered with trees and rocks,
With dirt and leaves and fossil histories,
And the road set out from plan, graded from point to point,
A doubled yellow line curving with it,
Its asphalt smooth and banked efficiently,
Following every degree of the built bed).
It does not describe the hill.

from The Way Out of the Wood

VII

   I crossed
Where chainlink fence, puckered and collapsing,
   Tackled by undergrowth,
Was beaten down into the mud; and stood
   At the edge of a junkyard.
Paths ran far ahead between stacks of cars

   And piles of tires; roads
Spread toward the hub of the field like a city plan.
   I passed,
Wading out of undergrowth, first
   Onto a wide skirt
Of junk beyond the boundary of the yard,

   Outside commerce,
Sold for the last time; there, in a waste of parts
   Too scattered for salvaging,

Whole cars straddled the property line,
   Their hoods gone, and leaned
Into new shapes across the thawing ground

   With bloated magazines, split cassettes,
Magnetic tape unspooled, creased, stripped
   Of information, inks long ago
Bled to one color as discarded ledgers
   Swelled and buckled
And all ownership was given back

   To materials
Resuming their own life in the open mud.
   Just beyond
Where the woods petered out, and just before
   The junkyard boundary,
I had come at last to the end of the marketplace.

   I walked the unmarked ground
Looking for some path in the high grass
   To lead me across the margin,
In among the tenement stacks of cars
   And on into
The great wealth of our waste;

   Here was everything
Marked down to nothing,
   And supply
Scattered out of stock,
   Beyond demand,
Entering the economy of snails.

   As I passed through
That rind between places, where anything
   Could fall unclaimed,
Forgotten except by weather
   Between untended properties,
The junkyard rose ahead through littered weeds,

269

And saw
My poor present refracted through the glass
    Of other times,
To other purposes:
    I thought I saw
A shattered windshield glinting whole again,

    Its hanging glass
Fill with a morning sky; and then I saw
    Things first
Give up their histories to noon light
    Then afternoon
Until at last, here by the fence of trees

    Darkening
In the oldest languages
    Of rust and glitter,
All things gave up their history
    To now.
Dusk followed me

    Coming out of the cool
Woods onto the broadness of the lot,
    Where I found
Long, geometric aisles in the high grass
    And littered mud,
Crackling with each step the dark ground's

    Literal glitter
Of jars and headlights, safety glass and mirrors
    Between cars, each
Preserving the after-instant
    Of its wreck
In cold shape of reaction.

Hermit with Landscape is a skillfully oblique book. Much of it is made up of love poems, but the love is rendered in glimpses only, in adumbrated vignettes. Hall is willing to be generous and ready to be frank, but he is not interested in anything so artless as being explicit. Instead, he proceeds by evocation, a poet deft in the description of transformative emotion. Hall's poetry is at heart Cavafyian, for he believes that in the acute sensitivities engendered by love lies our true vale of soul-making.

Daniel Hall was born in Pittsfield, Massachusetts, in 1952 and is largely self-educated. He was an Amy Lowell Traveling Scholar in 1992 93, and his second book, *Strange Relation,* was published as part of the National Poetry Series in 1997. He lives in Northampton, Massachusetts.

Dusting

Beautiful, visitors used to say
absentmindedly, glimpsing the figurine
(courtesan, bronze) ensconced in the fine
bay window. And it was, in a way
that the irises swaying outside
would never be, multitudes driven
unresisting from season to season,
year after year. When the old man died,
his favorite weathered the neglect
indifferently. The pose she held
had taken a lifetime to perfect,
would take a life, at last, to comprehend.
Dust fell, and her hand was filled,
awaiting the touch of a human hand.

Hardy's "Shelley's Skylark"

Maybe it throbs in the myrtle's green,
Maybe it sleeps in the coming hue

But its radiocarbon ticks
into eternity, and our caskets
silver-lined have been rung shut
and buried standing. A century,
you wouldn't know the place.
Our streets are quiet, not so much
as a hopscotch or an "Alouette"
where the projects finger up
into the hills; every shade
is drawn, and the TVs burning.

It doesn't matter how bitterly
we envy you your invisible
point of song, the melting
pale purple even, etc.,
etc. What we've inherited
is the daylit owl disheveling
its filthy feathers, piercing us
with a yellow glare we hope
never to have to answer.

Hermit with Landscape

Salvation bought, sin sold:
it was hell in the city of gold
until I remembered all roads led
away as well. I fled
with what I wore—travel
light, and live, upon arrival,
lighter still. But I'm being less
than candid: take a look at this

snuffbox, rosewood, worked
by knowing hands and packed
with a troy ounce of the glistering stuff—
worth nothing here, but enough
for a year's indulgence there. The day
I left, it found its way
into my shirt. Take it, you'll need it
where you're going—no, take it!
What are you, doing penance?
Don't be a fool: no one's
perfect.
          Places either, though
this one has done, will do:
whitewashed stone whose eight
corners gaze inward, contemplate
virtual emptiness, an airy cell
with table, chair and cot—the whole
set in a sunny, bird-woven
sky and water, tree and mountain.
Days follow nights like answers
to calm questions—could be worse.
Happiness? You come to me
for a purchase on serenity?
You are a fool—or just a slow
study in last things. No,
the question is, can you credit
Paradise's infinite
riches filling "a walled
enclosure," that's all.

X

If not for Uncle Li
I'd have no job at all. Part-time,
a few hours after school,
weekends—I do my best

to study here, but the room
is dark and chilly.

Out there's another story.
Dian ying, "electric shadows,"
is exactly right: what matters,
or seems to, is not the light
but the obstruction of it.
I sit here high above it,

horny and bored. So much flesh
just turns me off, and did
after a night or so.
What I can't sleep for dreaming of
is not a smiling flawlessness,
much less an ideal torso—

at some range everybody falls
short of the ideal anyway.
Which may be what the patrons
wait for, their fascination
sustained by a clattery
unreality. It's all

I can do to keep my mind
on tomorrow morning's test
in Physics 101 . . .
Another steps in, blinded
by the dark. Who thinks of me
alone up here? No one.

Bears Dancing in the Northern Air, 1991

Kyle's poetry pursues a Wordsworthian aesthetic of locating isolated moments of visionary transport among domestic and rural surroundings. While waiting to be so moved, the poet is occupied in a careful awareness of quotidian circumstance, viewing her world with an attention that implies belief in its inherent holiness.

Christiane Jacox Kyle was born in 1950 in Washington, D.C. She was educated at Mount Holyoke College and at Eastern Washington University, Spokane, where she teaches English and women's studies.

Fire in Early Morning

The men keep searching the room
for the culprit. I tell them
electricity, those glowing coils
of wire, this ironing board
with the cedar frame, my coat
flung over the board. I don't say
I came home late, silly from a night
spent in song. They ask me how—

The dream told me: a scream
lunged from the cliff where I
slept in my skull, white winds
swept the ridge of my spine, shrieked
down the nerve ends. I remembered
my legs: the dream roared out a tunnel,
the smoke found the soft membranes,
sucking into those sockets
that glowed in the hallway.

I think it's morning but no light
shoulders its way here. The ironing board
staggers, its crippled legs bucking.

The coat is all gone, the green vine
blackened, limp arms dangle in the window,
and the dust keeps sifting through the tissues
of walls, the cells shriveling. My house,
my home, everything I touch turns away,
and a keening rises on a wind that keeps on
searching the bare coils of my brain.

The Season of Locking-In

Now it begins. The sun plunges down
in circles through the trees. It spills
over stiff limbs, the fire crown
rising: a burning of the hills.

Now out of the heart something thrusts
deep into the brain, jamming up
against the skull, driving black gusts
of wind until the thin walls drop

wide open, and the winds rush
out over the hills in spasms.
Listen:
             Beyond the charred stumps the hush,
the fog, are crawling toward the chasm.

The Argument

So many days spent tracking the desert,
the white cliffs, so many checking the map,
reading the wind, birds scratching the dirt,
the slow shiver of light fingering the back
of the neck; so much blood and sinew and heart
spent in wild hope, stunned in the black

cavern air, dripping with sweat, under each heel
old bones: the promise, but never the fact

of gems. To come only to this, to come
to nothing. To kneel down in mud and cry
empty, empty, empty, and hear the stunned
shrieks of bats ring out in wild delirium,
the heart roaring outloud, the cold breath of sapphire
invisible, flowering underground.

This is a book inspired by the quick and the dead: by the poet's father, a Greek Orthodox priest, and by the memory of a lover who died of cancer. Samaras works instinctively toward the mysticism of the plain, the humble, the timeless. The poems are set both at home and abroad, but two landscapes predominate: that of Greece and that of grief.

Born in England at Foxton, Cambridgeshire, in 1954, Nicholas Samaras was raised both there and in Massachusetts. He was educated at Hellenic College in Brookline, Columbia University, and the University of Denver. The winner of a Taylor fellowship for study abroad in 1981–82, Samaras has taught at the University of South Florida and lives in New Port Ritchie, Florida.

Aubade: Macedonia

Χωρίς σύνορα εἴμεθα.
We are without borders.

The airstrip is soggy with humidity.
The dark's edgy light is washed of color:
the sky, the air itself,
glassy-blue, hallucinogenic
over a flat, tufted landscape.
Hellenism has a perfect
adjective for this liquidity,
this glassine quality of my leaving,
my skin sallow with the effort of separation.
          You are silent
as the harbor, brimmed
with alarmingly still blue
water, holds silence.
For our thin time, we lived in one vein.
We were two worlds, converged and tender,
unwilling to answer
a separate continent's call.
All last night, you spoke
in present tenses, spoke

to fill the bedroom's fluent air.
Your mouth darkened with the hours.
We made love fiercely,
           we walked the Macedonian wind.
Faced with distance, we vowed
we'd be inseparable, borderless.
But the single plane before us is real,
tarmac threads down to the mouthing bay,
marram stitches the earth to its end.
Now there is no longer land enough
for what could contain or define us.
           One may leave
but two are left. I board
with hollow, metallic footsteps,
your pleasant scent still on
my hands. My hands
resume their singular shape.
The prop-chug startles the air.
I see you on the runway, framed
by stiffening air, back to the wind,
shaking your cloak of my absence.
We mouth final words, our distinct
worlds resuming perspective.
Your face diminishes in the window.
I am lifted into a borderless horizon
and we are forever
           beautiful, haunting, gone.

Translation

The rock's grey place is precise
and phrases everything
else.

Be ginger.
Sit on the green hill, the high view
sloping in declension.

Watch the movement of trees.
The cursive branches.
Verb of the wind over a whitened plain.

I am home. And lost.
My hands on my knees.
This paper. These words.
Able to look like my father's father, squinting,
I am the hands of the Saddlemaker.

Rising up the olive slope,
the sound
of mule bells tonguing.

On the parchment of land, bodies,
what is rendered
by the creased text in a worker's palms,
the blunt eyes of ancient pictures.

I send this.
Your language
returned to you.

Gladding's book shows an interest in Zen Buddhism, and it may be said to share Zen's calm acceptance of surface. Her verse is tremulous and quiet, seeking a clarity she feels is to be found in a close examination of the natural surround. The poems in this volume are brief, designed to be lingered over line by line.

Jody Gladding was born in York, Pennsylvania, in 1955. She was educated at Franklin and Marshall College and at Cornell University, where she has also taught, and she held a postgraduate Stegner Fellowship at Stanford University. She lives in East Calais, Vermont.

Locust Shell

The locust thought
she'd die, she laughed
so hard.
She didn't
but her sides
split
Surprised
she lay
dazed, dazzling;
she was beside
herself
or what had
up till then
given her
definition.
It doesn't mean
anything. You
can take it
lightly.

Worsted Heather

What earth is like—as round
and blue and green and flecked with red,
held in midair, turning like this
(the shuttle of my husband's hands
letting fall by lengths the yarn
I wind), and just this lonely
(a makeshift warmth, a little light)—
no other life among the cooling stars,
nothing but love unraveling it.

The Fisherman's Wife

So the man went away quite sorrowful to think
that his wife would want to be a king.
　　　— BROTHERS GRIMM

You must understand how pinched she's been
this Alice
shivering in a ditch

needled by her desires
which have grown incrementally
from wistfulness, a little air moving

ripple of *wanting something else*
when the tiny invisible scales itch
when she minds the stink

and the fish eyes, glowering
at her ingratitude, and all day
imagining him out there with his lines

shining back at that generous, wifely sea.
So when he comes home empty-handed
except for a tale

they've risen to such a pitch
she has to send him back
despite his reticence

and hoping it will subside
he doesn't mention the sea change
the colors, the swells.

But don't you understand
she knows how it churns, she tosses
in her bed, outraged

by ditch, cottage, castle
dreaming she can be Pope
and no longer contained

in this brine, her blood
surges, she'll rise
one final wave of desire

to unman even the sun.

Wohlfeld is a self-possessed poet who employs a florid style and an extensive vocabulary. She works many catalogs into her poems, thereby giving her pleasure in language free rein. This volume is notable for its sexual imagery, so persistent as to become almost an end in itself. Crows, thighs, and the sea recur with regularity in Wohlfeld's verse, elements used often enough by other authors but nonetheless unusual in combination.

Born in Sacramento, California, in 1956, Wohlfeld spent time as a child in both American Samoa and Ecuador. She was educated at American University in Washington, D.C., as well as Sarah Lawrence College and Vermont College, and lives in Newburyport, Massachusetts.

Sea

1.

The unwritten whorls on a spire lead a mollusk forward to build its
        celestial course, its factory
of crooked corridors: sanctum and lobby;
flue and chute and canopy;
the aqueduct's suckled salt, its little house of tunnel. I can't
        understand each leaden syllable the dead thrust up to me
from out of husk and myrrh, though I've laid my head to gravestones
        like an infidel feeding on a mouthful of a lover's pearls — gluttony
of gem and argent neck which instructs the palate (that mute sentinel,
        that insomnious voyeur) in rehearsed repartee.
The sea breathes asthmatically, asymmetrically:
unfolding like a reverse origami
to its many creases on soiled paper. Lucretius thought the dead
        released their souls as smoke from out of the body's
spent valise. Under my sprawl of limbs then, a shawl of vapor, fume
        and soot, brushes along the body's
halls. The sea's entrances all foresee
the same threshold — like the weighty
breath of a revolving door, or the ineluctable asylum conferred on
        a bee

arriving like an overburdened angel bearing its five eyes and four
     wings, to the rose's inner cloister (Rose: supine courtesan in her
     tyranny
of petal and thorn). I took to the sea
once, I went into its peeling sides as into a toy box's wallpaper lining,
     stained with tea
and doll sleep. The sea is a box the key,
the little iron soul, has left. The sea
is like the body, it wants to run invisibly
on the autonomic machinery of capillary
and lung, stage whisperings of vertebrae and the organs' laconic
     company.
The sea longs to open and shut, not lock. I've the Atlantic sea,
cheap loot, tucked inside a souvenir I bought for its cedar pungency.
I can summon the sea
from out of my box like a servant rising from sleep in an old movie,
called by the touch of a bourgeoisie's
foot to bell under the dining table. The body
is like a crow that concedes its untenanted nests to mourning doves: a
     useless aviary
that weaves itself of wire, roots, paper, string. Lucretius, I am already
among the rushes as smoke rising to its axis of ordinates as it leaves
     the body
(as if mortality were a facsimile
of calculations yoked to their X coordinates, seized by the abscissae
as by the quick lash the genus *Corvus* uses to intersect with eye and
     tongue the venous berry
of the mellifluous, wild cherry).

2.

From out of its pharynx, out of its gullet, its heart,
entrails, kidneys; out of its sulphur and mercury;
its divine waters and divine dusts; its rot of brain
and refulgent coral; with its eyes sealed shut
in prayer; with its lit and salted raiments worn inside
out; pendulous in its gold and silver amulets inscribed

with the unpronounceable names of God; with the hangman's
rope encircling the neck of its cut-down body;
in its chemical vessels and baths; in its obscure female
anatomy which the Talmudic scholars would delineate
only as chamber, antechamber, upper chamber and hidden
chamber; with its long, perfumed arms hurling pots and china
dishes as to ward off the Angel of Death; with its 206 bones
the same as in the human skeleton; in its cadaverous
chromatics and nuptial veils; with its hook, grapnel, tongs,
pincers and forceps; in its false coming-ins and going-outs
like a child's heart sequestered in an iron lung;
as it turns in its bed like the idiot brother
Walt Whitman slept side by side with; as it waits to ignite
like the single red beard hair of a station agent tried
in Edison's search for a filament; as it sheds its glass
into color like the prism in Newton's hands; as it rises
like a golem pulling itself up from its knees: rises and rises
until you understand that it is meant for you;
that it has loosened its slips and lingerie,
let fall its unbound braids to move now like cirrus for you, rising and
    rising
until you cannot be kept from entering its cast-off silk
and unbridled hair to fill its floating throat
with your own voice, as though the vitreous stopper
of a still-molten vessel that rises
in a colorless heat to your open lips.

That Which Is Fugitive, That Which Is Medicinally Sweet or Alterable to Gold, That Which Is Substantiated by Unscientific Means

Earth, *Ephemera.*
Womb, *Elixir.*
Subject to its laws of development,
experience, observation and verification

of salted, borrowed blood: the given
name for the fetus must be *Empirical*.

Beaker of the body's warmth: pinprick,
secret ruby, transient blossom, Empirical.
The womb catches life like a well
harboring pennies, whatever's sent to it,
the water wise but untelling.

I lay on the table, my puerile
dress folded on a chair. Brought
with me a thesaurus, its outer covers lost.
My body moored, I watched the ceiling's white,
starless firmament and began my recitation
out of the injured book.

Cinnabar, cochineal, ponceau
Annatto, madder, ruddle, rouge
Scarlet, cardinal, vermilion
Claret-colored, flame-colored, rust-colored
Auburn, sandy, bay, sorrel, chestnut.
Again I was dark, green water
for the copper coins to hurry down to.

Crunk's work is written out of a Southern Baptist upbringing in semi-rural Kentucky. The poet seeks to balance the claims of memory with those of religion and a faith in the hereafter. Life as it has already been lived and the life to come compete with a present that is seen as shifting and unsatisfying, as something in which it is only intermittently possible to believe.

Tony Crunk was born in Hopkinsville, Kentucky, in 1956. Educated at Centre College of Kentucky, the University of Kentucky, and the University of Virginia, he lives in Huson, Montana, and teaches at the University of Montana, Missoula.

Visiting the Site of One of the First Churches My Grandfather Pastored

My mother said later that, to the shovel operators, we must have looked like some delegation from out of town that couldn't find the picnic. Or else the funeral. Not so bad my brother and me jumping the fence, and my father, but then my mother, and all of us helping my grandfather over, and finally my grandmother deciding she wanted to see, too.

Then all of us standing together at the rim of the pit in our Sunday clothes, sun reflecting off my grandmother's black patent purse, a few trees still hanging on nearby, roots exposed, like tentacles, like the earth is shrinking under them. The smell of sulphur.

The giant bucket scoops up through the rocks and dirt, the shovel swings around, the bucket empties, and the whole thing swings back, the noise taking an extra second to reach us. I am watching the two men inside, expecting them to notice us, to wave us away because we don't belong there, but they don't. They must be used to it.

Years later I will remember my grandfather saying that they strip away the land but all they put back is the dirt. Maybe plant a few scrub pine. "Good for nothing any more," he says now, turning to go back to the car. "Good for nothing except holding the rest of the world together."

It looks almost blue in the sun, the piece of coal I have picked up to take home for a souvenir.

Leaving

Were there such an end as destination
I could say that I was leaving,
could imagine friends gathered on the street below,
cheering maybe, waving maps tied to sticks.
But there isn't. There is only expansion and contraction
like infinity, or a dime on the sidewalk,
like a letter I found in a corner of the empty room
I am moving out of, a letter I didn't mail
that begins, "Dear S.—Guilt is the wound that never stops healing:
at times I want to look outside and see my daughter
standing beneath the ash tree and the stars,
a sparkler hissing blue and yellow in her two hands.
But the window is missing, lost,
lying in a field where someone passing
could look down into it and see the faces
rising up through the earth
and sinking back. . . ." A tiny, well-formed cloud
hovers in the space between my eye and the page.
I imagine I have inhaled the sky,
that I grow larger. I imagine that one day
I may grow large enough to fill my body.

Reunion

What we mistook for flight
was only the long struggle
to surface, and we arrive
at a place familiar as a socket—
sitting by a dirt road, watching wind
bristle the raw corn stubble,

discussing gravity and how,
with the invention of dust,
things began to pick up speed,
how October lays bare
the age of the world, how we
may yet find the word we seek,

which may be a labyrinth
with nothing at its center,
or a snowy egret that will rise
above the houses and the wires,
or which may again be the root
that, pulled up, lies twisting in our hands . . .

ELLEN HINSEY   *Cities of Memory,* 1996

Alert and atmospheric, Hinsey's verse is typical of a promising first book in that it finds artistic possibilities in the investigation of foreign culture. Less typically, history and scholarship are two of the alien terrains this poet sets out to explore. Her poetry shows poise and curiosity, although both qualities are filtered through a certain dreaminess. This is by intention an unhurried, even a solemn volume. The reader is intended to move through these dignified poems as along cathedral aisles.

Born in 1960, Ellen Hinsey was educated at Tufts University and the School of the Museum of Fine Arts in Boston. She lives in Paris.

The Art of Measuring Light

From the Pont-Neuf, Paris

The light here has begun to pass and as it passes
it will bend down to the Seine in the last of its
winter gymnastics: unwrapping its hands from
the white crevices of Saint-Germain-des-Prés,

giving a last honor to Sacré-Cœur. One will
turn one's eyes to the horizon, but there only
shadows lie, and the beams of cars that follow
the Seine northward toward Le Havre, their lamps

yellow like the pleasure boats that illuminate
the shores with serpentine eyes. But standing
in half-light, the mind devises a method,
and knows that distance is an arc, not a line;

it will follow light as it curves past the river
to meet its welcome in woods, distant from
the sphere of the thinker, yet distant only as
a pair of hands, clasping a tool in a far-off field.

The body in its accuracy cannot close the calipers
of space, but knows just the same that light
that has passed here is light that will contrive
to touch the white of wood on maple-lined streets,

deep in New Hampshire, where snow is piling
high, in the unbroken shadow of a new day.
Where for the difference of six hours, the hands
of the clock are unlocked, and Puritans progress

with morning. They will carve out a day, wrapped
in time, envisaged in the silence of apple and pine,
and of light curving to where it will break in the
suddenness of a windfall. Perhaps there one will

measure a quantum leap, where from pasture post,
to the end of the road, light will seize the form
of an animal breathless beneath the carcass
of a rusted frame; or watch as it breaks stride

at crossroads, finding figures passing surrounded
by the wreath of their breath. The sky is not a narrow
passage, and light is there to flex the ample arm of it.
On this side, the Pont-Neuf is dark, and the mind,

that lone traveler, comes back to rest like a cast
shuttle to a waiting palm. Across the bridges
night figures come, their loads weighted like
lanterns—swinging slowly in narrow arcs.

The Body in Youth

After rain, in the darkened room, the body
reed-like, marked by mysteries, hungered
to escape the rhythm of change, observed
nightly in the narrow bed.

Shadowless, the washed walls receded,
though benignly, in triptych, caught the
occasional beam's passing: such
the simple Annunciations

that taught limbs to reach, as if in passion,
into the near vagaries of space. Each part
resolutely delivered its tidings: ears
fanned and thickened like

muscular flowers, that thrive in the shade
of the water's edge; birthmarks, hidden,
spread, then darkened, inspected by fingers
for their singular shape.

Ribs betrayed the pulse's quickening pace.
Only dreams cradled imperfections —
rationalized the humidity of desires;
by day the body crept

to the mirror and under its scrutiny,
waited for change like an unseen horizon.
Just before rain it seemed the body
lingered transparent,

had carried one out under the firs, set
one free under the rotating spheres.
Now flesh was a constant breath
at one's ear, intoning

its litany of limitations. Yet how far the body
had to travel—when finally, after its shape
was fixed, and became one's signature
in the world of forms,

then faithlessly, like a ship tide-persuaded,
it drifted, abandoning what it sought
to become, the body in youth lingering
only a moment in its own folds.

The Roman Arbor

Suddenly you felt it. And under the white
    eye of afternoon, you turned

but could see nothing. Water flowed from
    the mouths of the stone heads,

that hung, as if sacrificed, above their basins
    in the trellised garden. You caught,

in an alcove of green, the quick movement
    of a lizard as it traced the sandal

of a departed goddess. The garden was so still
    that, apart from the shifting water,

you imagined sound had refused refuge there,
    preferring to venture out towards

where the islands broke the authority of the
    shoreline. Your calm was restored.

So when you met, face to face between the
    columns, you were not prepared—

he stood greater than you, his stone locks
    worn smooth as the tide's back,

his breast four times the hand's compass.
    Breathless before his bulk, you

failed to notice that afternoon was gaining
    territory. Then, slowly, under

the heat, a thought crept along the stone sills,
    leaving behind a thin trail of grief.

Who is not like him—you asked—your words
    sifting in the striated light,

and turning as the sand lifted once in
    the hot breeze, you said:

Who is not a witness of ruined places?

Ansel carries the young poet's fascination with unknown regions to an extreme, for her book records an excursion into the depths of the Amazon rain forest. Far from arriving at any heart of darkness, Ansel discovers a world so elemental and compelling as to render the civilization from which she had started insubstantial by comparison. To return from such remoteness is not easy—Ansel makes just this point in a sequence that imagines Caliban in Shakespeare's London—and one finishes this volume feeling we are fortunate to have gotten the author back.

Born in Madison, Wisconsin, in 1964, Talvikki Ansel was raised in Mystic, Connecticut. She was educated at Mount Holyoke College and Indiana University and was the recipient of a Stegner Fellowship in creative writing at Stanford University. In 1997 she was a resident at the Djerassi Resident Arts Program in Woodside, California.

from In Fragments, In Streams

i

The *Teatro Amazonas,* remnant
from the rubber barons, who sent
their laundry to France. Turn of the century
embroidered hanky in this city—
scrape in the jungle, once embellished:
the opera house, a fish market designed
by Alexandre Eiffel, dark and cool.
Inside, the piranhas and pirarucu
smooth and twitching on the marble counters.
Outside in the bright heat, the vendors
hawking watches, the radios and stereos,
and always the *Teatro,* calm as cream. Stone
from Italy, and plush seat covers within,
a painted ceiling, once—Jenny Lind.

iv

At night, coolness like water lapping
around our hammocks, wrapped in a woolen
blanket, I'd rock, listen for the laughing-
frogs, the potoo's "poor-me-all-alone,"
one foot pushing off from the ground. I
never expected this: a bird's small, pale
eggs in a laced-up palm frond, how easily
trees would fall, tilting up from the fine earth,
coming down with a tangle of vines.
Afloat in the green island of forest,
slipping into the stream each evening
minnows would nudge my shoulders and spine.
A happiness as complete as belief,
suspended midair, the nest in the leaf.

vi

Halley's Comet crossed the jungle sky
that April, six mornings in a row
I woke to hike out to a clearing
and never saw it. Somewhere above the low
clouds, the constellations: *Cruzeiro do*
sul, all wings and tail like a giant
macaw. Dust and rain puddles. Who knows
what comes before, or trails after;
my first night in the city, a sloth
on the headboard, my sudden fear: *what have I*
done this time? A bat in the net at dawn,
leaf nosed, the ancient face familiar,
inscrutable, like the eroded trail,
the mute sloth's remnant stub of tail.

vii

Before first light, we would open the nets
for birds and wait, half dozing on a log,

slapping tapir-flies, pulling out
their tongues. A number for each bird, a dog-
eared field guide, a scale, and a ruler
for measuring wings. They hung upside down
until we took them out: first feet, then shoulders
and head, an aluminum band around
one leg: the *Galbulas'*, soft and yellow,
hummingbirds' too short for bands, the heart's
flicker in the palm of your hand. To know
their names: antbird, antshrike, *Myrmetherula,*
wren. Familiar plumage, song—it stirs—
flies, and I can't follow where it has gone.

xiv

Along the road, the bright painted crosses
on the steepest banks, overturned buses,
people waiting in the rain. A deep
gouge with smaller rivers running down it,
mud slick as ice, and driving we slide
sideways. My last day in the forest
I tilt my head back in the stream, the palms
silhouetted against the sky, under
my butt the water hollows out sand;
why did I come here? Everything slips
away. On the road, the man with a gun,
a dead chachalaca slung at his waist;
back in the city, rain clouds stud
the grey sky, my clothes are reddened with mud.

xviii

Waking, months after I leave the jungle,
I have lost something in sleep; I curl
under my blankets. My toes numb,
I push a foot against the wall until
I rock slightly in my bed. New England
spring, the crocuses bloom and freeze. Brazil

is like a bird in watercolor I thought
I saw a long time ago, a fading ceiling;
I try to remember one thing, a blue
winged moth, sun filtering through the trees,
the spiders spinning their threads across
the paths; when I wake again I am
freezing, and my remembering,
the web I walk through every morning.

Credits

Index